TRANSNATIONAL FEMINISMS AND ART'S TRANSHEMISPHERIC HISTORIES

In this second book of her trailblazing trilogy, Marsha Meskimmon proposes that decolonial, ecocritical, feminist art's histories can unravel the anthropocentric legacies of Eurocentric universalism, to create transformative conversations between and across many and more-than-human worlds.

Engaging with the ecologies and genealogies – worlds and stories – that constitute the plural knowledge projects of transnational feminisms and art's transhemispheric histories, the book is written through two critical figurations: *transcanons* and *trans-scalar ecologies*. Materializing art's histories as radical practices of disciplinary disobedience, the volume demonstrates how planetary feminisms can foster interdependent flourishing as they story pluriversal worlds, and world pluriversal stories, *with* art.

This is essential reading for students and researchers in art history, theory and practice, visual culture studies, feminism and gender studies, environmental humanities and cultural geography.

The Trilogy:

Transnational Feminisms, Transversal Politics and Art: Entanglements and Intersections
Transnational Feminisms and Art's Transhemispheric Histories: Ecologies and Genealogies
Transnational Feminisms and Posthuman Aesthetics: Resonance and Riffing

Marsha Meskimmon is Professor of Transnational Art and Feminisms, and Director of the Institute of Advanced Studies at Loughborough University (UK). Her publications include *Transnational Feminisms, Transversal Politics and Art: Entanglements and Intersections* (2020), *Contemporary Art and the Cosmopolitan Imagination* (2010), *Women Making Art: History, Subjectivity, Aesthetics* (2003), all with Routledge.

TRANSNATIONAL FEMINISMS AND ART'S TRANSHEMISPHERIC HISTORIES

Ecologies and Genealogies

Marsha Meskimmon

LONDON AND NEW YORK

Cover image: Boxed plinth with graffiti following Rhodes Must Fall demonstrations, University of Cape Town, South Africa, August 2015. Image courtesy of the author

First published 2023
by Routledge
4 Park Square, Milton Park, Abingdon, Oxon OX14 4RN

and by Routledge
605 Third Avenue, New York, NY 10158

Routledge is an imprint of the Taylor & Francis Group, an informa business

© 2023 Marsha Meskimmon

The right of Marsha Meskimmon to be identified as author of this work has been asserted in accordance with sections 77 and 78 of the Copyright, Designs and Patents Act 1988.

All rights reserved. No part of this book may be reprinted or reproduced or utilised in any form or by any electronic, mechanical, or other means, now known or hereafter invented, including photocopying and recording, or in any information storage or retrieval system, without permission in writing from the publishers.

Trademark notice: Product or corporate names may be trademarks or registered trademarks, and are used only for identification and explanation without intent to infringe.

British Library Cataloguing-in-Publication Data
A catalogue record for this book is available from the British Library

ISBN: 978-1-138-57975-0 (hbk)
ISBN: 978-1-138-57976-7 (pbk)
ISBN: 978-0-429-50781-6 (ebk)

DOI: 10.4324/9780429507816

Typeset in Bembo
by SPi Technologies India Pvt Ltd (Straive)

CONTENTS

List of Figures	*vi*
Acknowledgements	*ix*
Introduction	1

PART I
Storying Pluriversal Worlds   17

1 *Transcanons*: Transhemispheric Stories for Pluriversal Worlds 19

PART II
Practice and Flourish   63

2 *Poetic Stories*: Genealogies of Work and Survival with Audre Lorde 65

3 *Pedagogical Worlds*: Expansive Ecologies of Connection and Care 86

PART III
Worlding Pluriversal Stories   109

4 *Trans-Scalar Ecologies*: Worlding Planetary Feminist Stories *with* Art 111

Afterword: On *Trilogics* *148*

Selected Bibliography	*150*
Index	*162*

FIGURES

1.1 Phil Sayers and Rikke Lundgreen, installation view, *Changing Places*, Liverpool, Lady Lever Art Gallery, 2007–08. Image courtesy of the artists — 25

1.2 *Statuette of Standing Hermaphrodite*, 70–100 AD. Image courtesy of National Museums Liverpool — 26

1.3 Frederick Leighton, *The Bath of Psyche*, 1890. Image courtesy of Tate Gallery, London — 27

1.4 Phil Sayers, *On Reflection*, 2007. Image courtesy of the artist — 29

1.5 Phil Sayers, *Captivated*, 2007. Image courtesy of the artist — 34

1.6 *Les Sauvages de la Mer Pacifique* designed by Jean-Gabriel Charvet for the firm of Joseph Dufour et Cie, c.1805. Image courtesy of the National Gallery of Australia, Canberra — 36

1.7 Lisa Reihana, *In Pursuit of Venus [infected]*, 2015–17. Ultra HD video, colour, 7.1 sound, 64 min, Auckland Art Gallery. Photo: Jennifer French. Image courtesy of the artist — 38

1.8 Lisa Reihana, *In Pursuit of Venus [infected]*, detail: *Stars*, 2015–17. Ultra HD video, colour, 7.1 sound, 64 min. Image courtesy of the artist — 41

1.9 Lisa Reihana, *In Pursuit of Venus [infected]*, detail: *Mourning*, 2015–17. Ultra HD video, colour, 7.1 sound, 64 min. Image courtesy of the artist — 42

1.10 Mariana Castillo Deball, *Between making and knowing something*, Modern Art Oxford, installation view, 2020. Photographer:

Figures **vii**

Ben Westoby. Museum case courtesy of the Oxford University
Museum of Natural History.
Image courtesy of the artist and Modern Art Oxford   47

1.11   Mariana Castillo Deball, *A_____LL Around I*, installation view,
from *Between making and knowing something*, Modern Art Oxford,
installation view, 2020. Ceramic vessel made of red stoneware
painted with engobe slip. Hand-woven textile dyed with an ikat
pattern and displayed with backstrap looms produced in the state of
Michoacán, Mexico by Ukata. Ceramics produced with the assistance of ceramicist Silvia Andrande. Photographer: Ben Westoby.
Image courtesy of the artist and Modern Art Oxford   49

1.12   Mariana Castillo Deball, *Between making and knowing something*,
Modern Art Oxford, installation view, 2020. Photographer:
Ben Westoby. Museum case courtesy of the Oxford University
Museum of Natural History. Elsie McDougall fieldwork
photography, parts of wooden backstrap looms. Fieldwork photo-
graphs courtesy of the Pitt Rivers Museum, University of Oxford.
Image courtesy of the artist, Modern Art Oxford and Pitt Rivers
Museum, University of Oxford   53

2.1   Lana Lin, still from *The Cancer Journals Revisited*, 2018.   79

3.1   Lala Rukh, *Mirror Image: 1*, 1997. Mixed media on graph paper,
48 × 60 cm. Collection of the Metropolitan Museum of Art,
New York (2019.260a–c).
Image courtesy of the Estate of Lala Rukh and Grey Noise Dubai   92

3.2   Lala Rukh, *River in an ocean: 6*, 1993. Mixed media on
photographic paper 24.8 × 20.9 cm.
Image courtesy of the Estate of Lala Rukh and Grey Noise, Dubai   93

3.3   Boxed plinth with graffiti following Rhodes Must Fall demonstrations,
University of Cape Town, South Africa, August 2015.
Image courtesy of the author   98

3.4   Graffiti shadow of Rhodes at the base of the covered plinth
following Rhodes Must Fall demonstrations, University of Cape
Town, South Africa, August 2015.
Image courtesy of the author   98

4.1   Wu Mali, Breakfast event with local residents (2010), from *Art as
Environment: A Cultural Action at the Plum Tree Creek*, 2010–12.
Image courtesy of the artist and Bamboo Curtain Studio, New
Taipei City   119

4.2   Judith F. Baca, copyright 1983. Detail 'Mrs Laws' to 'Louisa
Moreno', several panels from the 1940s section of the *Great Wall
of Los Angeles* mural.
Image courtesy of the SPARC Archives SPARCinLA.org   122

viii Figures

4.3   Wu Mali, Shaping the village, *Art as Environment: A Cultural Action at the Plum Tree Creek*, 2010–12.
Image courtesy of the artist and Bamboo Curtain Studio, New Taipei City   124

4.4   Judith F. Baca, copyright 1983. Detail 'Chinese Build the Railway' to 'Chinese Massacre, 1871', several panels from the first 1000 ft. section of the *Great Wall of Los Angeles* mural.
Image courtesy of the SPARC Archives SPARCinLA.org   131

4.5   Wu Mali, Walk along the Plum Tree Creek, *Art as Environment: A Cultural Action at the Plum Tree Creek*, 2010–12.
Image courtesy of the artist and Bamboo Curtain Studio, New Taipei City   136

4.6   Judith F. Baca, copyright 1983. Detail 'Jewish Arts and Sciences' to 'Indian Assimilation', several panels from the 1950s section of the *Great Wall of Los Angeles* mural.
Image courtesy of the SPARC Archives SPARCinLA.org   137

ACKNOWLEDGEMENTS

This volume would not have been completed without the generous engagement of a number of colleagues, friends and family, not to mention the support of a range of institutions. It is a pleasure to thank them here for their care and attention – two terms that have come to be more fully appreciated over the past few years, as the ethico-political acts that they are.

The arguments in this book unfold as conversations with artworks and I owe a huge debt of gratitude to the artists who have granted permission to reproduce their work across its pages, not to mention the many who engaged with early versions of the chapters, bringing insights and nuances to the conversations that only they could offer. The book is better for this generous dialogue. My thanks, in particular to Phil Sayers and Rikke Lundgreen, Lisa Reihana, Mariana Castillo Deball, Lana Lin, Wu Mali and Judith Baca. In addition, I was extended exceptional courtesy and assistance from individuals working with the artists and in institutions holding their estate, or in key collections, and I would like to recognize this, as it was crucial to the realization of the volume. My thanks to Nathan Pendlebury, Keith Sweeney and Heather McCabe at National Museums Liverpool; Chris Sutherns at Tate Images; Madison Du at the National Gallery of Australia; James Pinker at artprojects, Auckland; Amy Budd and Jessie Robertson at Modern Art Oxford; Remko at Studio Castillo Deball in Berlin; Mark Dickerson at the Pitt Rivers Museum, University of Oxford; Elaine Lubguban at Grey Noise Gallery, Dubai; Cristina D'Alessandro at Scala Archives, Florence; Svea Josephy at the Michaelis School of Art, University of Cape Town; Bamboo Curtain Studio in New Taipei City, and Pilar Castillo at the Social and Public Art Resource Center (SPARC) in Venice, California.

Dialogues with trusted friends and colleagues, many having to be continued at long distance and digitally for the past few years, underpin this volume. Loughborough University is a good home for my thinking and, in particular, my

x Acknowledgements

intellectual momentum over the course of writing this book was sustained by the care and wit of Marion Arnold, Rachael Grew, Hilary Robinson, Steve Rice and Steve Rothberg. I await many more conversations to come, 'IRL'. I enjoy the pleasure of leading Loughborough's Institute of Advanced Studies, with the aid of an amazing team: Helen Tighe, Laura Dale, Katy Wing, Kieran Teasdale and Bhavna Patel. They make it possible to create the space for dialogue so needed in the Academy and it is an honour to work closely with them. Likewise, I have enjoyed close working friendships for many years with Amelia Jones, Emma Brennan and Dorothy Price, whose commitment to reimagining the limits of art's histories remains a constant source of inspiration. Draft chapters of this volume were read by an exceptional group of colleagues, including Nikos Papastergiadis, Jane Chin Davidson, Alpesh Patel and Anne Ring Petersen, each of whom made valuable contributions to the final version of this book and did so with a huge generosity of spirit – thank you! Thanks also to three of my sharpest doctoral students who commented on aspects of the project: Hazel McMichael, Marlous van Boldrick and Agostinho Pinnock. My editor at Routledge, Natalie Foster, and the two Editorial Assistants who worked with me on this volume, Kelly O'Brien and Jennifer Vennall, have been wonderfully supportive throughout the project and I am very much obliged to them.

Much of this volume was written during the course of various lockdowns, and while I am ever grateful to my husband, Phil, and son, Davy, for their love, care, and endlessly vibrant, unexpected (even surreal!), turns of conversation, their presence over the past two years was a lifeline. They make our house a home.

My final thoughts turn to Martin L. Davies, my teacher, mentor and friend for more than 35 years, who died in December of 2021. It was Martin who first introduced me to the idea of an 'ecology of knowledge' some two decades ago, and whose thinking was always on the move, refusing the complacency of merely miming the knowledge already known. Martin was brilliant, intellectually, but he was also profoundly generous, modest and supportive of others' work, not to mention funny, joyous and musical. For the majority of my adult life, I enjoyed conversations with Martin that challenged and changed, for the better, the way I understood the world. We often read drafts of one another's writing and, before he died, he had read two chapters of this volume, which we discussed over Zoom, a technology he loved to hate. I miss him immensely and hope that I can continue to *give forward* the gift of his friendship and scholarly guidance. This book is dedicated to his memory.

INTRODUCTION

What would a decolonial, ecocritical feminist art history be like?
Arguably, plural and planetary, but never pure.

This is a book about the ecologies and genealogies – worlds and stories – that constitute the plural knowledge projects of transnational feminisms and art's transhemispheric histories. As this introduction unfolds to explore these terms, and the ramifications of their critical imbrication, my rhetorical opening gambit shifts from singular to plural and object to process: *what will decolonial, ecocritical feminist art's histories do?* The shift is meaningful; there is material-discursive[1] method in its semantic madness.

The grammatical change recognizes a critical difference between *art history*, conceived as an object/discipline, a singular episteme designed (and destined) to uphold (and police) an exclusive 'Western canon', and *art's histories*, material-discursive knowledge practices,[2] through whose multiple, iterative, and potentially transformative intra-actions, both 'art', and its 'histories', emerge in mutuality. More simply, it is not the aim of my argument to secure (or salvage) canonical art history as an object,[3] but to explore art's transhemispheric histories as radical practices of materialization that can enable multiple epistemic worlds to flourish. I concur with the insight of Argentinian decolonial theorist Walter D. Mignolo that the 'universalization of Western Universality was part of its imperial project',[4] and that the extractive, silencing and universalizing logic of categorical purification that underpins canonical art history, is a logic thoroughly entangled with the very legacies of European imperialism, heteropatriarchal nation-building and colonial conquest that decolonial feminist scholarship and activism seeks to challenge and change.[5] My argument further emphasizes that the anthropocentric and monocultural knowledge project that Eurocentric universalism set into motion continues to be maintained by interconnected violences – genocide, femicide, ecocide and epistemicide.

DOI: 10.4324/9780429507816-1

2 Introduction

It is the premise of this volume that epistemic transformation is both possible, and imperative, if the violent legacies of social, economic and ecological injustice that continue to dominate the present are to be countered. More strongly, I am arguing that the creative and collaborative knowledge projects that constitute transnational feminisms and art's transhemispheric histories, effect significant epistemic and imaginative transformations as they materialize plural and planetary (but never pure) ecologies and genealogies, with and through, not just *about*, art. Transnational feminisms' decolonial, race-critical, queer/trans, and ecological thinking dismantles the Eurocentric universal narrative of One world, to facilitate contingent conversations between and across many and more-than-human worlds. My reformulated question thus begins to garner a response:

> *What will decolonial, ecocritical feminist art's histories do?*
> Arguably, story pluriversal worlds, and world pluriversal stories, *with* art.

Transnational Feminisms, Transhemispheric Histories

Although the term 'transnational feminisms' is neither fixed nor static, a recognizable and coherent body of thought and global activist praxis tends to coalesce under the heading, aspects of which I delineated in the first volume of this trilogy in a form that remains relevant here:

> Intellectually, transnational feminist theory describes a multidimensional field of thought that commonly moves across and between disciplines, engaging intersectional, decolonizing and race-critical analysis, queer, ecological, Indigenous and 'slow' activisms, and, increasingly, a vital materialist move away from solely human-centred understandings of the world.[6]

Transnational feminisms commonly eschew the 'blood and soil' logic of essentialist identity politics, along with binary models of gender/sex and simplistic centre/periphery constructs of geopolitical and transcultural exchange, tending instead to favour thinking focused on flows, connectivities and affinities in difference.[7] The decolonial and race-critical trajectories of transnational feminisms are deeply indebted to the exceptionally rich and long-standing intellectual legacies of Black, Indigenous and women/queer of colour research and activism, produced principally in the Global South and/or the metropolitan centres of the 'West'.[8] This body of critical praxis has long offered stunning analyses of the nexus of racialized, spatialized, gendered and genocidal power that underpins the old and new world orders of Western imperial globality and their central protagonist, 'Man'.[9] Adding to this, an increasingly vibrant field of decolonizing trans and non-binary thought has further extended the critical engagement of transnational feminisms with concepts of the 'human', and with how to think in post- and more-than-human times and spaces.[10] This is not easy; as political philosopher Shireen Roshanravan has argued, '...rejecting coloniality's violent heteropatriarchal, gendered normalization of being human requires collectively imagining ways of being human that do not reproduce this violence'.[11]

Shifting scale to collectively re-imagine the 'human' as a species is a profoundly creative act of epistemic transformation that brings the planetary[12] into transnational feminisms, and engenders a dialogue with insights taken from critical ecofeminisms, Indigenous and vital materialist thought, political ecology, and environmental justice activism. My argument follows ecofeminist scholar Greta Gaard's compelling formulation of these links:

> Critical ecofeminism benefits from past lessons about gender and racial essentialisms, as well as from the more contemporary critical dimensions of economic, posthumanist, and postcolonial analysis. ... it grows in dialogue with queer ecologies [and]... advances on the earlier findings of feminist animal activists, feminist peace and antinuclear activists, feminist environmental justice activists and queer feminist environmentalists as well as antiracist ecofeminists.[13]

Transnational feminisms reject universal discourses of mastery and domination in all of their forms, and routinely practice disciplinary and epistemic disobedience by bringing decolonial, race-critical, queer/trans and ecological thinking together to know differently, imagine otherwise and engender a world in which many worlds can flourish. In positing this plural, planetary and impure approach to storying worlds and worlding stories, I am proposing that transnational feminisms are, at their best, 'epistemologies of the South'.[14]

My proposition does not take 'South' to be a geographical point or magnetic pole, though I remain cognizant of the leading contributions made by scholars, artists and activists living and working in the Global South to the conceptual and creative dynamism of 'Southern theory'.[15] South, used here, indicates, instead, a critical politics of epistemic location, and a form of resistant intellectual positionality that does not obscure its locus of enunciation. Thinking with and through the South challenges the normative epistemic centrality of the Global North/West by taking active responsibility for the *how*, *why* and *where* of knowledge production, asking not 'what' is known, but from whose vantage point, for what purpose and to what ends. To understand the stakes of engaging with epistemologies of the South as a form of knowing *from somewhere*, so to engage ethically and relationally with others, *elsewhere*, I turn to Indigenous feminist and literary scholar Jodi A. Byrd, whose thinking on 'the Souths' speaks of entangling complex intimacies across the globe:

> The Souths and non-Souths might finally (re)turn against conquest to pattern the intimacies of geographic relationalities in ways that account for the historical violences of slavery and removal, racialization and colonization. Without requiring purity or demanding innocence, such patterned intimacies request a willingness to be responsible to people and to land as well as to the geographies beyond nation-states and other such Norths.[16]

4 Introduction

I am convinced and compelled by Byrd's argument – convinced by her analysis, in this text and elsewhere,[17] of the violent and iniquitous geographic relationalities forged by five centuries of 'Northern' nation- and empire-building, and compelled by her wager that patterning the impure and complicit intimacies created by this project might enable more equitable futures to be materialized. Byrd's cogent take on the 'Souths' persuades me all the more because her voice is not alone, but part of a powerfully resonant chorus of decolonial feminist interventions into the gendered and racialized geopolitics of colonial conquest, (neo)imperialism and globality, that focus on re-imagining intimacies as a catalyst for change.[18]

Without collapsing the differences of direction taken by this rich and varied work, there are two overarching insights on the intimate and intimacies that are of particular relevance to the argument I am pursuing in this volume. The first is that analysing intimacy cuts across conventionally-conceived binary boundaries between subjects and social worlds, demonstrating the entanglements of, for example, the personal with the political, affective experience with public culture, and/or bodily autonomy with economic exchange. The second is that mapping trans-scalar intimacies between times, spaces and bodies is an act of epistemic disobedience with deeply transformative potential. The imperial project of Western Universality was also anthropocentric; it relied upon creating distinct and discrete scales of knowing, that reinforced a One world tale of the progress of 'Man'. Exploring and articulating the patterned intimacies that constitute a global world of many (human) worlds, existing interdependently with/in a vibrant and more-than-human cosmos, entangles human history and agency with planetarity, and reconnects us, intimately, with our dependence upon, and responsibility to, the earth.

But what has this to do with transhemispheric histories and art? It is my contention that thinking transhemispherically provides the possibility of engaging productively with the differential, yet deeply interconnected, intimacies of geo/chrono/ bio power and agency at, and between, human/historical and species/planetary scales. Transhemispheric thinking is not binary; it defies the logic of centre/periphery, focusing instead on the intrinsic and long-standing entanglements between the hemispheric configurations of the West and the East, the Global North and South, the 'developed' and 'developing' worlds. The crossings and connections made by transhemispheric thinking are horizontal,[19] multidimensional and durational, complicating linear narratives of 'progress'[20] by mapping the complex and differential patterns of power that constitute the global present as the palimpsestic effect of multiple historical and epistemic imbrications of space, time, and bodies in the past.

My use of the term transhemispheric brings in two further shades of meaning that make it especially apt for the arguments being pursued over the pages of this volume. The first is its emphasis on ways of thinking about crossings and connections that bear greater resemblance to the shape and form of the planet as a watery sphere, than to the more conventional anthropocentric logic of bounded continents and countries. There is, throughout this volume, a turn to oceanic histories, archipelagic thinking, and the epistemic fluidity signalled by the terraqueous spaces of the shoreline and the shoals.[21] These ways of thinking create connections between

Introduction **5**

human and environmental/geologic understandings of space and time, as well as bringing non-human agencies into anthropocentric epistemes – a singular universal world yielding to the pluriverse.

The second valence of the term transhemispheric is less strictly geographical, but no less a material mapping, or figuration, of radical connections across and between corporeal and spatial boundaries of scale. In neurology, 'transhemispheric' signals the intrinsic interdependence between left and right brain thinking, a mutuality that is critically connected to cognition, creativity and subjectivity. For me, the transcorporeal resonances are compelling – our bodies, mutually material and cognitive, function as vital transhemispheric systems. They, in turn, are entangled within larger, multiple, but similarly transhemispheric systems that comprise many and diverse worlds. The trans-scalar, transcorporeal and transhemispheric imbrication of bio/geo/chrono that runs throughout this volume provokes thinking again about worlds and stories, and the responsibility we have for our 'loci of enunciation' with/in them.

Loci of Enunciation: Complicity, Response and Responsibility

Setting out their case for gender theory as southern theory, Pallavi Banerjee and Raewyn Connell point out that:

> Most gender theories and feminist research paradigms circulating around the world are developed in the global north. … The problem is not that these writings erase local histories or social context. What extraverted writings suffer from is a reductive epistemology, where the southern context is reduced to a case study, providing data that reaffirms or modifies a northern conceptualization.[22]

Banerjee and Connell are not alone in their critique. For decades, transnational feminists have demonstrated the complicity of White/liberal feminism with the epistemic violence of narrow Eurocentric thought, arguing that its privileged position in the academy creates both striking intellectual blindspots and an insidious form of 'pious universalism' premised upon 'White solipsism'.[23] These are ways of thinking that obscure their loci of enunciation and silence diverse knowledges, only to extravert a reductive episteme through a process of assimilative mirroring, a process memorably described in the sharply ironic observation of feminist philosopher Elizabeth V. Spelman, 'How lovely: the many turn out to be one, and the one that they are is me.'[24]

These critiques are more than a 'call-out' designed to chasten White/Western feminists, they are a *call* for radical and transformative change and they seek a *response*. The logic of call-and-response[25] builds an ethical relation between active speakers and listeners premised upon mutual *responsibility*, not only for what is said, but from where and to what ends. It is striking how many well-known critiques of White/liberal feminism were framed precisely as directed 'calls' – from Hazel Carby

6 Introduction

in 1982 hailing her readers with 'White woman listen!' to Audre Lorde, addressing the majority White graduating class at Oberlin College in 1989 with the words: 'I am a Black feminist lesbian warrior poet doing my work, and a piece of my work is asking you, how are you doing yours?'[26]

I find it impossible to hear these words and not respond. How might *my* work best heed these calls? I take the coordinates of my response from *listening*. And with Spelman's words still ringing, the first thing I hear is that it is not all about *me*. These calls for change are neither answered by individual 'confessions' of personal complicity with privilege, nor, worse yet, by engaging in a competitive 'oppression Olympics'.[27] Both strategies serve to reinforce the ego-centric individualism on which Western liberal epistemologies (and their legacy – the neoliberal academy) are built, by focusing attention on personal guilt and contrition, rather than structural change. In the worst-case scenarios, they default to essentializing identitarian positions that deflect criticism and refuse change by 'piously' arguing for solipsistic scholarship under the guise of 'authenticity'. But to these conceits, my response hears Lorde's clarion call: 'We have many different faces, and we do not have to become each other in order to work together.'[28] And there is work to be done.

As a White cis-gender feminist writing from the heart of the Anglosphere, my locus of enunciation inherits the privileged and complicitous coordinates of Euro- and anthropocentric universalism, but my work does not need to continue to foster the self-same silencing logic and extractive practices of epistemic violence that maintain its hold.[29] Following Spelman – '... how one starts, in thinking and in acting, has everything to do with where one might go'.[30] I begin by taking responsibility for my locus of enunciation, and setting my course to *listen* to, *learn* from,[31] and *walk* worlds into being with,[32] many and diverse earth others. In many ways, this volume is about making knowledges differently, and these methodological concerns are reiterated and amplified in each and across its chapters, as they unfold by storying pluriversal worlds, and worlding pluriversal stories, *with* art. But I want to make two points of praxis explicit here: the first concerns plurality and partnership in the production of knowledges, and the second, contingency.

Banerjee and Connell make the point that while extraverted epistemes may address diverse local contexts, they all too often mine them for case studies. This point is exceptionally pertinent to scholarship focused on global art, including feminist projects centred on art produced beyond the limits of the Global North.[33] While there has been an extraordinary response to the decolonizing call amongst feminist art historians, theorists, curators and critics throughout the world, much of this work still focuses on Western-centric feminist theory being extended/applied to case studies of Global Majority artists/works. This replicates the extractive and mastering logic of Eurocentric universalism and does very little, in practice, to challenge the kinds of histories and theories engendered by mainstream feminist art scholarship, *both* because it occludes and silences the theoretical/critical epistemes produced by 'non-Western' scholars, *and* because it continues to maintain the binary logic of theory over practice. I seek in this volume to unsettle both of these forms of epistemic mastery, by setting out alternative modes of storying and worlding *with* art, in the hope of creating multi-epistemic dialogues that take seriously

Introduction **7**

the knowledges produced by the visual, material and spatial registers of art, as well as the creative poetics of diverse practices of making 'theory'.

Working towards plural and multi-epistemic practices of knowing,[34] is not a matter of willing them into being through mastering omniscience. This volume seeks rather to engender its arguments alongside a multiplicity of other knowers and knowledge projects through connective and contingent practices of close reading, attentive looking, vulnerable listening and thick description. Its pages are replete with the echoes and traces of partner discourses, dialogues and encounters (including copious citation),[35] whilst remaining alert and attentive to the inevitable gaps and incommensurabilities that relational knowledge practices entail. I am convinced by those who argue that listening and attending are crucial to collaborative survival and flourishing in more-than-human worlds.[36] The plural, planetary and impure agencies of decolonial and ecocritical feminisms make it possible to materialize transnational feminisms and art's transhemispheric histories otherwise, so to embrace complexity, contingency and collaboration. This project will never be complete and my contribution to it here is most certainly not the last word. Charting this course will continue to require new competencies and those engaged in this work will continue to rethink the value of its diverse knowledge projects. But if this project does not produce positivist, market-driven, fast knowledge, designed to be consumed easily,[37] it is, nonetheless, an earnest response to the call to transform knowing and imagining limited by One world universality into the ecologies of knowledge through which a world of many worlds might yet flourish.

Ecologies and Genealogies: Worlds and Stories

This volume is built around the concepts of ecologies and genealogies – worlds and stories – and their critical entanglement with/in the knowledge projects that comprise transnational feminisms and art's transhemispheric histories. I return to each of these terms at greater length in later chapters, but offer here some brief propositions as coordinates to help readers chart the terrain that is this book. In delineating these coordinates, I remain mindful of the apposite words of feminist philosopher of science Donna Haraway: 'It matters what worlds world worlds. It matters what stories tell stories.'[38]

Ecologies suggest ways of knowing and flourishing in many and more than human worlds.

Ecologies, as used in this volume, is a term related to the environment, from anthropogenic environmental destruction, to social justice and ecological activisms. But it also exceeds that singular use, turning especially towards 'ecosophy'[39] and concepts such as ecological thinking[40] and the development of ecologies of knowledge.[41] These are multi-epistemic practices of thinking that call for imaginative transformation and material change. They are profoundly plural, trans-scalar and dynamic. They articulate the critical and complex entanglement between human and non-human agency in materializing vibrant worlds, and bring knowledge practices into close connection with imagination and an extended responsibility for the flourishing of many and diverse communities of 'kin'.[42]

8 Introduction

Worlds are plural, and the practices through which they are made, are never pure

This volume explores the implications of shifting from One world thinking, signalled by the parochial universalism of the European imperial project, towards thinking with and through a world of many worlds, or a pluriverse.[43] Not surprisingly, questions of *worlding* and *worldmaking* emerge as these discussions unfold and, whilst I am committed to arguing for art's potential[44] to participate in projects that seek to make worlds 'otherwise',[45] it is not the case that I envisage worldmaking as an easy or simple task. In using the terms worlds and worldmaking, I am cautious to retain both the plurality of *worlds* (not just *one* 'new' world), and the profundity of *unworlding*, a position that challenges the adequacy of the present 'world' as a space from which to make anything at all.[46] Worldmaking across these pages is always understood as contingent, complicit and resistant – every making is an *un-* and a *re-making* – but, as I also argue, it remains a practice that is nonetheless worth the trouble.[47]

Worlds point beyond the globe towards the planet and the cosmos

This volume addresses questions of globalization and globality, but it does not collapse the idea of the world into the much more limiting and anthropocentric framework of the globe. The globe is an abstraction for the managed space of human history and technology; it signifies mastery, possession and extraction. This is in sharp contrast to thinking the world through the scalar logic of the planet and the cosmos, a scale of thought that refuses the dominance of human agency, resists conceptualization through anthropocentric forms of history, and introduces 'alterity' and species-logic into the equation.[48] The planet is not possessed, but inhabited, by humans and we are most certainly not in control. Moreover, the cosmos is vibrant and pluriversal, and offers the potential to reconceive relational ethics and sociality as an embedded and more-than-human mode of cosmopolitanism.[49]

Genealogies matter to transnational feminisms

Genealogy has long been significant to transnational feminisms, for a number of different reasons.[50] Excavating histories and mining archives to materialize counter-narratives of the past that challenge contemporary gender norms, has been one of the central activities of feminist scholarship for generations.[51] Practices of genealogy facilitate non-linear and multidimensional engagements with the historical residues, traces and absences that constitute the past, making it possible to materialize a palimpsestic present, differently. Moreover, despite the familial overtones of the word, feminist genealogies do not demonstrate filial duty to heteropatriarchal conventions, nor do transnational feminisms adhere to mainstream White liberal discourses of the human.[52] Transnational feminisms and practices of genealogy have thus become fast and firm friends, creating the potential to story queer and kaleidoscopic kinships in more-than-human worlds.

Stories can be(come) theory

It is only a matter of convention whether attentive listeners hear a story *or/as* a theory. That solidus introduces a demarcation that hovers in the shoals, a space of resolute indeterminacy that has been occupied with exceptional creative and

Introduction **9**

intellectual power, particularly by Black, Indigenous, feminist/queer of colour scholars, artists, and activists from around the world.[53] Ranging from Indigenous claims that story is theory, to the 'insurgent poetic revolt' of Black feminisms, and ecofeminist ventures into the realm of speculative fiction and polyamorous sci-fi, stories and storying are increasingly demonstrating the potential to know differently and articulate otherwise, as part of a transformative, affective politics. This volume is indebted throughout to the stunning insights of story as theory, and engages with the provocative qualities of poetic fiction, feminist figuration[54] and critical fabulation[55] as means by which to story pluriversal worlds *with* art.[56]

Storying opens the future to possibility

Storying is active and relational; in the space between the telling and the listening, imaginative possibilities open. More to the point, storying is not merely 'reflective' of the world, but part of its making.[57] My argument throughout the pages of this volume is that 'feminism is a politics of the possible'.[58] Storying is intimately intertwined with how we come to know, imagine and inhabit a world in which many worlds fit, and that worlding, with and through art, is crucial to the knowledges we can story towards collaborative survival with more-than-human earth others. The structure of the volume is intrinsic to the materialization of its argument, to which I turn in the final passage of this introduction.

Storying Pluriversal Worlds, Worlding Pluriversal Stories

This is the second volume of a trilogy on transnational feminisms and art. The first volume opened the trilogy by examining how transnational feminist thought and activism had reconceived politics and the terrain of political engagement towards creative, non-identitarian, and transversal alignments, positing art as an active, contributing participant within a transversal politics, rather than a mute reflection or 'representation' of the political. Its central focus coalesced around the phrase 'knowing, imagining and inhabiting, earthwide and otherwise', a phrase that continues to resonate across the pages of this second volume. The third and final book in the trilogy will take up the challenge of articulating a transnational feminist aesthetics of the post- and more-than-human. The present volume, then, resides in the charged middle ground between politics and aesthetics – a nexus, a crossing, an inflection point, *neplanta*.[59] As a volume focused on materializing the knowledge projects that constitute decolonial, ecocritical feminisms and art's transhemispheric histories, that space could hardly be more appropriate.

This volume continues to understand art as active in processes of making meaning, and as a material-discursive assemblage that dynamically mobilizes affective and multi-sensory modes of knowing. In many instances across the pages of this volume, I use the grammatical configuration '*with* art', even where the sound/read of this might be slightly awkward, in preference to the default positions of writing *about* art, or suggesting that meanings are held *in* art. Exploring the knowledge projects through which transhemispheric histories and 'art' emerge in mutuality, focuses attention on partner discourses, ways in which *making* – making stories, making

10 Introduction

worlds, making meaning, making 'art' – is always plural and never exhausted. It also focuses critical attention on crossings and connections; in this volume, figured most consistently through the multidimensional prefix 'trans'.

First, of course, my argument takes 'transnationality' seriously as a way of making feminist knowledges, and in this I echo the crossings and connections made so eloquently by anthropologist Aihwa Ong, who described transnationality as: 'the *trans*versal, the *trans*actional, the *trans*lational and the *trans*gressive aspects of contemporary behaviour and imagination that are incited, enabled, and regulated by the changing logics of states and capitalism.'[60] As discussed earlier in this introduction, this volume adds to its focus on *trans*national feminisms, a turn to thinking *trans*hemispherically, by means of engaging with the complex, asymmetrical and intimate patterns of power and relation between spaces, times and bodies that constitute globality and point towards planetarity. But that is not all; in the first and final chapters, two figurations are developed: *transcanons* and *trans-scalar ecologies*. These again bring the crossings and connections between geo/chrono/bio logics, politics and power into sharp focus, while providing the potential to tell tales that are plural and planetary, but never pure. As the arguments unfold, these focal, 'trans-prefix' terms meet others to extend the work of moving across and between seemingly fixed categories of meaning, to open the radical potential of non-linear thinking in multi-epistemic worlds: translocal, transregional, transcultural, transdisciplinary, transversal, transtemporal, transcorporeal and transformative. It is important to point out that the emphasis on the prefix here is not an indication that the text occludes the contemporary stand-alone use of the term *trans* to signify non-binary, gender-fluid and diverse individuals and the productive and generative epistemic refusal of fixed binary gender/sex norms. Indeed, many of the arguments in the text unfold with and through just such explorations and are indebted to the groundbreaking work of trans artists, scholars and activists.

This introduction opened with a rhetorical question: *What will decolonial, ecocritical feminist art's histories do?* The structure of the volume hinges on its elliptical answer: Arguably, story pluriversal worlds, and world pluriversal stories, *with* art. The volume is comprised of four chapters organized in three parts. Part I embarks upon storying pluriversal worlds by means of an opening chapter that develops a model for writing decolonial, ecocritical feminist art's histories through an inventive, connective, transhemispheric material praxis I configure under the term *transcanons*. Transcanons are a plural heuristic for unraveling the extractive, silencing, One world logic of categorical purification that underpins canonical art history. The chapter focuses specifically on how practices of collecting and curating fine and decorative art, ethnographic objects, and scientific specimens, might be storied differently, with and through art, to create plural and transhemispheric tales of contact history. Part III sets out to world pluriversal stories, focusing on a chapter that explores *trans-scalar ecologies*, ways of bringing human-scale histories of globality into vital connection with planetary feminisms, ecological thinking and the arts. In this case, the worlding stories are materialized through encounters with messy rivers that create flourishing ecological communities in spaces otherwise blighted by

Introduction **11**

anthropogenic climate change. Transcanons and trans-scalar ecologies, as feminist figurations, are not exhausted by these particular engagements, but, rather, indicate the potential to converse with, and walk alongside, many more worlds in future.

Part II, set between these two non-linear stories and worlds, attends more particularly to method – what do we mean by stories and worlds if we set out to pursue the decolonial, race-critical, queer/trans and ecological thinking of transnational feminisms and art's transhemispheric histories? Two chapters sit within this section to explore the question of method – the first focused on poetics, and the second on pedagogies.[61] Critically, this charged middle, the second of three parts with its paired chapters, goes under the heading of Practice and Flourish, meant precisely to counter the logic of One world epistemic violence identified with such eloquence nearly half a century ago in the titular words: *Discipline and Punish*.[62] This is not a book designed to maintain Western-centric universals, anthropocentric monocultures of knowledge, disciplinary purity or the logic of interconnected violences – genocide, femicide, ecocide and epistemicide – that underpin them. Decolonial, ecocritical feminist art's histories are plural, planetary, but never pure. They are tales told in more-than-human worlds. But that is the very space of opportunity – the opportunity to work otherwise, with many and diverse others, to story pluriversal worlds and world pluriversal stories *with* art.

Notes

1 My use of 'material-discursive' here is deliberate and follows feminist philosopher and physicist Karen Barad's formulation of materialization as: '…an iteratively intra-active process whereby material-discursive bodies are sedimented out of the intra-action of multiple material-discursive apparatuses through which these phenomena (bodies) become intelligible.' NB: Barad's text was in dialogue with the work of Judith Butler. Barad, 'Getting Real: Technoscientific Practices and the Materialization of Reality', *Differences: A Journal of Feminist Cultural Studies* 10:2, 1998, pp. 87–128, p. 108 (italics in original).
2 Elizabeth Grosz, *Space, Time and Perversion: Essays on the Politics of Bodies*, London and New York: Routledge, 1995, p. 37.
3 Indeed, I am aware that some would argue that decolonizing art history is inherently impossible.
4 Walter D. Mignolo, 'Foreword: On Pluriversality and Multipolarity', in Bernd Reiter, ed. *Constructing the Pluriverse: The Geopolitics of Knowledge*, Durham, NC and London: Duke University Press, 2018, pp. ix–xvi, p. x.
5 These ideas are developed throughout the present volume, but suffice to say they are not 'new', even within my own work, *cf. Women Making Art: History, Subjectivity, Aesthetics*, London and NY: Routledge, 2003:

> The rise of the modern, bourgeois, Euro-centric individual and the progressive, linear historical models which accompanied his autonomy and power in the world, was the corollary of European colonial expansion and imperial domination, as well as the so-called scientific and industrial revolutions. The geopolitical dominance of the 'west' over its 'others', the rise of the modern nation-state and the systematic assimilation or destruction of difference are related phenomena. … Disentangling these complex strands… is difficult but possible.
>
> (p. 7)

12 Introduction

6 *Cf.* Marsha Meskimmon, *Transnational Feminisms, Transversal Politics and Art: Entanglements and Intersections*, London and New York: Routledge, 2020, p. 3.

7 These ideas have long been central to transnational feminisms, see: Inderpal Grewal and Caren Kaplan, eds, *Scattered Hegemonies: Postmodernity and Transnational Feminist Practices*, Minneapolis, MN and London: University of Minnesota Press, 1994; M. Jacqui Alexander, *Pedagogies of Crossing: Meditations on Feminism, Sexual Politics, Memory and the Sacred*, Durham, NC and London: Duke University Press, 2005; Cheryl Suzack, Shari M. Huhndorf, Jeanne Perreault and Jean Barman, eds, *Indigenous Women and Feminism: Politics, Activism, Culture*, Vancouver and Toronto: UBC Press, 2010; Madina Tlostanova, Suruchi Thapar-Björkert and Redi Koobak, 'Border Thinking and Disidentification: Postcolonial and Postsocialist Feminist Dialogues', *Feminist Theory* 17:2, 2016, pp. 211–28; Sylvanna M. Falcón, 'Transnational Feminism as a Paradigm for Decolonizing the Practice of Research', *Frontiers: A Journal of Women's Studies* 37:1, 2016, pp. 174–94; Julia Roth, 'Feminist Politics of Connectedness in the Americas', in L. Rehm, J. Kemner and O. Kaltmeier, eds, *Politics of Entanglement in the Americas: Connecting Transnational Flows and Local Perspectives*, InterAmerican Studies vol. 19, Trier: WVT, 2017, pp. 1–22.

8 *Cf.* Anneeth Kaur Hundle, Ioana Szeman and Joanna Pares Hoare, 'What Is the Transnational in Transnational Feminist Research?', *Feminist Review* 121 (Special Issue on Transnational Feminisms), 2019, pp. 3–8. Note, in addition, the tripartite focus of the excellent journal *Meridians: feminism, race, transnationalism*, https://www.dukeupress.edu/meridians.

9 I return to the thinking of both Sylvia Wynter and María Lugones throughout this volume, but suffice at this point to note two key texts: Wynter, 'Unsettling the Coloniality of Being/Power/Truth/Freedom: Towards the Human, after Man, Its Overrepresentation – An Argument', *CR: The New Centennial Review* 3:3, 2003, pp. 257–337; Lugones, 'Toward a Decolonial Feminism', *Hypatia* 25:4, Fall 2010, pp. 742–59.

10 *Cf.* Aren Z. Aizura, Trystan Cotton, Carsten Balzer/Carla LaGata, Marcia Ochoa and Salvador Vidal-Ortiz, 'Introduction', special issue: 'Decolonizing Transgender', *TSQ: Transgender Studies Quarterly* 1:3, August 2014, pp. 308–19; Jinthana Haritaworn, 'Decolonizing the Non/Human', in 'Dossier: Theorizing Queer Inhumanisms', *GLQ: A Journal of Lesbian and Gay Studies* 21:2–3, 2015, pp. 210–13; Susan Stryker, 'Transing the Queer (In)Human', also in 'Dossier: Theorizing Queer Inhumanisms', *GLQ*, pp. 227–30; Rosi Braidotti, 'A Theoretical Framework for the Critical Posthumanities', *Theory, Culture and Society*, special issue, 'Transversal Posthumanities', May 2018, pp. 1–31.

11 Shireen Roshanravan, 'Motivating Coalition: Women of Color and Epistemic Disobedience', *Hypatia* 29:1, Winter 2014, pp. 41–58, p. 53.

12 Gayatri Chakravorty Spivak, *Death of a Discipline*, New York: Columbia University Press, 2003 (on planetarity, see chapter 3, pp. 71–102).

13 Greta Gaard, *Critical Ecofeminism*, Lanham, MD: Lexington Books, 2017, p. xxiii.

14 *Cf.* Boaventura De Sousa Santos, *Epistemologies of the South: Justice against Epistemicide*, London and New York: Routledge, 2014.

15 These 'Southern' coordinates are traced again at greater length later in this volume, but suffice to say that the insightful work of Raewyn Connell, Nikos Papastergiadis and Pallavi Banerjee, in addition to Boaventura de Sousa Santos, has been especially significant to my thinking. See: Connell, *Southern Theory: The Global Dynamics of Knowledge in Social Science*, Cambridge: Polity, 2007, Papastergiadis, 'What is the South?', *Thesis 11* 100, February 2010, pp. 141–56, and Banerjee and Connell, 'Gender Theory as Southern Theory', in Barbara J. Risman, Carissa M. Froyum and William J. Scarborough, eds, *Handbook of the Sociology of Gender*, London, Berlin and New York: Springer, 2018, pp. 57–68.

16 Jodi A. Byrd, 'A Return to the South', *American Quarterly* 66:3, September 2014, pp. 609–20, p. 619.

17 Jodi A. Byrd, *The Transit of Empire: Indigenous Critiques of Colonialism*, Minneapolis and London: University of Minnesota Press, 2011.

Introduction **13**

18 *Cf.* Lauren Berlant, ed., *Intimacy*, Chicago, IL: University of Chicago Press, 2000; Ann Laura Stoler, *Carnal Knowledge and Imperial Power: Race and the Intimate in Colonial Rule*, Los Angeles and London: University of California Press, 2002; Geraldine Pratt and Victoria Rosner, *The Global and the Intimate: Feminism in Our Time*, New York: Columbia University Press, 2012; Lisa Lowe, *The Intimacies of Four Continents*, Durham, NC and London: Duke University Press, 2015; Hazel Carby, *Imperial Intimacies: A Tale of Two Islands*, London and New York: Verso, 2019.

19 'Horizontal' per Piotr Piotrowski, 'Toward a Horizontal History of the European Avant-Garde', in Sascha Bru and Peter Nicholls, eds, *European Avant-Garde and Modernism Studies*, Berlin: De Gruyter, 2009, pp. 49–58.

20 NB: some of these are implied by the temporal or positional hierarchies of the 'Western-centric' terminology itself – e.g. from 'developing' to 'developed', and 'First', Second' and 'Third' Worlds.

21 *Cf.* On oceanic histories: David Armitage, Alison Bashford and Sujit Sivasundaram, eds, *Oceanic Histories*, Cambridge: Cambridge University Press, 2018, and Sivasundaram's *Waves across the South: A New History of Revolution and Empire*, London: William Collins, 2020. On archipelagic thinking: Édouard Glissant, *Poetics of Relation* (1990), trans. Betsy Wing, Ann Arbor: University of Michigan Press, 1997; Epeli Hau'ofa, 'Our Sea of Islands', *The Contemporary Pacific* 6:1, Spring 1994, pp. 148–161; Elizabeth de Loughrey, *Routes and Roots: Navigating Caribbean and Pacific Islander Literatures*, Honolulu: University of Hawai'i Press, 2007; Tatiana Flores and Michelle A. Stephens, eds, *Relational Undercurrents: Contemporary Art of the Caribbean Archipelago*, Durham, NC and London: Duke University Press, 2017; Paul Carter, *Decolonizing Governance: Archipelagic Thinking*, London and New York: Routledge, 2019. On shoals, see: Tiffany Lethabo King, *The Black Shoals: Offshore Formations of Black and Native Studies*, Durham, NC and London: Duke University Press, 2019. 'Shoreline' echoes Audre Lorde, whose work is the focus of the second chapter of this book.

22 Banerjee and Connell, 'Gender Theory as Southern Theory', p. 58.

23 'Pious universalism' from Tiffany Lethabo King, 'New World Grammars: The "Unthought" Black Discourses of Conquest', in Tiffany Lethabo King, Jewell Navarro and Andrea Smith, eds, *Otherwise Worlds: Against Settler Colonialism and Anti-Blackness*, Durham, NC and London: Duke University Press, 2020, pp. 77–93, p. 87, and White solipsism from Adrienne Rich, 'Disloyal to Civilization: Feminism, Racism, Gynephobia', in *On Lies, Secrets, and Silence*. New York: W. W. Norton, 1979, pp. 275–309.

24 Elizabeth V. Spelman, *Inessential Woman: Problems of Exclusion in Feminist Thought*, Boston, MA: Beacon Press, 1988, p. 159. It is significant that María Lugones collaborated in 1983 with Spelman (María C. Lugones and Elizabeth V. Spelman, 'Have We Got a Theory for You! Feminist Theory, Cultural Imperialism and the Demand for "the Woman's Voice"', *Women's Studies International Forum* 6:6, 1983, pp. 573–81) and later lauded Spelman's address to White feminist privilege in 'On the Logic of Pluralist Feminism', in *Pilgrimages/Peregrinages: Theorizing Coalition Against Multiple Oppressions*, Lanham, MD, Boulder, CO, New York and Oxford: Rowman and Littlefield Publishers, 2003, pp. 69–76.

25 Patricia Hill Collins discussed the significance of call-and-response in *Black Feminist Thought: Knowledge, Consciousness and the Politics of Empowerment*, London and New York: Routledge, 1990; this formed part of the first chapter (on Post-Truth) of the first volume of this trilogy, *Transnational Feminisms, Transversal Politics and Art*.

26 Hazel Carby, 'White Woman Listen! Black Feminism and the Boundaries of Sisterhood', in Centre for Contemporary Cultural Studies, eds, *The Empire Strikes Back: Race and Racism in '70s Britain*, London and New York; Routledge, 1982, pp. 212–35; Audre Lorde, 'Commencement Address: Oberlin College' (1989), in Rudolph P. Byrd, Johnnetta Betsch Cole and Beverly Guy-Sheftall, eds, *I Am Your Sister: Collected and Unpublished Writings of Audre Lorde*, Oxford: Oxford University Press, 2009, p. 214.

27 Nira Yuval-Davis, 'Dialogical Epistemology: An Intersectional Resistance to the "Oppression Olympics"', *Gender and Society* 26:1 (Patricia Hill Collins Symposium

14 Introduction

Issue), February 2012, pp. 46–54. This also brings to mind conversations with my friend and colleague Dorothy Price on bell hooks and White women's tears.

28 Lorde, 'I Am Your Sister: Black Women Organizing across Sexualities', in *A Burst of Light and Other Essays* (1988), Long Island: Ixia Press edition, 2017, pp. 10–17 (p. 10).

29 And there is work to be done – I heed Tiffany Lethabo King:

> There is so much work that could be done on whiteness and how its coherence requires parasitism in order to survive. I think white folks have so much to do in that respect. … White people should pay attention to this genocidal process of disavowal in their own epistemic systems. That's a project.

From Frank Wilderson III and Tiffany Lethabo King, 'Staying Ready for Black Study: A Conversation', in King, et al., eds, *Otherwise Worlds*, pp. 52–73, pp. 56–7.

30 Spelman, *Inessential Woman*, x–xi.

31 Responding to Boaventura de Sousa Santos' comment that after five centuries of teaching the world, the Global North cannot seem to learn from it; *cf. Epistemologies of the South*, p. 19.

32 Responding to Ruana Kuokannen, *Reshaping the University: Responsibility, Indigenous Epistemes, and the Logic of the Gift*, Vancouver: University of British Columbia Press, 2007 and Juanita Sundberg, 'Decolonizing Posthumanist Geographies', *Cultural Geographies* 21:1, 2014, pp. 33–47.

33 Not to mention scholarship that eccentrically applies the label 'transnational' or 'global' only to those artists/works produced outside the Euro-North American axis, and principally by artists of colour.

34 Banerjee and Connell use the descriptor 'world-centred, solidarity-based' theory and note the idea of 'braided' theory developed by Chilla Bulbeck. *Cf.* 'Gender Theory as Southern Theory', p. 57.

35 On citation, I share the point made so eloquently by Astrida Niemanis in *Bodies of Water: Posthuman Feminist Phenomenology*, London and New York: Bloomsbury Academic, 2017:

> In a book that argues for the relationality necessary for living well with all measure of embodied others, it seems important to press the point that no one ever thinks alone, and that gratitude is worth deliberately, even meticulously, cultivating.

(p. 9)

36 See, particularly, Julietta Singh on 'vulnerable listening': *Unthinking Mastery: Dehumanism and Decolonial Entanglements*, Durham, NC and London: Duke University Press, 2018, pp. 138–40; and Greta Gaard on trans-species listening: *Critical Ecofeminism*, pp. xvi–xxii. I develop some of these ideas more in the first chapter of the first volume of this trilogy, *Transnational Feminisms, Transversal Politics and Art*.

37 Gearoid Millar outlines well the difficulties of working against the grain of conventional knowledges in his 'Trans-scalar Ethnographic Peace Research: Understanding the Invisible Drivers of Complex Conflict and Complex Peace', *Journal of Intervention and Statebuilding* 15:3, 2021, pp. 289–308; 294, 295, 302.

38 These evocative lines were themselves part of a dialogue – of Haraway's with anthropologist Marilyn Strathern – from the essay 'Tentacular Thinking: Anthropocene, Capitalocene, Chthulucene', in *Staying with the Trouble: Making Kin in the Chthulucene*, Durham, NC and London: Duke University Press, 2016, pp. 30–57, p. 35.

39 Felix Guattari, *The Three Ecologies* (1989), trans. Ian Pindair and Paul Sutton, New York and London: Continuum, 2008.

40 Lorraine Code, *Ecological Thinking: The Politics of Epistemic Location*, Oxford: Oxford University Press, 2006.

41 My mentor and friend, the late Martin L. Davies, was the first scholar to introduce me to the idea of the ecology of knowledge in his ground-breaking work on the moribund logic of conventional historical thought. See his 'Thinking Practice: On the Concept of an Ecology of Knowledge', in Martin L. Davies and Marsha Meskimmon, eds, *Breaking*

the Disciplines: Reconceptions in Knowledge, Art and Culture, London: I.B. Tauris, 2003, pp. 9–34. See also, De Sousa Santos, *Epistemologies of the South*.

42 Chris J. Cuomo, *Feminism and Ecological Communities: An Ethic of Flourishing*, London and New York: Routledge, 1998.

43 This language echoes the influence of the Zapatistas, and their dynamic invocation of Indigenous thought, across many platforms. *Cf.* https://globalsocialtheory.org/topics/zapatismo/.

44 I am not alone in this: Caroline Turner and Michelle Antoinette, eds, *Contemporary Asian Art and Exhibitions: Connectivities and World-making*, Canberra: ANU Press, 2014; Michelle Antoinette, *Reworlding Art History: Encounters with Contemporary Southeast Asian Art after 1990*, Amsterdam and New York: Rodopi, 2014.

45 Ashon Crawley, 'Stayed/Freedom/Hallelujah', in King, et al., eds, *Otherwise Worlds*, pp. 27–37.

46 *Cf.* Claire Colebrook, 'Creative, Speculative and World-Ending Ecologies', *Public* 32:63, September 2021, pp. 46–55.

47 Isabelle Stengers, 'The Challenge of Ontological Politics', in Marisol de la Cadena and Mario Blaser, eds, *A World of Many Worlds*, Durham, NC and London: Duke University Press, 2018, pp. 83–111; Lauren Berlant, interviewed by Hans Demeyer, 'Lauren Berlant on Intimacy as World-Making', in *Extra Extra* 16, Spring 2021, https://extraextramagazine.com/talk/lauren-berlant-on-intimacy-as-world-making/.

48 Spivak, *Death of a Discipline*.

49 Although I do not take up the question of cosmopolitanism directly in this volume, its potential as a 'posthuman' project is deeply provocative and related. Nikos Papastergiadis has begun to develop this thinking, arguing for 'a form of cosmopolitanism that embeds human rights with aesthetic, ecological and cosmic connectedness', 'Cosmos and Nomos: Cosmopolitanism in Art and Political Philosophy', *Journal of Aesthetics and Culture* 13:1, 2021, pp. 1–14, pp. 1–2.

50 Indicative, but by no means exhaustive: Grewal and Caplan, eds, *Scattered Hegemonies*; M. Jacqui Alexander and Chandra Talpade Mohanty, eds, *Feminist Genealogies, Colonial Legacies, Democratic Futures*, London and New York: Routledge, 1996; Ella Shohat, ed. *Talking Visions: Multicultural Feminism in a Transnational Age*, Cambridge: MIT Press, 1999.

51 Lowe, *The Intimacies of Four Continents*.

52 Brendan Hokowhitu, 'Monster: Post-Indigenous Studies', in Aileen Moreton-Robinson, ed., *Critical Indigenous Studies: Engagements in First World Locations*, Tucson: University of Arizona Press, 2016, pp. 83–101; Nasheli Jiménez del Val, 'A Conceptual Genealogy of "The Indigenous" in Mexican Visual Culture', in *Revista de Estudio Globales y Arte Contemporáneo* 7:1, 2020, pp. 55–90.

53 The second chapter of this volume takes these issues up at length, focusing on the work of Audre Lorde.

54 Rosi Braidotti, initially in dialogue with Donna Haraway's work and notions of feminist genealogy, developed the idea of the figuration with exceptional clarity in her *Nomadic Subjects: Embodiment and Sexual Difference in Contemporary Feminist Theory*, New York: Columbia University Press, 1994, pp. 275–80 and later in her Rosi Braidotti, *Metamorphoses: Towards a Materialist Theory of Becoming*, Cambridge: Polity, 2002, pp. 2–8. Figurations have been very important to my work: *Women Making Art*, pp. 117ff. and *Contemporary Art and the Cosmopolitan Imagination*, London and New York: Routledge, 2010, pp. 9–10.

55 Saidiya Hartman, 'Venus in Two Acts', *Small Axe* 26, June 2008, pp. 1–14.

56 On the implications of storytelling, creative writing and art's histories, see: Catherine Grant and Patricia Rubin, eds, 'Special Issue: Creative Writing and Art History', *Art History* 34:2, 2011; Alpesh Kantilal Patel and Yasmeen Siddiqui eds, *Storytellers of Art Histories: Living and Sustaining a Creative Life*, Bristol and Chicago, IL: Intellect, 2022.

57 Birgit M. Kaiser and Kathrin Thiele speak evocatively of this making as creating a temporal flux that runs counter to linear narrative: 'The future will first have to be

16 Introduction

remembered, *imagined.*' See their: 'What Is Species Memory? Or, Humanism, Memory and the Afterlives of "1492"', *Parallax* 23:4, 2019, pp. 403–15, p. 410. On powerful social fictions, responsibility and cultural transformation, see: Moira Gatens and Genevieve Lloyd, *Collective Imaginings: Spinoza Past and Present*, London and New York: Routledge,1999.

58 Transcultural art historian and feminist scholar Monica Juneja coined this great phrase in a lively conversation we enjoyed and it has stayed with me since – my thanks are offered here.

59 Inflection points and Gloria Anzaldúa's notion of *neplanta* will come to the fore in the first chapter; see her 'Border Arte: Nepantla, el Lugar de la Frontera' (1993), reprinted in *The Gloria Anzaldúa Reader* edited by Analouise Keating, Durham, NC and London: Duke University Press, 2009, pp. 176–86.

60 Aihwa Ong, *Flexible Citizenship: The Cultural Logics of Transnationality*, Durham, NC and London: Duke University Press, 1999, p. 4.

61 Although I had not seen it until the poetics and pedagogy work in the present volume was complete, I take heart from the remarkable resonance in the sub-title of the anthology edited by Joni Adamson, Mei Mei Evans and Rachel Stein, *The Environmental Justice Reader: Politics, Poetics and Pedagogy*, Tucson: University of Arizona Press, 2002.

62 Michel Foucault, *Discipline and Punish: The Birth of the Prison*, New York: Random House, 1977.

PART I

Storying Pluriversal Worlds

1

TRANSCANONS

Transhemispheric Stories for Pluriversal Worlds

Canons tell stories that make new worlds from old. Their stories have the potential to fashion a world of many worlds,[1] as yet unimagined, but too often they tell teleological tales of the ever-same, mask parochial perspectives as universal truths, and naturalize acts of epistemic violence designed to make all 'possible worlds' in the image of One. Engaging with canons and the histories of their formation is thus of critical significance in exploring the ecologies and genealogies, worlds and stories, that emerge at the nexus of transnational feminisms and the arts. This chapter proposes a shift from the canon to *transcanons*, to pluriversal and speculative practices of conversing with multi-epistemic worlds that connect the decolonizing agency of transnational feminisms with art's ability to materialize new and many worlds not just from, but with and through, the old and the One.

Canons are complex discursive structures that are embedded in, and made manifest through, institutions, knowledges and disciplines. Canons of art and literature have shaped both professional and passionate writing about the arts, have defined which works were (and are) read, shown, commissioned, collected, curated, archived and preserved for posterity, and, of course, have been integral to the formation of the disciplines of art history and literary criticism, and the teaching of the arts at all levels. Canons of art are structurally entangled with the art market, museums, galleries and archives, art schools, universities and academies, publishing houses and contested public spaces.

Canons and institutions are neither static nor neutral, but mobile and profoundly political. Following transnational feminist scholar Gayatri Spivak: 'There can be no general theory of canons. Canons are the condition of institutions and the effect of institutions. Canons secure institutions and institutions secure canons.'[2] Pointing to the mutual constitution of canons and institutions, Spivak demonstrates the partial, political and plural nature of both. The Canon thus recedes in favour of canons,

DOI: 10.4324/9780429507816-3

20 Storying Pluriversal Worlds

their value judgements subject to contest. Writing from within the US academy at the height of what came to be called there the 'culture wars',[3] Spivak's succinct take on canons and institutions interrogated the structural logic that continues to connect colonial histories of genocide and epistemic violence with anthropocentric, masculinist and heteronormative power politics under the rubric of universal systems of value.

Canons purport to be universal by occluding the material conditions of their own histories. In 1999, internationally renowned feminist art historian Griselda Pollock published a compelling study of the sexual politics underpinning the canon of European modernist art and its histories, entitled *Differencing the Canon: Feminist Desire and the Writing of Art's Histories.*[4] The canon of which Pollock wrote was, as she recognized, a modern European construct and not an eternal truth. The institutional practices that secured the canon's structural pre-eminence in the period, and for some time before and after, were both exclusive and normative.[5] Pollock's decisive feminist counter to the canon demonstrated its deeply-ingrained logic to be partial, patriarchal and parochial; the modernist canon naturalized the male European (and, by extension, White, middle-class, cisgender and heterosexual) subject in and as culture, rendering women, people of colour, queer and colonized subjects as nature/other. It did so through mythic stories, particularly about the makers of art, those subjects privileged to create sanctioned knowledges: 'The canon is held in place by the stories it tells about artists. The mythologies are not all the same.'[6]

The universality of 'the canon' renders it as timeless and placeless, yet applicable to all times and places. Near the start of *Differencing the Canon*, Pollock provided a concise and cogent definition of canons that emphasized their function rather than their content: 'Canons may be understood, therefore, as the retrospectively legitimating backbone of a cultural and political identity, a consolidated narrative of origin, conferring authority on the texts selected to naturalise this function.'[7] Her assessment of the power of Eurocentric canons to retrospectively legitimate cultural identity (privileging sameness over difference) through teleological narratives, which, simultaneously, naturalize their own authority, has proved both apposite and enduring.

In the decades that have passed since Spivak and Pollock levelled their feminist critiques against the role of Eurocentric literary and artistic canons in naturalizing nationalisms, colonial violence, and iniquitous racial and sexual power politics, the canonical legacy of 'the Western Universal'[8] has been reinforced by the economic and cultural success of the 'global' art market. The dominance of Eurocentric/ Western art history, a discipline strongly bound to Europe's colonial past, persists in the present through practices of cultural heritage and assimilative, 'global', canon formation.[9] Calls to decolonize art history[10] and its limited canon in favour of more inclusive, equitable and intellectually rich genealogies of the arts across the world are urgent and much needed, but the practices that can and will facilitate the emergence of these new stories and worlds must be capable of engaging with extant canons that are not easily 'unsettled'.[11]

What to do with canons is not a new question for feminist artists, historians, theorists and curators, nor for scholars pursuing decolonial and queer projects in the arts. Tellingly, their arguments commonly coincide around three core points, the first of which is that merely dispensing with, ignoring or displacing canons does not stop them from exerting institutional and intellectual force. The second point is that an 'additive' approach to canons (entering more and different names of artists and artworks into extant canonical inventories) serves only to reinforce their normative power. The third point of correspondence is that the construction of 'alternative' or 'counter' canons, however important, suffers from the inherent limitations of all 'separate but equal' strategies.[12] These points of confluence have led decolonial feminist artists and scholars to propose various strategies for rethinking canons and canon formation, ranging from psychoanalytic 'differencing' and deconstructive 'unsettling', to intersectional 'troubling' and transcultural 'creolizing'.[13] Assembling transhemispheric histories with/in a pluriversal (art)world, the concept of *transcanons* being elaborated here builds upon productive dialogues with each and all of these.

In her editorial introduction to the critical anthology, *Re-envisioning the Contemporary Art Canon: Perspectives in a Global World*, Ruth E. Iskin asked the pivotal question: 'Are pluriversal canons possible?' Going on to delineate the concept of pluriversal canons, Iskin argued incisively that:

> To conceive of a single pluriversal canon would be to mimic the idea of the Western canon and remain beholden to many of its limitations… pluriversal canons can only exist in the plural. They are distinct from the recent so-called global art canon insofar as the latter is still primarily composed of male, Western artists with more or less token additions of women artists, artists of color in the West and non-Western artists… With pluriversal canons, we are no longer limited by a paradigm based on the political fiction of a 'universal' canon.[14]

I am compelled by Iskin's call for pluriversal canons and also by her reasons for asking whether such canons are possible. As an art historian whose work has long engaged with the gender politics of 19th-century French art and graphic design, Iskin is positioned ideally to identify the limitations and political exclusions underpinning the structures of national canons and Eurocentric approaches to non-Western art. What I find especially exciting about her writing on pluriversal canons, however, is that she remains convinced that they are not merely utopian promises, but generative possibilities already beginning to emerge. And, in asking how this emergence might be fostered, Iskin is clear: through 'more experimentation – artistic, scholarly and curatorial…'[15]

What does 'more experimentation' look like, in practice? That is the central question driving this chapter and its exploration of transcanons as a form of artistic, scholarly and curatorial experimentation that facilitates the emergence of transnational feminist genealogies of art. If canons tell stories that make new worlds from

22 Storying Pluriversal Worlds

(and as) old, then transcanons tell stories that converse with, and walk alongside, pluriversal worlds.

In using the formulation 'conversing with and walking alongside', I am in dialogue with feminist geographer Juanita Sundberg, who has called for new forms of epistemic practice to decolonize the Eurocentric universalism underpinning the discipline of geography, and Western thought more generally.[16] As a scholar focused on feminist political ecology, environmental destruction, border control and militarization, Sundberg does not engage directly with Western canons of art, yet her thinking on the 'knowledge performances' that naturalize Eurocentric perspectives as universal, and her practical strategies for decolonizing posthumanist geographies, are remarkably resonant with the experimental practices of thinking-in-making that I want to suggest coalesce through transcanons.

Sundberg, herself in dialogue with Sami feminist scholar Ruana Kuokannen, argues that 'ongoing processes of ontological purification' close off possible worlds through a double performance of silence: silencing the situatedness of Eurocentric thought to naturalize it as universal, and silencing any other epistemes through the performance of 'sanctioned epistemic ignorance'.[17] This is the self-same silencing performance that supports the privilege of the Western canon of art. Sundberg's argument not only exposes these silencing performances; it also suggests methods by which to move beyond them. Critically examining her own naturalized epistemic practices, Sundberg demonstrates that a commitment to decolonizing universalizing worldviews requires both self-reflexive *unlearning* (of silence, of privilege, of the sanctioned ignorance of epistemic mastery[18]), and ethically engaged forms of *learning with and from* other 'epistemic worlds' – conversing with and walking alongside.

Sundberg's apt invocation of 'ongoing processes of ontological purification' resonates powerfully with the work of the late decolonial feminist philosopher and activist, María Lugones. Across a substantial body of critical and creative writing, Lugones argued that the self-same practices of ontological purification and categorical separation that secured Eurocentric epistemes as 'universal', justified global forms of social, economic and ecological injustice and violence as part of the European imperial project. Importantly, Lugones did not separate decolonial critique from race-critical, ecofeminist and queer perspectives on what she termed 'the coloniality of gender', but rather pointed to the connections between diverse forms of domination:

> ... the colonial imposition of gender cuts across questions of ecology, economics, government, relations with the spirit world, and knowledge, as well as across everyday practices that either habituate us to take care of the world or to destroy it.[19]

The logic of purity, for Lugones, was dangerous, divisive and destructive of anyone or anything defined as outside the normative, colonizing and *fictional* limits that centre White, male, cisgender subjectivity. The 'lover of purity', as Lugones called this normative subject, 'shuns impurity, ambiguity, multiplicity as they threaten his own fiction'.[20] Diverse bodies and dissonant voices must be expelled and silenced to protect the partial, parochial and patriarchal narrative through which the impoverished Western canon prevails as *the* story that makes new worlds in the image of the old and the One.

But if Lugones constructed a formidable, transnational feminist argument *against* purity, her work was not a discourse of negativity.[21] Time and again she reaffirmed the power of generosity, coalition, community and love, advocating *mestizaje* practices of 'hybrid imagination' and 'world traveling', as critical to transformational change.[22] As Lugones described it, 'world traveling' is a pluriversal practice of learning with and from, of walking alongside, others' many and different worlds. It is a practice that takes risks, unravels the certitude of mastery that characterizes universalizing knowledges in favour of fashioning 'a new feminist geopolitics of knowing and loving'.[23] Inhabiting the borderlands, crossings and points of inflection, 'world travelling' forges coalitions between and across difference, and stories multi-epistemic worlds.[24]

Transcanons tell impure and plural stories, fashioning feminist figurations and critical fabulations that connect, rather than separate, times, spaces and bodies. As practices of hybrid imagination, transcanons engender transnational feminist genealogies of art in/as transhemispheric contact zones, spaces of encounter, and mutually interdependent 'centres' and 'peripheries'. Transcanons do not, however, purport to be universal, they do not occlude their 'loci of enunciation',[25] they do not essentialize origin stories or teleologies, they do not set in place hierarchies of greatness between artists, nor do they make normative/purifying value judgements about the quality of art works. As transnational feminist practices of *learning with and from*, transcanons attend to the embodied, situated and affective dimensions of knowing and imagining, and the power of creative forms of close reading, attentive looking, vulnerable listening, and thick description to materialize connections between the 'global and the intimate'.[26] For 'lovers of purity', contact is crisis, but for subjects who inhabit the borderlands, contact provides the possibility of telling long-silenced stories and inhabiting an interdependent and pluriversal world, otherwise. In the dialogues that follow, critical transcanons are materialized through experimental forms of transnational, transcultural, transgender, transmedial, transdisciplinary and transgressive storying that bring forth new and many worlds, with and through the old, revealed as always, already, more than One.

Strange Encounters with Lady Lever: Turning Points and Moments of Crisis

Over the course of 2007–08, artists Phil Sayers and Rikke Lundgreen installed a series of exhibition-interventions in municipal museums, galleries and special collections in the north of England, under the collective title *Changing Places*.[27] This ambitious collaborative project took shape as a body of still and moving-image works in which Sayers and Lundgreen literally 'changed places' with the subjects

24 Storying Pluriversal Worlds

from a number of fine and decorative artworks held in the collections. Using their own bodies to re-imagine the visual economies of late Victorian paintings, sculptures and photographs, classical statuary, Chinese and European ceramics and decorative arts, *Changing Places* staged encounters with individual artworks and collections, such that both were opened to new and, potentially, very different readings. I want to suggest that these encounters might be understood as 'strange encounters', in dialogue with Sara Ahmed's invocation of the same phrase in her thinking on transnational feminisms, as:

> ... ways of encountering what is already encountered – in order to engender ways of being and acting in the world that open the possibility of the distant in the near, the unassimilable in the already assimilated, and the surprising in the ordinary.[28]

The strange encounters created by *Changing Places* revealed the inherent complexity of the objects and artworks with which Sayers and Lundgreen engaged. More strongly, *Changing Places* disrupted the seamless logic of the canonical narrative that underpinned the formation of an extensive network of provincial art museums, galleries and public collections at the height of the British Empire. It is to these strange encounters that we now turn.

While not a uniform group of institutions, the museums with which *Changing Places* conversed collectively demonstrate the entanglement of cultural, economic and social capital with the successful expansion of British industrial and imperial power on a grand scale.[29] Established through the Museum Acts of 1845 and 1850, municipal museums' collections were, in the main, initiated through bequests from local industrialists and frequently comprise significant, if idiosyncratic, bodies of material ranging from classical sculpture and artefects (more often Roman than Greek), to Chinese and European ceramics, glass, textiles, furniture, jewellery and fine metalwork. In the majority of cases, the most substantial collections of fine art are of British painting and sculpture from the 18th and 19th centuries, the work most avidly collected by newly-wealthy industrialists in the latter half of the 19th century.

The Lady Lever Art Gallery, which will be the focus here, exemplifies these collection patterns. The Gallery was opened in 1922 to house the fine and decorative art collection of William Hesketh Lever, first Viscount Leverhulme, the son of a Bolton grocer who amassed a fortune from manufacturing and selling domestic soap products. By 1884, Lever's company was global, sourcing raw materials and trading throughout the British Empire and beyond. A shrewd businessman, Lever's art collection was formed through a mixture of investment and interest.

In 1893, Lever purchased his first work of art, a painting by Edmund Leighton intended to be used in an advertising campaign for Sunlight Soap. Not surprisingly, many early acquisitions held by the Lady Lever Art Gallery are focused on bathing, but, as the cultural critic Anne McClintock has so cogently argued, the trade and advertising of soap in the Victorian period could be a dirty business.[30] In her work on the imbrication of gender, race and class in the expansion of the British Empire, McClintock demonstrated that commodity racism and imperial advertising went hand-in-hand. In particular, the languages of bodily purity associated with domestic cleaning products were swiftly transformed through the visual tropes of Victorian art and advertising into discourses of racial and sexual purity in a domesticated empire. In addition, art collecting and public philanthropy themselves played a part in social and cultural 'whitewashing' for newly-wealthy and upwardly-mobile industrialists such as Lever, whose access to the higher echelons of British society were facilitated through the acquisition of sufficient cultural capital to transcend his humble origins.

Sayers and Lundgreen produced and installed a number of works in the galleries of Lady Lever as part of *Changing Places*, including a video montage focused on a sculpture by Edward Onslow Ford, photographic interventions within the displays of Greek vases and Chinese porcelain, and two large-scale digital re-workings of paintings of languorous women in Roman baths by Lawrence Alma Tadema. Sayers and Lundgreen effected their strange encounters with the gendered and racialized dynamics of the collection many times over through a compelling combination of finely-tuned technical expertise and sharply-observed wit, but one instance is particularly resonant with the argument being pursued here.

In the Classical and 18th-century sculpture rotunda, a large-scale digital print by Sayers, *On Reflection* (2007), was set within a decorative arched niche (Figure 1.1).

FIGURE 1.1 Phil Sayers and Rikke Lundgreen, installation view, *Changing Places*, Liverpool, Lady Lever Art Gallery, 2007–08.
Image courtesy of the artists.

26 Storying Pluriversal Worlds

On Reflection epitomizes the transcanonical conversation that *Changing Places* opened through its experimental artistic and curatorial articulation of a trans view of the histories of British art collections as they intersected with race, gender and Empire. *On Reflection* converses with a first century Roman figure of Hermaphrodite, restored in the 18th century and on display in the same rotunda, bringing that figure into an imaginative re(-p)lay with the 1890 painting by Frederick Leighton, *The Bath of Psyche*, a textbook example of late Victorian neo-classicism from the Tate Gallery (Figures 1.2 and 1.3).[31]

FIGURE 1.2 *Statuette of Standing Hermaphrodite*, 70–100 AD.
Image courtesy of National Museums Liverpool.

In a very direct sense, *On Reflection* describes a turning point, a moment of transition and a locus of open undecidability. In the work, Sayers literally 'changes places' with the youthful, White female figure of Psyche, ushering in a complex relay of visual turning points.[32] The pose of Leighton's Psyche derives from the Roman sculpture known as the Venus Callipyge, who lifts her robes to look down upon her 'beautiful buttocks',[33] and in so doing, invites others to do the same. Looking is never neutral. The allegorical story of Cupid and Psyche encoded vision within a sexed economy that rendered woman as a passive object to be viewed by an active masculine, heteronormative subject. As told by Apuleius, the blissful, but forbidden, love affair between Cupid and Psyche culminated in a moment of crisis,

FIGURE 1.3 Frederick Leighton, *The Bath of Psyche*, 1890.
Image courtesy of Tate Gallery, London.

when, rejecting her prescribed role within a heteronormative visual economy, Psyche lifted her lamp to look at the body of her sleeping lover in the darkness. Changing places with Psyche in *On Reflection*, Sayers knowingly enacted another visual point of inflection, turning their gaze outward to catch the viewer's eye, rather than inward to invite a voyeuristic look.

There is much at stake in this disobedient sexual politics of vision. In a compelling analysis of *Changing Places* that drew together psychoanalysis, performativity and postcolonial discourses around difference, feminist art historian Dorothy Price made the investment clear:

> Their re-enactment of visual sites of beauty and desire problematise the normative heterosexual gender politics of looking and being looked at that is at stake in the staging of the visible within the realm of the phallocentric Symbolic field. To rupture this field is to open the possibility for other kinds of sexual identities and gender identifications to be in play.[34]

As the relays of looking increase, the imaged body becomes less stable, and the possibility that alternative sexual and gender identifications will emerge, becomes

28 Storying Pluriversal Worlds

more probable. These alternatives emerge not only through the work's obvious disruption of the voyeuristic Victorian fantasy of watching nubile young women bathe, unseen, but through the placement of a very different and far less determinate body into the centre of the image. Sayers' work is not a direct copy from Leighton's; where Leighton indicates a reflecting pool at Psyche's feet that acts as a mirror, Sayers creates an *inflection*, a critical turning point, at the centre of the work, inverting the lower imaged body such that it does not simply reflect the upper. In the upper half of the work, Sayers' middle-aged body, posed as Psyche, with prosthetic breasts, long coiffured hair and soft white drapery, looks out to viewers and gestures in the feminine; at the inverted visual fold, the figure's gaze averts, and the pose turns frontal to 'reveal' male genitalia. Psyche meets Hermaphrodite at the inflection point that performs gender/sex as endless, (re)iterative becoming, focused unflinchingly on the body of Sayers, a White British artist who identifies across gender fluid positions as trans (Figure 1.4).

In their closely-argued text on recent and contemporary trans artists and self-imaging, Eliza Steinbock noted the significance of the figure of Hermaphrodite, and of aesthetic strategies that destabilize corporeal boundaries, to intersex and trans practitioners seeking evidence of what they call 'transcestors', historical precedents for queer and trans artists and art making.[35] Steinbock argued that, for trans artists, imaging the body frequently falters around the problematic imperative to display or reveal the 'truth' of the trans subject, but the figure of Hermaphrodite offers a productive refusal of such reductive binary truths, suggesting, instead, a perpetual state of transition and becoming, or, in the terms being developed here, a means by which to figure trans subjectivity as/at the point of inflection.

In the *Changing Places* catalogue, Lindsay Smith also noted the significance of Hermaphrodite to late-Victorian literature and visual cultures.[36] Like Steinbock, Smith understands Hermaphrodite as a cipher for 'irresolution, of not simply settling for one thing or the other', but in addition, as a scholar of Victorian culture and photography, Smith connected the visual strategies of *Changing Places* with the histories of the collections with which the project conversed:

> They [Sayers and Lundgreen] are using the performance of gendered identities, whether anonymous or identifiable, to make original interventions in the history of art, and of collecting and connoisseurship. Sayers and Lundgreen remind us that the way we remember, cease to remember and display English collections is rooted in concepts of the body. But they signal for us too that those myriad bodily forms are forever past, passing and to come.[37]

Smith's brief comments are apt; *Changing Places* was more than a series of discrete *tableaux vivant* in which Sayers and Lundgreen reversed spectatorial expectations by donning costumes and performing drag versions of past works of art. Their engagements with past works are complex aesthetic reconfigurations that play with and against the 'originals' through carefully executed exchanges of bodies, objects, images, spaces, visual technologies and compositional norms. Their

FIGURE 1.4 Phil Sayers, *On Reflection*, 2007.
Image courtesy of the artist.

30 Storying Pluriversal Worlds

work materialized a transgender and *transcorporeal* encounter with the art of the past, where transcorporeality is understood as an entangled 'contact zone' between emergent, and radically open bodies,[38] that variously compose, decompose and recompose the material legacies of the past with/in the present. The artists' trans performances, to paraphrase Elizabeth Freeman on queer histories' challenge to what she calls 'chrononormativity', are practices of 'temporal drag', allegorical encounters designed to 'reincarnate the lost, nondominant past in the present and to pass it on with a difference'.[39]

The temporal drag effected by siting *On Reflection* within the sculpture rotunda at Lady Lever is precise. The work disrupts the normative temporal flow of the displayed collection, a flow that is complicit with a canonical narrative connecting Roman imperial sculpture to the art of the ascendant British Empire vis-à-vis a masculine, heteronormative politics of vision. Reading the collection through the dissonant bodies in the works of Sayers and Lundgreen creates a transcanonical flux that reincarnates nondominant pasts to complicate normative gender identifications in the present. The notion of 'nondominant pasts' is critical here; *Changing Places* neither simply 'reversed' its sources (replacing 'female' with 'male' but maintaining an underlying heteronormative binary logic), nor created a 'new' (read 'original, authentic') corporeality, with which to replace the old. Rather, *Changing Places* 'stayed with the trouble',[40] animating the hybrid mutabilities of the bodies (and the collection) that were always, already present, through *trans*canonical conversations – critical fabulations effected by transgender, transcorporeal and transformative transpositions.

That High Victorian nudes, and the retrospective construction of a 'classical tradition' by 18th- and 19th-century British collectors, were riven by complex and contradictory messages about race, class, sex, sexuality and gender norms, would not be news to scholars of the period.[41] It is also visually apparent. Take, for example, Lady Lever's Hermaphrodite, with which *On Reflection* conversed. The 18th-century restoration is not seamless; the joins where the new head, arms and legs were connected to the fragmentary torso of the Roman work are clearly visible. Nor is the restoration conceptually seamless; the pose is stilted, the head is generic and the resultant figure fails to obscure the fact the stylistic tropes for imaging gender/sex in two very different times and places did not coincide. While this may seem, from a contemporary standpoint, to produce a wonderfully apt hybridity for the figure of Hermaphrodite, it was not the object of the restoration.

Changing Places revealed neither the truth of the body, nor the stability of canonical stories; rather, it pointed to hybrid bodies, gendered tropes of viewing and interwoven temporalities that were always already present, if silenced, by the public performance of normative histories in Victorian museums and galleries. This horizontal and transcorporeal genealogy unbinds time from history. Returning briefly to Freeman:

> [U]nbinding time and/from history means recognizing how erotic relations and the bodily acts that sustain them gum up the works of the normative

structures we call family and nation, gender, race, class and sexual identity, by changing tempos, by remixing memory and desire, by recapturing excess.[42]

Changing Places changed tempos, remixed memory and desire, and recaptured excess, to facilitate rich dialogues with public canons of art established at a critical turning point in the histories of family, nation, gender, race, class and sexual identity in Britain. But critical turning points can also provoke moments of crisis, and the Western canon, secured by ongoing processes of ontological purification, is not easily unsettled.

When *Changing Places* was shown at Lady Lever in 2007, the site of crisis was the Gallery's Visitors' Book. Amongst the comments were a number of unusually virulent responses to the project, anonymously voiced in malicious, and telling, language. Some of the comments centred on the status of the works from *Changing Places*, refusing to acknowledge them, without qualification, as art:

> Beautiful – an inspiration. Only blot was PHIL SAYERS revolting images – typical of modern 'Art'
> <u>Wonderful</u> apart from the awful transvestite pornography

Many comments focused on distinguishing the 'beautiful', 'wonderful' and 'inspiring' permanent collection from the 'awful' or 'degrading' images from *Changing Places*:

> Putting on degrading photos such as this does no justice to other great works – so sad!
> I have visited this gallery many times and am distraught to find modern photos of transvestites + homosexuals as part of such a unique + inspiring collection! The gallery is devalued.

Significantly, a proportion of the commentary suggested moral corruption:

> Shame about the perverse transsexual photography. Homo.
> Did not like the 'transvestite art' and asked how anyone could explain it to their children.
> Inappropriate picture of transgender old man/woman Get it down/think of the kids.

While it might be tempting to ignore these crude transphobic responses to contemporary art as a proverbial storm in a teacup, I want to take them seriously, as the artists themselves did a year later through their responses to the commentary in the installation and catalogue for *Changing Places* at Leeds.[43] To begin to unravel the moment of crisis provoked in the Visitors' Book, it is useful to turn back to the Western canon.

In 2001, Nigerian-born postcolonial art historian and curator Olu Oguibe published a short article in *Art Journal* entitled 'Whiteness and "The Canon"'.[44] The

32 Storying Pluriversal Worlds

article is framed as an answer to a question posed by a student, 'Selina', who is concerned about over-exposure to the 'Western canon'. In his response, Oguibe is clear that exposure to knowledge, even of a limited 'Western canon', is to be preferred over the egregious state that is ignorance. However, he makes a final, salient point about the dangers of the canon that are resonant here:

> Yet, like the sand dune of whiteness, the 'canon' is but a limited enclave in a vast universe. Those who bury their heads miss the immense vista that is the world... Selina, there is merit to your concern, for that which is impoverished may prevail and self-perpetuate only through a system of violence – not necessarily of the visible, physical kind, but a stealthy and more dangerous violence whose target is the mind.[45]

The comments in the Visitors' Book at Lady Lever precisely perform this more dangerous violence in seeking to protect an impoverished 'canon' from the dialogues opened by *Changing Places*. It is a stealthy violence, premised upon a tacit knowledge that is both partial and fictive. The 'transvestites + homosexuals' are already in the 'unique + inspiring collection', along with some of the 19th century's most explicitly erotic painting and sculpture. Take the sculpture rotundas; the centrepiece of the Classical and 18th century rotunda is the Roman figure of Antinous, the young friend and lover of Hadrian, appropriately restored as Ganymede, and the focal point of the 19th-century rotunda is Desiré Maurice Ferrary's *Salambo* (1899). Depicting the moment that Salambo prepares to yield her virginity to the 'barbarian' Matho to save the people of Carthage, Ferrary's work is still known for its 'blatant emphasis upon raw sexuality' and the racialized overtones of the scene are rendered clearly by the contrast between the white marble body of Salambo and the dark bronze used for the figure of Matho.[46]

The Visitors' Book comments thus beg the question – what were these viewers *seeing* when they looked at the collection? I want to suggest that they saw the collection through the universalizing Eurocentric lens of the Western canon, where Art (with a capital A) is ontologically purified as a 'unique and inspiring' category of objects and images that secure cultural capital as privileged knowledge of the world and certitude of one's significant place within it. I want to argue further that *Changing Places* provoked a crisis for these viewers by demonstrating that the 'canon' that they had normalized is not a universal norm, but rather, per Oguibe, a limited enclave in a vast universe. With their heads buried in the sand and threatened by a glimpse of other epistemic worlds, the visitors called for the silencing performance of purity – get rid of these dissonant and contaminating bodies!

And this returns us to Lugones' powerful point that in the coloniality of gender, bodies do matter. More than once, Lugones invoked trans and queer subjects as a primary counter to male, heteronormative colonizing knowledge: 'Hermaphrodites, sodomites, viragos and the colonized were all understood to be aberrations of male perfection.'[47] The display of Lever's collection at Lady Lever Art Gallery centred the mastering gaze of the male industrialist to create a fictive universal narrative of heteronormative, Eurocentric power. Its 'canon', implicitly sanctioned as 'pure' as well as powerful, was profoundly challenged by the trans bodies and hybrid imagination introduced into the space by *Changing Places*. These bodies, conversing with and walking alongside the fragile and impoverished Western Universal, created a crisis for viewers in 2007 because the tensions between bodies, times and spaces – the epistemic power of bio/chrono/geo politics – that were created by European imperialism have yet to be resolved. But if the 'canon', and the coloniality of gender, are embedded in the histories, theories, institutions and practices of art, so too are critical points of inflection where decolonizing feminist transcanons can emerge to begin the work of walking other worlds into being.

Connections and Contaminations: Fine and Decorative Intimacies

Sayers and Lundgreen did not limit their transcanonical conversations with Lady Lever Art Gallery to the collections of classical sculpture and European fine art, but engaged in similarly provocative transpositions with work from the Gallery's extensive holding of decorative art, including the collection of Chinese porcelain and enamels.[48] In two digital photographs, Sayers 'changed places' with the central female figures from a pair of 18th-century Chinese painted mirrors, depicting women in domestic interiors. Made for a European market, the mirrors' painted scenes, framed by opened curtains, implied privileged visual access to female bodies in private spaces from far distant lands.

In *Captive* and *Captivated* (both 2007), Sayers' transgender transpositions troubled the voyeuristic display of Chinese women as a seamless exotic fantasy for a European consumer, by emphasizing the structured fiction of the images, and their studied performance of racial and sexual difference as a desirable commodity.[49] There is no authentic body revealed by the photographic encounters. Rather, the works' elaborate props and prostheses – costumes, make-up, ornaments, swathes of drapery, carefully-staged poses – rendered visible the transcultural visual economy that underpinned the coloniality of gender at the height of European imperial engagements with Asia (Figure 1.5).

Based on Italian miniatures popular in China from the 1680s, the mirrors in the collection at Lady Lever were part of a lucrative circular trade between China and Europe that began, at latest, during the 13th century, and flourished until the middle of the 19th. Chinese porcelain and decorative art, along with silks, fine metalwork and tea, were at the centre of this trade and, during the Victorian period, a number of newly-wealthy industrialists formed substantial collections of Chinese decorative arts.

The majority of Lever's Chinese collection was acquired in bulk on the death of James Orrock, an artist and dealer who had advised Lever on his collection over many years. Orrock was a 'self-made man' and it is significant that large parts of Lever's collection in both fine and decorative art were purchased in similar circumstances, including Lever's other major collection of ceramics, the Wedgwood jasperware purchased from Dudley Coutts Marjoribanks, First Earl Tweedmouth.

Marjoribanks was a Scottish businessman, whose father had been a senior partner in Coutts Bank. It was through the connections between the bank and the Darwin

FIGURE 1.5 Phil Sayers, *Captivated*, 2007.
Image courtesy of the artist.

family, that Marjoribanks had come to own the jasperware. As is well known, the Darwin and Wedgwood families had strong ties and wide influence. Friends and members of the Lunar Society of Birmingham, Erasmus Darwin and Josiah Wedgwood, were central to the 'Midlands Enlightenment', a body of 18th-century political, economic and scientific thought pivotal to the expansion of British industrial power in tandem with its Empire.

Marjoribanks' own fortune was likewise amassed through a combination of industry and Empire, as the owner of the Meux Brewery and as a Director of the British East India Company from 1853 to 1894. He was also a Liberal MP, as was his son, the Second Earl Tweedmouth, and both were key supporters of William Ewart Gladstone. It was their shared support of Gladstone, liberalism, free trade, industry, social reform and self-improvement, that connected the Marjoribanks with Lever, and it was wholly in keeping with their interests, particularly with Lever's passion for Samuel Smiles' book *Self-Help* (1859), that they would invest in Wedgwood pottery.

In the year that *Self-Help* was published, Britain and France were embroiled in what has come to be called the Second Opium War (1856–60), an ugly act of military conquest supporting the influx of British-Indian opium into China to destabilize the trading success of the Chinese and their products in Europe. In 1857,

British forces en route to China were diverted to India to violently quash the Indian Rebellion (1857–58). The lynch-pin between these two infamous military acts was the British East India Company, whose access to Indian and Chinese markets and labour was making liberal industrialists in Britain very wealthy. By 1860, the Chinese had been defeated; their reparations included the regulation by Britain of the movement of Asian labourers, a movement that would ultimately support the colonizing expansion of the United States to its Pacific coastline along with the continued decimation of its Indigenous population.[50] Gladstone and his Liberal supporters were strongly opposed to the Opium Wars, yet Marjoribanks continued to profit as a Director of the East India company whilst both India and China were 'subdued'.

The Wedgwood pottery and the Chinese porcelain in the Lady Lever Art Gallery are thus connected by a thread that entangles the Victorian fashion for decorative arts within a knotty paradox that weaves European liberalism, reform and free trade with scientific exploration, art, industry and imperial violence on a world scale.[51] These entanglements are occluded by the silencing performance of the Western canon. *Captive* and *Captivated*, by contrast, materialize a transcanonical tale of possession[52] that refuses to obscure the cross-contaminations between the fine and decorative arts, industry and commerce, narratives of human progress and colonial genocide, imaged through the looking glass – the viewer seeing only himself on one side and the world as his rightful possession, on the other.

The Chinese collection amassed by Orrocks was a financial investment. The Wedgwood jasperware followed a circuitous path from the Darwin family to the Lady Lever Art Gallery via Coutts Bank. That banking and finance underpinned colonial expansion, trade, industry, the arts and scientific exploration, is no surprise. Nor should it be surprising that the founder of the Coutts Bank acquired in 1793 an exceptional work of Chinese decorative art in the form of a hand-painted panoramic wallpaper, brought back by Earl Macartney following one of Britain's earliest ambassadorial trade missions to China. From his office in London, Coutts and his clients could view the world, a possession rendered visible through their distant contemplation and control.

Spiral Time and Tide: On the Spherical Infections of Transcanons

In 2017, the artist Lisa Reihana represented Aotearoa New Zealand at the Venice Biennale with *Emissaries*, an exhibition that called into question the construction of a singular narrative of the Pacific world, told from a Eurocentric point of view. Sited in the Arsenale, the former hub of Venetian naval power, and part of Europe's earliest and most enduring 'international' art fair, Reihana's show opened a critical conversation between the many worlds that collided as people from the Pacific encountered Europeans coming to their shores as explorers, traders, colonizers and, in the worst cases, emissaries of death. The centrepiece of the show was Reihana's panoramic video installation *In Pursuit of Venus [infected]* (*iPOV[i]*, 2015–17), a work of exceptional aesthetic and technical sophistication, developed over the course of a decade's experimental practice. Significantly, Reihana's panorama was in direct conversation with an earlier representation of European encounters with the Indigenous inhabitants of the Pacific, the French panoramic wallpaper *Les Sauvages de la Mer Pacifique*, designed by Jean-Gabriel Charvet for the firm of Joseph Dufour et Cie, c.1805.[53]

During the course of the 19th century, panoramic wallpapers produced in France and Britain overtook the Chinese trade in both the European and burgeoning US markets, and instituted a very different point of view for their bourgeois consumers. The Chinese wallpapers presented scenes of China to a European market; by contrast, the European panoramas focused mainly on non-European scenes re-presented through a controlling optic, a lens ground by colonial encounter and possession.

Charvet's designs for the wallpaper were themselves based largely on the engraved *Tableau of the Discoveries of Captain Cook and La Pérouse* (1798–99) by Jacques Grasset de Saint-Saveur, one of a number of engravings of 'peoples of the world' that Saint-Saveur produced between 1784 and 1806 recounting the travels of 18th-century European explorers in Asia, the Americas and Oceania (Figure 1.6)[54]. It has not gone unnoticed that Saint-Saveur's tableaux depicted the people encountered by James Cook and Jean-François de Galaup, comte de La Pérouse using classical tropes, and that these likewise pervade the panoramic wallpaper designs of Charvet. Visually, *Les Sauvages* is both spectacular and dissonant; hung on the walls of a European or federal-style US drawing room, the paper surrounded its viewers with an Arcadian vista,[55] born of colonial exploration, mediated by the classicizing tropes of the Western canon, and displayed for the visual pleasure of the bourgeois consumer. The point of view is all-seeing, yet unseen; from this singular and universal vantage point, a story is told of many worlds rendered in and as the image of One.

FIGURE 1.6 *Les Sauvages de la Mer Pacifique* designed by Jean-Gabriel Charvet for the firm of Joseph Dufour et Cie, c.1805.

Image courtesy of the National Gallery of Australia, Canberra.

Significantly, it was the spectacular visual dissonance created by the wallpaper that provided the initial impetus for *iPOV[i]*. As Reihana tells the tale, she first encountered *Les Sauvages* in 2005 on display at the National Gallery of Australia and was struck both by its ambitious format – printed using more than 1,000 blocks, then hand-painted, a full set of 20 panels measures over 10 metres across, with a drop of 2.5 metres – and by the classicizing depiction of Pacific subjects in ways that bore little resemblance to her experience either of Pasifika friends and colleagues, or of her own Māori heritage.[56] Reihana's panoramic video installation tells its tale of European contact with Oceania from a very different point of view, one that emphasizes the mutuality and complexity of transcultural exchange and implicates contemporary viewers within the frame of the histories it materializes.[57] Critically acclaimed, *In Pursuit of Venus [infected]* has already generated an excellent scholarly literature, particularly focused upon the work's ability to story European/Pacific contact histories from multiple perspectives, its address to gender and sexual politics, its deployment of Indigenous Pacific conventions of time and space, and its compelling visual and sonic qualities, rendered through the technical feat of its realization as a seamless, 64-minute moving-image loop, deploying 1,500 individual digital layers and 7.1 surround sound, to facilitate its projection at more than 20 metres across and 2.5 metres high.[58]

It is not my intention here merely to replicate, in condensed format, the arguments that others have made so eloquently about Reihana's video installation, but, rather, to converse with the work, its historical and aesthetic contexts, and the critical commentary it has generated, in order to explore how its reconceptions of space, bodies and time contribute to transnational feminist genealogies of art that move beyond the hemispheric limits inscribed by both the epistemic hegemony of the North and the fictive universals of the West. If *Les Sauvages* represented other worlds through the assimilative lens of the Eurocentric canon, *iPOV[i]* articulates emergent transcanons, material forms of conversing with and walking alongside contact histories, to story plural and transhemispheric worlds otherwise. These figurations require careful navigation and strategic reorientation, processes we shall start by thinking through the dynamic relations between land, sea and sky.

In Pursuit of Venus [infected] brings the Arcadian viewpoint of *Les Sauvages* into dialogue with accounts of Cook's three Pacific expeditions (1768–71, 1772–75, 1776–80) derived from both European and Pacific sources. The work takes its main title from the primary purpose of Cook's first Pacific voyage, to chart the Transit of Venus, a celestial event whose occurrence in 'pairs of pairs' happens only every 243 years, and whose accurate recording in 1769 was critical both to the development of European science, navigation and exploration, and to the extension of European imperial interests throughout the Pacific.[59] Significantly, the spectatorial position in *iPOV[i]* is from the land, looking across the shore, to the sea, from whence the emissaries of the old world would come to meet the new. The work thus radically disperses a Eurocentric vantage point from the outset and this continues in other, equally critical, ways.

Before the moment of first contact depicted in *iPOV[i]*, we see the Whitby ship, *Endeavour*, on the horizon. However, *before* we see the British vessel, and again three times following the arrival of its emissaries, we see Pacific canoes navigating the waters with ease. And these are specific and different vessels hailing from a wide geographical range – Māori, Tahitian, Hawaiian and Nootka Sound canoes. Pacific sea-faring technologies were exceptionally advanced centuries before the arrival of Europeans, and Pacific peoples were well-connected and networked across Oceania, which was conceived by them more as a fluid archipelago than a vast space peppered by isolated islands.[60] In *iPOV[i]*, Europeans do not bring navigational knowledge to the Pacific; the Ra'iatean navigator and astronomer Tupaia, who accompanied Cook on his first journey, is included in the work on a par with Cook and the British naturalist Joseph Banks, and the Tahitians who host Cook and his men during the sighting of Venus, take an active interest in the European optical technology and share their knowledge of navigation and the Southern skies (Figure 1.7).

FIGURE 1.7 Lisa Reihana, *In Pursuit of Venus [infected]*, 2015–17. Ultra HD video, colour, 7.1 sound, 64 min, Auckland Art Gallery.
Photo: Jennifer French. Image courtesy of the artist.

Contrary to the title of Charvet's wallpaper design, in Reihana's work Cook and his fellow travellers do not meet an homogenized group of 'savages' on 'desert islands',[61] but rather, as Lugones wrote of earlier European colonizers' contact with Indigenous people in what came to be called the Americas, they meet 'complex cultural, political, economic, and religious beings: selves in complex relations to the cosmos, to other selves, to generation, to the earth…'[62] Reihana's panorama introduces just such selves, enacting complex relations to other selves and the cosmos, through some 70 vignettes, many of which were co-authored and enacted by Pacific Island, Māori and Aboriginal Australian performers invited by Reihana to collaborate on the work.[63] The vignettes consistently portray the complicated and mutual agency of Pacific/European contact, characterized by a mixture of wonder, generosity, desire, intimacy, understanding, misapprehension, shock, betrayal, anger and violence.

From the vantage point of the foreshore, *In Pursuit of Venus [infected]* reimagines and stories colonial histories from the South. In arguing this, I am using 'South' less as a fixed point on the map and more as a locus from which to rethink the centre–periphery models of space that privilege the partial, but powerful, viewpoint of the Global North articulated through the Western canon. In doing this, my thinking aligns with what Nikos Papastergiadis has elsewhere called a 'spherical consciousness from the South', a way of understanding the profound transhemispheric entanglements that colonization set into motion and that continue to ground geopolitics in a 'naturalist discourse of magnetic polarities'.[64] This is the spherical South through which *iPOV[i]* materializes its fluid and mutable space of contact, a space in which many vibrant worlds coexist and interact. But if colonial contact may be reimagined otherwise, its effects cannot simply be nullified. In Reihana's words: 'Once people have encountered each other, history is changed forever... and that's the infection.'[65]

Infection brings bodies back into the narratives of colonial contact and conquest with force. European emissaries brought both infectious diseases to the Pacific, and an integrated system of scientific and social categorization, underpinned by political, economic and military subjugation, that instituted enduring forms of colonial biopower across the Pacific.[66] That bodies matter is made abundantly clear by *iPOV[i]*. Take, for instance, the inclusion of Aboriginal Australians in the final version of the work,[67] an inclusion that Reihana emphasized as being of particular significance because the brutalities suffered by Indigenous people in Australia at the hands of British colonial authorities were justified by appeals to hierarchical 'racial science' and the myth of an uninhabited land.[68] Siting a performance by the Koomurri dance troupe adjacent to the first instance of European contact in the work, the video juxtaposes radically divergent worlds as coincident and connected, countering any lingering fiction that Cook, Banks, Tupaia and the crew of the Endeavour met *Terra Nullius* on their quest for *Terra Australis (incognita)*.

It also hearkens to the role played by Joseph Banks in the development of biological science through the materials and insights gleaned during his Pacific journeys. Banks was part of a network of European learned men, led principally by French, British, German and Swedish naturalists, who collected and traded vast quantities of Pacific specimens – specimens which included dried plants, seeds, minerals and body parts, both human and nonhuman. Skulls of Indigenous Australians were particularly prized for their scientific use. As president of the Royal Society for 41 years, Banks would later advise the British Crown on the establishment of Botany Bay as a penal colony, as well as on the development of the botanical gardens at Kew, and, as a member of the Society of Dilletanti, the founding of London's Royal Academy. With Banks, it becomes clear how politics, science and the arts converged at the nexus of Pacific bodies and British colonial biopower.[69]

And if colonial biopower was racialized in the Pacific, so too was it critically marked, per Lugones, by the 'coloniality of gender'. As a number of trans-Indigenous feminist and decolonial queer scholars have argued, the construction of sharp, binary concepts of gender and sexuality was one of the most profound impacts of European colonization globally, and its enforcement facilitated both genocidal acts of sexual violence against colonized women and gender-diverse subjects, as well as manifold forms of cultural epistemicide.[70] *In Pursuit of Venus [infected]* does not fail to grasp this point, emphasizing the significance of Indigenous women's agency, and the central roles they played within social and ritual activities, as well as recognizing the esteemed position of gender-diverse people in Indigenous societies in the Pacific, such as Samoan fa'afafine and Māori takatāpui, who appear in the work. Additionally, the work's vignettes include customary practices later banned

40 Storying Pluriversal Worlds

by colonial administrators, such as the ceremonial birthing performance in which a male figure bears an adult 'infant' following an elaborate ritualized labour.[71]

But there is more. If *iPOV[i]* acknowledged the historical existence and significance of women and diverse gender expression in the Indigenous cultures of the Pacific, it did not leave the normative, heteropatriarchal position of the European emissaries unchallenged. This point is significant; the colonizing and categorical logic of Eurocentric racial science, in tandem with the disciplined production of binary gender/sex norms, was imposed upon the bodies of women, gender-diverse and colonized subjects, who were in turn produced as 'monstrous others'[72] in relation to a White, male, cisgender norm that was thus rendered invisible and unmarked. But Eurocentric heteronormativity was itself an effect produced through mutual encounter; demonstrating that the bodies of White, male subjects were not 'naturally' the normative centre of visual and epistemic power is a profound challenge to the coloniality of gender and to the global production of 'race' through European imperial biopower. It also begins to open a transcanonical dialogue with the imbrication of bodies and time in another key worlding effect of European colonial power, the inauguration of the Anthropocene, with its sharp categorical separation of the human from the nonhuman.[73]

And here we meet the body of Captain Cook, redrawn through a trans point of inflection in *iPOV[i]*. During a sociable scene between Cook, some of his men and a group of Pacific Islanders, there is an attempt to debag the Captain to ascertain whether he is male or female. It is recounted that his fastidious sexual abstinence (and 'illegible' costume) rendered him corporeally ambiguous to his hosts, who, in addition, did not assume that revered leaders must, by definition, be male.[74] In *iPOV[i]*, the 'Gender Cook' vignette signals, conceptually, a transgender transposition, further emphasized by the fact that Cook is played in the video both by a male actor and a female lead. The introduction of this gender/sex transposition acts as a point of inflection, effectively transforming the narrative sequencing of the video from a linear loop to a 'doubled' helix or, a spiral repetition with a transcorporeal twist. Many critics have noted the significance of the spiral in Māori cosmology, and its temporal entanglement with a flexible and contingent concept of genealogy (*whakapapa*), connecting humans with each other, but also with the earth and the cosmos. This is not eternal or unchanging time (chronos), but an unfolding temporal helix that repeats and ascends, creating futures with and through pasts, without fixing times, spaces or bodies in the process.[75]

Signalling a spiral (re)turning point in the work through the radical gender/sex fluidity of Cook is a bold stroke, and one that critically infects other representations of Cook, and of White, male European subjects, across *iPOV[i]*. Take, for instance, the scenes of Cook's men being tattooed, or of Banks' body being ritually marked before donning his costume to join the raiding party of the Chief Mourner (Figure 1.8). These encounters materialize White male bodies as open, inscriptive surfaces awaiting Pacific agency to render them meaningful in new ways within different worlds. These subjects are not all-seeing, yet disembodied, masters of the universe, but one element within an animated cosmos understood to be comprised of many and more than human worlds.[76] Cook's participation in the Hawaiian

FIGURE 1.8 Lisa Reihana, *In Pursuit of Venus [infected]*, detail: *Stars*, 2015–17. Ultra HD video, colour, 7.1 sound, 64 min.
Image courtesy of the artist.

Lono ceremony, the focus of another vignette, is an especially poignant instance of this, since it is clear with hindsight that Cook and his hosts did not read his inscription within an Hawaiian cosmos in the same way – a fact that presages later violence and death on both sides.

The coexistence, and sometimes collision, of many and different epistemic worlds in the spiral time and space evoked by *iPOV[i]* is signalled both sonically and visually. The work's multi-layered soundtrack enmeshes ambient Pacific sounds of weather, tide and native animals, with human dialogue, song and the sounds of both Pacific and European instruments – including the ticking of the very clock that accompanied Cook on his journeys, now housed at the Royal Society, having returned to London along with some 30,000 specimens and countless Pacific artefacts, not least the costume of the Chief Mourner.[77] Visually, the measured pace of the movement of *iPOV[i]* across the screen from right to left is countered by the appearance of the four Pacific canoes travelling left to right. The presence of the Pacific canoes precedes and outlasts the European narrative span, but more pointedly, their movement produces a temporal vortex experienced visually. The work's time signature is neither linear nor teleogical, but multidirectional and emergent, a continuum spiralling between the past and the present, duration and new arrival, that opens the possibility to story past, present and future differently. And here, returning to the cipher of Cook is especially apt.

More than once, Reihana commented that the appearance of the scene of Cook's death in Charvet's wallpaper was, for her, 'THE site of rupture' in *Les Sauvages*.[78] Simply, it is difficult to make sense of the scene within an arcadian panorama inhabited by 'noble savages' and 'dusky maidens' displayed for the pleasure of the empowered European capitalist.[79] Cook's death is also included in *iPOV[i]*, but rather than rupture the narrative, its complex aftermath is played out over time, materialized through a fluid interchange between sonic and visual phenomena (Figure 1.9).

42 Storying Pluriversal Worlds

FIGURE 1.9 Lisa Reihana, *In Pursuit of Venus [infected]*, detail: Mourning, 2015–17. Ultra HD video, colour, 7.1 sound, 64 min.
Image courtesy of the artist.

Following the scuffle in which Cook is killed, the first sound heard is of Hawaiians singing in mourning. This opens a sequence that culminates with Hawaiian emissaries bringing Cook's cleaned thigh bone and hat back to his crew, whose shock, horror and misunderstanding of the offer of these 'grisly gifts' is registered vocally. But there is no 'break' created in the spiral time and tide of the work, sonically or visually. Rather, in the aftermath of these death rites, where Cook's body is inscribed, irreducibly, within many and different worlds at once, the infection of contact opens the possibility to inhabit and story pluriversal worlds otherwise – through a radically redrawn chrono/bio/geo logic of entanglement rather than mastery.

There are no human masters of the pluriverse; mastery is created by canons that make many worlds in and as the image of One. *In Pursuit of Venus [infected]* materializes transcanons, contingent genealogies for futures created with and through the spherical contaminations of the past. This is not a tale for Lugones' 'lover of purity', but an 'impure' ethics that posits 'complicity and compromise as a starting point for action'.[80] It is an ethics in pursuit of Venus, always, already infected. It is an ethics signalled by the radical trans/position of Cook's fe/male body, that confounds the 'prick tale of Humans in History'.[81] Moving beyond the ongoing ontological purification of the canon through the experimental registers of art, we reach another kind of contact story, where the decolonial possibilities of transnational and Indigenous feminisms meet queer ecologies to engender kindred spirits from the past as they story new and many worlds for the future. This is a transcanonical genealogy of contact, defined by conversation and care, and, as Indigenous feminist scholar Kali Simmons argued so eloquently, in decolonial reorientations, much broader notions of time, contamination and kinship will pertain.[82]

Collections and Contaminations: Art, Artefacts and World Traveling

In Pursuit of Venus [infected] was shown in 2018 in *Oceania*, a major exhibition of the arts of the Pacific, held at London's Royal Academy to mark 250 years since Cook's first voyage. *Oceania* was advertised as continuing the Royal Academy's tradition of hosting outstanding exhibitions of material from world cultures, such as *Africa: The Art of a Continent* (1995), *Aztecs* (2002) and *China: The Three Emperors, 1662–1795* (2005). The exhibition brought together more than 200 objects spanning 500 years, placing contemporary works of art such as *iPOV[i]* into dialogue with texts, maps and textiles, carvings and canoes, 'living treasures' and human remains.[83] In a recorded interview with curator Tim Marlow, Reihana turned to the subject of the powerful, animate objects co-located with *iPOV[i]* in the show, making the salient point that many of the most precious Pacific objects, 'traded or stolen', are now in collections in Europe, and that this has far-reaching implications for the living heirs to those cultures.[84]

The tales of how objects from colonized cultures came to reside in European collections are most commonly stories of cultural conquest and extractive epistem-icide. In some instances, the histories of acquisitions have been obscured in the archives; in others, we know the tale – the costume of the Chief Mourner shown in *Oceania*, for example, was brought to London on Cook's ship and donated to the British Museum through Banks' negotiations. The British Museum, along with the British Library and London's Natural History Museum, were themselves enmeshed in British colonial expansion; the institutions were established through the bequest of the physician and collector Sir Hans Sloane, whose wealth and social elevation came through deep connections with 17th-century British plantations in Jamaica, worked by enslaved Africans.

By the middle of the 19th century, museums were being established throughout Britain and Oxford rivalled London for collections associated with the study of nat-ural history, archaeology and the new science of anthropology. Oxford's Museum of Natural History was founded in 1860 and hosted, that same year, the famous Oxford Evolution Debate between the Darwinian Thomas Huxley and the Bishop of Oxford, Samuel Wilberforce. In 1884, British Army officer and archaeologist, Augustus Pitt Rivers, left his extensive collection to the university on the condi-tion that a permanent lectureship in anthropology be established, and a museum of anthropology and archaeology be built to house the collection – this would become the Pitt Rivers Museum.[85]

The first curator of the Pitt Rivers Museum, Henry Balfour, was, like Pitt Rivers, an expert on firearms and weapons, but also musical instruments. Following a Darwinian approach to material culture and development, Balfour organized the Pitt Rivers collection typologically, rather than geographically, the better to demonstrate how the complexity of instruments and objects 'reflected' the racial/

44 Storying Pluriversal Worlds

cultural complexity and development of their makers.[86] Not surprisingly, British technological superiority demonstrated British cultural superiority; better guns led 'naturally' to the destruction of 'less developed' people, whose cultures needed to be studied, documented and collected urgently by anthropologists before they 'died out'.[87] This quest for urgent knowledge and categorization fostered the collection/theft of non-European cultural materials on a grand scale as a crucial part of 'the science of colonial administration', incidentally, a subject in which Oxford University came to excel, running summer schools that drew on their extensive ethnographic collections throughout the 1920s and 1930s.

A substantial body of Māori material, ranging from photographic documentation to cloaks, skirts and carvings, was given to the Pitt Rivers collection by a fascinating liminal figure, Makereti (aka Margaret Pattison Thom). Makereti was the daughter of a Māori woman (Te Arawa/Tuhourangi/Ngāti Wahiao) and a Pākehā man, who moved between her Indigenous and settler roots with relative ease. At the turn of the 20th century, Makereti guided European visitors through Aotearoa New Zealand, and later organized tours with members of her family to Australia, the United States and Britain as a 'cultural concert party'. Marrying an Oxfordshire man in 1912 and settling in Britain, Makereti soon became involved with the work of Pitt Rivers curators Balfour and T.K. Penniman, and with the activities of the Anthropological Society. In 1927, she studied for the Oxford Diploma in Anthropology and her dissertation was published posthumously as *The Old-Time Māori* in 1938.[88] Makereti did not pursue her studies without the knowledge, assistance and blessing of her elders, and the manuscript of her book was edited in close consultation with Te Arawa. Her approach to ethnography was a careful and complex balancing act between responsibility to Māori genealogy and a desire to bring her knowledge to an anglophone audience through an institutional apparatus of exceptional power.

Whilst Makereti was bringing Māori songs, stories and canoe demonstrations to British audiences, William Hesketh Lever was travelling the world for business and pleasure. His first world tour (1891–92) took him to Australia, Canada and the United States where he was building soap factories. By 1910, he was travelling through Africa and the Pacific in search of raw materials for its manufacture. He acquired objects throughout his trips, with a particular interest in ethnographic artefacts and 'curiosities', the most remarkable being two Pacific canoes brought back from the Solomon Islands in 1913 at great expense.

Lady Lever Art Gallery was commissioned in 1913 and opened in 1922. It would not be an overstatement to say that it was founded at a moment of crisis for Lever and for British imperial interests. In 1911, Lever came close to losing Sunlight Soap when it came to light that the company was using forced labour to produce palm oil in the Belgian Congo; the ensuing scandal also damaged his reputation as a Liberal social reformer. In 1913, his beloved wife Elizabeth, to whom the Art Gallery was eventually dedicated, died. For most of the time during which the Gallery was being planned and built, Britain was at war, and by the time it opened, the old imperial order of Europe had been rocked by political upheaval at home and abroad.

Although Lady Lever Art Gallery came to house the major part of Lever's diverse collection, it only housed fine and decorative art.[89] His ethnographic artefacts and 'curiosities' were located elsewhere – mainly in his business premises and private houses. Though not definitively articulated by Lever, the treatment of his collection implied a hierarchy between works of art and ethnographic artefacts, the former carefully selected and catalogued for the Gallery (the arrangement of which was Lever's major passion in the last years of his life), and the latter poorly recorded and widely dispersed.

Art or artefact, history or ethnography? The materials collected from colonized peoples were never easily contained by the limiting logic of the Western canon, and their exclusion from Lady Lever speaks volumes. This past continues in our present; a full century after Lever's first world tour, curator Edward Morris penned an Introduction to a special issue on Lever's collections for the *Journal of the History of Collections*, published by Oxford University Press, in which he commented on the ethnographic objects thus:

> The impact of Lever's business career on his collections can be seen most clearly in the context of his ethnography. This was largely collected from those under-developed areas where his companies operated in their quest for the raw materials needed for soap manufacture by Lever Brothers, and it reflected Lever's respect for and interest in the life and culture of those primitive peoples whose lives he sought to improve.[90]

The partial, parochial and paternalistic world created by the Western canon will not be unsettled easily.

The Middle Place, in between Knowing and Making

In October 2020, the artist Mariana Castillo Deball opened the exhibition *Between making and knowing something* at the Museum of Modern Art, Oxford. The exhibition was conceived following work undertaken by the artist in the archives of the Pitt Rivers Museum and with the Smithsonian Collection in Washington, DC. *Between making and knowing something* took as its starting point images and objects in the Oxford and Washington collections acquired through the anthropological work of four extraordinary individuals: Makereti, the Māori/Pākehā anthropologist discussed briefly above; White British anthropologist Elsie Colsell McDougall, who, for some three decades from 1926, documented the Indigenous textile cultures of Mexico and Guatemala, leaving an extensive collection of objects, photographs and detailed fieldnotes to the Pitt Rivers Museum; and finally the pair of We'wha, the Zuni *Lha'mana* (Two Spirit) weaver and potter and Matilda Coxe Stevenson, a White US American anthropologist whom she met in 1879, and with whom she worked closely. Stevenson's photographs, documenting We'wha's working methods, led to their collaboration with the Smithsonian, who accessioned for their collections a number of pieces by We'wha, including pottery, woven textiles and hand looms. In various ways, these four historical figures each occupied a liminal

46 Storying Pluriversal Worlds

space between making and knowing, and it is this vibrant space between that was so eloquently realized by Deball's installation.

Deball is no stranger to spaces between making and knowing. Born and educated in Mexico, the artist has lived since 2002 in Europe, currently residing in Berlin. Deball frequently works across conventional boundaries between academic disciplines, creating conversations between art and its canonical histories, archaeology, anthropology, cultural geography and the human sciences, focusing on how knowledges are made and how they are conveyed, consumed and challenged.[91] Much of her work engages with cultural institutions, such as museums, galleries and archives, and their role as producers and mediators of contested forms of knowing, particularly contests between Eurocentric and Indigenous understandings of pre-Columbian artefacts from what has come to be called Mexico.

Between making and knowing something continued the earlier trajectory of Deball's creative interdisciplinary enquiry, conversing with two significant ethnographic collections to focus attention on the multifaceted processes by which artefacts are acquired, studied, categorized, labelled, placed on display and/or packed away from view. At the same time, the show walked alongside European and Indigenous women and Two Spirit makers and knowers, exploring the complexity of racialized and gendered cultural agency articulated at the borders of nations, institutions and disciplines, with and against the grain of the canons they normatively secure. But *Between making and knowing something* did more than document the histories of two collections and bring to light some 'hidden figures' from the early years of anthropology.[92] *Between making and knowing something* was an artistic, scholarly and curatorial experiment – a transcanonical intervention – that demonstrated, paraphrasing Australian feminist philosopher Elizabeth Grosz, that 'knowledge is a practice', and that knowing something cannot be separated from making and re-making it.[93] In doing this, Deball's exhibition emphasized feminist figurations as a vibrant space between making and knowing, a middle place where imaginative and material practices meet. Arguably, it is in just such a vibrant middle place that transnational feminist genealogies of art can emerge and flourish.

Between making and knowing something was installed in three rooms in Oxford MOMA – a large and open gallery space into which viewers first walked, followed sequentially by two, smaller and more intimate rooms. In the second room, the middle space of the show, four wall-mounted vitrines, borrowed from the Oxford Museum of Natural History, displayed fieldwork donated by Makereti to the Pitt Rivers Collection, including a number of professional photographs taken of her, images of her Aotearoa New Zealand home (whare), and her posthumously published thesis. The materials displayed in the vitrines are evocative documents of a life led between two cultures and Makereti's story is a compelling tale of women's agency emerging within and across the boundaries of many worlds. As a *display*, however, Makereti's material was not at first sight visually remarkable, but rather replicated conventional display case arrangements that can still be found in any number of European historical museums and collections. But the space of the exhibition was not a museum of natural history, archaeology, ethnography or anthropology – it was a museum of modern art – and the cases mounted on two walls in the corner of the room thus appeared as a fragment from another time and place.

At a small distance from the cases containing Makereti's fieldwork, on its own in the centre of the room, was another vitrine. This one was free-standing and empty, its 'display' consisting of a two-minute sound piece. The work was titled *his heart rested at the site named the middle place* (2020) (Figure 1.10).[94] The short sound piece was spoken by Deball, but the storyteller in the first-person narrative is the vitrine: '*I have been waiting in dusty storage for many, many years…*' As the tale unfolds, we share in the excitement of the case being prepped to show an object, but alas, no object appears: '*Probably the object that I was supposed to exhibit couldn't be shown.*' The final lines complete the thought as they name the show:

> That is why this vitrine is left empty, as a symbol of respect to all the objects that have been taken without consent, and not asking the original makers, the proper conditions or even the possibility to exhibit it to a wider audience. Between making and knowing something.

FIGURE 1.10 Mariana Castillo Deball, *Between making and knowing something*, Modern Art Oxford, installation view, 2020.
Photographer: Ben Westoby. Museum case courtesy of the Oxford University Museum of Natural History. Image courtesy of the artist and Modern Art Oxford.

48 Storying Pluriversal Worlds

In this second room, we encounter multi-epistemic worlds meeting one another in a middle place – the gallery between the other spaces of the exhibition, a room in which furniture and objects from the past converse with contemporary audio technologies and the conventions of the white cube, cases in which photographs from halfway around the globe tell a tale of Edwardian England. This is a middle place of material gestures and dialogue, but also of profound 'incommensurability',[95] spaces where any pretense to instrumental scientific/technological mastery of the world fails and where knowledge emerges instead in the imaginative acts of re-making the in-between, which is allowed its silence. Engaging well with multi-epistemic worlds does not simply entail knowing *more*, or falling into the ethnographic project that seeks to *know all*, but instead, engaging with the practices and production of what counts as knowledge, by and for whom, and to what ends.

Makereti's work was sometimes criticized by later European scholars for being too domestic, too anecdotal, and too collaborative with her 'objects' of study, but this misses the point of the middle place and its precious incommensurability. Her knowledges were not of dominated 'objects' understood from afar, but of subjects with agency to whom she was responsible, both human and more than human. That responsibility included the generative possibility of a silence that confounds the epistemicide borne of colonial domination and its objectifying extraction of knowledge. Placing these vitrines together in the middle place of the exhibition created a dialogue that denaturalized the conventions of museum collection, categorization and display such that the institutional practices through which knowledges are made (and re-made) came into view. At the site of the empty vitrine, we meet, yet again, a point of inflection – in this instance, a vibrant middle place between making and knowing something.

In the first and main room of *Between making and knowing something*, a different encounter with the middle place emerged. The large and open gallery was articulated spatially by abstract forms comprised of replicas of objects from the archives, re-created in new versions for the show (Figure 1.11). Three hand-woven rebozos, dyed with an ikat pattern, produced in Michoacán, Mexico by the textiles collective Ukata, were suspended in eight-metre lengths across the space. Entitled *all around to the oceans* (2020), the 'unfinished' rebozos were shown still connected to the hand looms on which they were made, and were interconnected with a second work, *when the arms legs stretched*, consisting of 19 red stoneware vessels, painted with engobe slip, perforated and strung together with a hundred metres of black cotton rope trailing above, across and along the floor of the room.

Both the rebozos and pottery vessels were strategic forms of 're-making' that conversed with the Pitt Rivers and Smithsonian collections of textiles and pottery from the Indigenous people of what once was, or yet remains, Mexico. Working with ceramicist Silvia Andrade, using patterns and techniques derived from the work created by Zuni weaver and potter We'Wha, Deball produced the ceramic vessels in her studio in Berlin and transported them to Oxford to be perforated and installed in the gallery. Likewise, the rebozos were produced off-site, in Mexico, using the very technologies that McDougall spent her life documenting through

FIGURE 1.11 Mariana Castillo Deball, *A_____LL Around I*, installation view, from *Between making and knowing something*, Modern Art Oxford, installation view, 2020. Ceramic vessel made of red stoneware painted with engobe slip. Hand-woven textile dyed with an ikat pattern and displayed with backstrap looms produced in the state of Michoacán, Mexico by Ukata. Ceramics produced with the assistance of ceramicist Silvia Andrande.
Photographer: Ben Westoby.Image courtesy of the artist and Modern Art Oxford.

photographs and fieldwork notes, themselves displayed in vitrines borrowed from the Oxford Natural History Museum in the third room of the exhibition. Arguably, the first space of the installation staged a dynamic tension between the re-made objects and their mode of display that posed a categorical question: are these objects artworks or artefacts, and where do they belong: in the modern art gallery or the ethnographic collection of a natural history museum? It is my contention that Deball's installation refused a simple, canonical answer: the replicated objects are always, already both and neither, the materialization of a vibrant middle place of re-making that cuts across categorical knowledges that cannot admit of the impure contingencies of hybrid imagination.

This invocation of hybrid imagination, border crossing and the creative potential of the in-between is profoundly resonant with transnational feminist approaches to decolonizing canonical histories of art, and, in particular, with the eloquent

50 Storying Pluriversal Worlds

writing of the late Chicana scholar Gloria Anzaldúa on the concept of 'neplanta', a liminal in-between state of dwelling in/on the border. In 1993, Anzaldúa published the essay 'Border Arte: Neplanta, el Lugar de la Frontera' in response to her experience of seeing the exhibition, *AZTEC: The World of Moctezuma* at the Denver Museum of Natural History.[96] That the concept of neplanta, a term that came to be used widely in explorations of Chicana art, Latinx feminist and queer theory, and decolonial 'epistemologies of the South', originated in response to an exhibition of pre-Columbian art and artefacts from one of the living Indigenous traditions of Mexico, makes it exceptionally resonant here.[97] But more than that, as Anzaldúa used it, neplanta is a compelling formulation for the experience of a vibrant middle place, an in-between state of continual transformation that makes connections between geopolitical borders, fluid and mobile forms of subjectivity, and the power of creative agency and the arts:

> Art and la frontera intersect in a liminal space where border people, especially artists, live in a state of 'neplanta'. Neplanta is the Náhuatl word for in-between state, that uncertain terrain one crosses when moving from one place to another, when changing from one class, race, or sexual position to another, when traveling from the present identity into a new identity. ... [It is] the one spot on earth which contains all other places within it.[98]

Neplanta is pluriversal. Anzaldúa's argument was sharply critical of the continuation of colonial narratives into the present in *AZTEC*, from the billing of the exhibition as an act of 'good will' between North America and Mexico, to the extraction, decontextualization and commodification of objects, images and knowledges from a living culture, treated as if dead, and 'regurgitated' by White scholars through Eurocentric institutions. But the strength of her critique did not sentence her argument to hopelessness. Asking what it meant, in her words, '... for me, esta jotita, this queer Chicana, this mexica-tejana to enter a museum and look at indigenous objects that were used by her ancestors',[99] Anzaldúa understood her position as simultaneously complicit and empowered by a knowledge that provides the material through which to make change. 'Though I, too, am a gaping consumer, I feel that these artworks are part of my legacy.'[100] Her mobilization of the state of neplanta provided a far-reaching and productive understanding of the complexity of complicity and contingency as a basis for a political, ethical and aesthetic challenge to the logic of ontological purification and categorical separation, that recognizes how making and re-making are at the heart of knowing differently and imagining otherwise. And in this re-making, the art of the border, forged in the middle place, plays a crucial role.

The re-made objects in *Between making and knowing something* conversed with and walked alongside the colonial and canonical disciplines and practices that distinguished sharply between art and artefact in order to define, hierarchically order, and control the people who made them. But occupying the middle place enabled different forms of knowing to be made and re-made with and through the materials and practices of the past, countered, but not excised. Transcanons make stories that can be both critical *and* generative, a vital combination for transnational feminist genealogies seeking to explore the complex agency of women and gender-diverse subjects from the past, as *Between making and knowing something* did so creatively.

In Deball's project, histories, institutions and practices of art and anthropology intersected with critical questions of race, class, gender and sexuality. At this intersection, there was, of course, a tale to be told of powerful nations and institutions fostering canonical knowledges as they expanded markets and empires across the globe. That tale subtended Deball's installation, demonstrating how the power of the British Empire in the 19th and early 20th centuries was supported by Britain's museums and universities, whose collections and courses developed British anthropology alongside the 'science of colonial administration'.

Shared interests in the Pacific brought Britain broadly into alignment with burgeoning US American imperial expansion as the two nations tensely negotiated the settlement of 'Oregon Country' in 1846. The Oregon Treaty was signed just as the United States, under the presidency of James K. Polk, a slave-holding Jacksonian Democrat, was pursuing the aggressive imperialist annexation of Texas from newly-independent Mexico. Violent expansion into Mexican territories westward to the Pacific under the banner of Manifest Destiny would lead to the Mexican–American War (1846–48), exacerbate US racial and political divides, increase genocide against Indigenous people, and foster the invidious development of race science and eugenics in the early years of the 20th century. The entanglement between the Pitt Rivers and the Smithsonian is in part derived from this special relationship; James Smithson, the British scientist whose legacy founded the institution that bears his name, was a Fellow of Pembroke College, keen to foster 'the increase and diffusion of knowledge'. After much debate, his legacy was accepted by the United States government under the administration of James K. Polk, ushering in a period where the Smithsonian Institution played a vital role in the development of US American science, not least anthropology. Much of the fieldwork done by early US American anthropologists was amongst Indigenous groups in the western United States and Pacific Islands.

As Nasheli Jiménez del Val argued in her work on the genealogy of 'the Indigenous' in Mexican visual culture, colonizing the imaginary of dominated people requires transforming difference to hierarchy, exscinding related histories from one another and then reproducing that resultant impoverished logic.[101] The hybrid connectivities that flowed 'all around to the oceans' in *Between making and knowing something*, re-made relationships between the histories of institutional and disciplinary connections between British and US imperialism apparent. But it did not end simply by demonstrating that historical collections of art and artefacts in the metropolitan centres of the Global North have been formed through iniquitous relationships with the Global South and the legacy of Indigenous conquest within. Deball's show focused on the complexity of the middle place, a space in which other tales, critical fabulations and counter-narratives of worlds within One world, might be told. Like Reihana's installation *In Pursuit of Venus[infected]*, and Sayers'

52 Storying Pluriversal Worlds

and Lundgreen's project *Changing Places*, there is a recognition that knowing cannot but be a re-making, after contact, acknowledging infection, yet working with and through the material of the past to reimagine untold or silenced tales the better to story new and different futures.

Makereti, We'Wha, Stevenson and McDougall inhabited histories already over-determined by the logic of European conquest, settler colonialism and the predominance of the Western universal, and there are elements of their works and of their biographies that replicate those dynamics – most pointedly perhaps, Stevenson's photographs of secret and sacred Zuni activities taken against the wishes of the group, now rarely displayed. But in many ways, the lives and work of each of these figures also posed a challenge to the normative tales of sex, gender, race and power, in their own times and through historical narratives persisting into ours. This is perhaps most obvious in the case of the Zuni *Lha'mana* We'Wha, whose works in the Smithsonian are only now beginning to be correctly attributed and whose feminine pronouns are being reinstated in the archive – feminine pronouns that her friend and collaborator Stevenson never failed to use in her fieldwork notes and correspondence. It is, perhaps, truly fitting that the Zuni name for homeland, Halona Idiwan'a, translates as the Middle Place.

The insistence on *making* within Deball's project is critical to the different knowledges that are able to be materialized through the exhibition, and Deball herself consistently emphasized that her understanding of the work in the archives had been transformed by her experience of the material practices of re-making demanded by the installation.[102] Anthropological fieldwork was in its infancy in the period in which so many women emerged as protagonists in the discipline, both in Britain and in the United States. Conventional hierarchies of knowledge production were not yet wholly established and there was scope to make interventions into both the collection methods and the interpretation of material gathered *in situ*. The significant presence of White, Indigenous and women of colour scholars in anthropology's early years, fostered a climate of intellectual and practical experimentation that often ran counter to normative conventions of race and gender.[103] Two of the most important anthropologists to work closely with Zuni Pueblo communities in the inter-war years, for example, were Ruth Fulton Benedict and Ruth Leah Bunzel. Both women focused, albeit in different ways, on women's roles, creativity and culture in Indigenous societies, Bunzel, in particular, exploring the social significance and artistry of Zuni pottery.

Benedict and Bunzel studied and taught at Columbia University in the circle of Franz Boas, whose many women students and colleagues included anthropologist and author Zora Neale Hurston, who would later become a pivotal figure in the Harlem Renaissance, Indigenous ethnographer and linguist Ella Deloria, whose studies of the Sioux language remain key texts, and one of the most well-known public scholars of the period, Margaret Mead. This circle of diverse female scholars and their German-Jewish émigré mentor, Boas, were some of the strongest voices raised against the emergence of US and European racist eugenics promoted as 'science' in the years leading to the rise of the Nazi party. This circle of women academics inhabited the creative ground of neplanta, making knowledges in the borderlands. Academic disciplines, like the knowledges they seek to foster, are never wholly fixed, but fluid forms, capable of transformation, *in the making*.

The final room of *Between making and knowing something* brought these questions from the archive to the present in a direct and material way. The third space in the gallery contained vitrines of McDougall's extensive fieldwork notes on Indigenous textiles from Mexico and Guatemala. Looking at this material, I was reminded of Anzaldúa's writing on a museum in Guatemala City that held an extensive collection of Indigenous clothing displayed as if a relic from a dead culture, making no mention of the living women who inhabited the city '… weaving the same kind of clothing and using the same method as their ancestors'.[104] The Ukata collective who wove the rebozos suspended across the gallery in the first space of Deball's exhibition used the very methods documented by McDougall in the photos displayed in the vitrines. But when they shipped their textiles to Oxford, they wrapped them in current Mexican newspapers. In a wonderful moment of serendipity, not initially planned as part of the exhibition, Deball unfolded the newspapers and mounted them on the wall behind McDougall's encased fieldwork (Figure 1.12).

FIGURE 1.12 Mariana Castillo Deball, *Between making and knowing something*, Modern Art Oxford, installation view, 2020.

Photographer: Ben Westoby.Museum case courtesy of the Oxford University Museum of Natural History.Elsie McDougall fieldwork photography, parts of wooden backstrap looms.Fieldwork photographs courtesy of the Pitt Rivers Museum, University of Oxford.Image courtesy of the artist, Modern Art Oxford and Pitt Rivers Museum, University of Oxford.

54 Storying Pluriversal Worlds

The vibrancy of a continuing, living tradition could hardly have been more evident than through this juxtaposition, and the fact that the papers carried stories of the thousands of Mexican women who were marching for International Women's Day frames the point more poignantly than any material from the archive ever could. In a state of neplanta, many new worlds can be (re-)made with and through even the most precarious materials left over from the old and the One.

This chapter opened by demonstrating that the institutional power of the Western canon still secures an artworld dominated by the Global North.[105] Over its course, examples of *transcanons* – decolonial feminist genealogies of art, decidedly plural and impure – were seen to be capable of unravelling naturalized epistemic hierarchies and categorical distinctions, and to run counter the partial and patriarchal fictions of Eurocentric universalism. These transcanons suggest ways in which feminist figurations can chart transhemispheric histories, that, in their turn, materialize pluriversal worlds. This is more than an abstract intellectual challenge, it is a political imperative, mobilized through transnational feminist practices of poetics and pedagogy, to which this volume now turns.

Notes

1　I take the phrase 'a world of many worlds' from the anthology of the same name edited by Marisol de la Cadena and Mario Blaser (Durham, NC and London: Duke University Press, 2018), who are in turn glossing the Zapatistas' call for 'a world in which many worlds fit' (p. 1). Introducing their rich collection of essays, the editors define a 'pluriverse' as: 'heterogeneous worldings coming together as a political ecology of practices' (p. 4). The emphasis they place on 'storying' (following Marilyn Strathern) is also significant here.

2　Gayatri Spivak, 'The Making of Americans, the Teaching of English, and the Future of Cultural Studies', *New Literary History* 21, 1990, pp. 781–98, p. 784.

3　The term 'culture war' had been used in other contexts and periods, but passed into common political parlance in the US during the 1990s with the publication of *Culture Wars: The Struggle to Define America*, by James Davison Hunter (New York: Basic Books, 1991). It is significant that African-American scholar and cultural critic, Cornel West, entered what he called 'the battle' between 'male WASP cultural homogeneity' and 'those constituted as others' in 1987 with an article similarly focused on the politics of literary canons and canon formation: 'Minority Discourse and the Pitfalls of Canon Formation', *Yale Journal of Criticism* 1(1), Fall 1987, pp. 193–207, p. 194–5.

4　Griselda Pollock, *Differencing the Canon: Feminist Desire and the Writing of Art's Histories*, New York and London: Routledge, 1999.

5　Also published in 1999, as part of the Open University course series, *Academies, Museums and Canons of Art*, edited by Gill Perry and Colin Cunningham (New Haven, CT and London: Yale University Press) focused on Britain and France between the 18th and early 20th centuries, demonstrating the intrinsic connections between nation-building, the institutional politics of art and the contested establishment of European canons in the period.

6　Pollock, *Differencing the Canon*, p. 39.

7　Pollock, *Differencing the Canon*, p. 3.

8　This is Walter D Mignolo's term and it chimes well with the term 'Western canon' that decolonial art scholars are now using with increasing frequency. Mignolo makes the following salient point: 'The universalization of Western Universality was part of its imperial project.' See 'Foreword: On Pluriversality and Multipolarity', in Bernd Reiter, ed., *Constructing the Pluriverse: The Geopolitics of Knowledge*, Durham, NC and London: Duke University Press, 2018, pp. ix–xvi, p. x.

9 The relationship between art history, canon formation and the geopolitics of globalization has been addressed by a number of scholars, see, especially: *Partisan Canons*, edited by Anna Brzyski, Durham, NC and London: Duke University Press, 2007; Jennifer Rahim with Barbara Lalla, eds, *Beyond Borders: Cross Culturalism and the Caribbean Canon*, Jamaica: University of the West Indies Press, 2009; and, more recently, rethinking 'world art canons' in earlier historical periods, Béatrice Joyeux-Prunel, 'Art History and the Global: Demonstrating the Latest Canonical Narrative', *Journal of Global History* 14:3, 2019, pp. 413–35.

10 Under the editorial direction of Dorothy Price, the UK journal *Art History* has taken a leading role in decolonizing Anglophone scholarship in art history. The desire to decolonize the field is palpable; in the first month after publication, the collective essay 'Decolonizing Art History', *Art History* 43:1, February 2020, pp. 8–66, co-edited by Price and Catherine Grant, was downloaded more than any other article in the journal's long history. Calls to decolonize have also been taken up in the cognate terrain of curating: see Dorothee Richter and Ronald Kolb, eds, *Decolonizing Art Institutions*, issue 35 of *On Curating*, December 2017.

11 The notion of 'unsettling' comes from Lize van Robbroeck, 'Unsettling the Canon: Some Thoughts on the Design of *Visual Century: South African Art in Context*', *Third Text Africa* 3:1, November 2013, pp. 27–37.

12 A few examples will suffice: Pollock's argument in *Differencing the Canon*, is well-defined on all three points (pp. 23–5); James D'Emilio raised the spectre of rejecting canons completely as complicit with colonizing knowledges in 'Decolonising Art History', Price and Grant; in 'Minority Discourse', West addressed the problems with an additive approach; Ruth E. Iskin addressed 'counter-canons' in the introduction to her edited anthology, *Re-envisioning the Contemporary Art Canon: Perspectives in a Global World*, New York and London: Routledge, 2017, pp. 1–42.

13 Pollock, *Differencing the Canon*; van Robbroeck, 'Unsettling the Canon'; Pauline Boudry and Renate Lorenz in Helena Reckitt, 'Troubling Canons: Curating and Exhibiting Women's and Feminist Art', in Iskin, *Re-envisioning the Contemporary Art Canon*, pp. 252–71; Charles H. Geyer, 'Creolizing the Canon: Manuel Puig, Junot Diaz, and the Latino Poetics of Relation', *The Comparatist* 43, October 2019, pp. 173–93.

14 Iskin, *Re-envisioning the Contemporary Art Canon*, pp. 1, 28.

15 Iskin, *Re-envisioning the Contemporary Art Canon*, p. 28.

16 The phrase comes from Juanita Sundberg's compelling article 'Decolonizing Posthumanist Geographies', *Cultural Geographies* 21:1, 2014, pp. 33–47, p. 35; in addition, exploring the construction of feminist knowledges in/as conversation also alludes to the elegant arguments of Elke Krasny on feminist curating and to my methodological deployment of conversation in *Transnational Feminisms, Transversal Politics and Art: Entanglements and Intersections* (2020), the first volume of this Trilogy.

17 Sundberg, 'Decolonizing Posthumanist Geographies', p. 34. Rauna Kuokannen's pivotal writing on Indigenous epistemologies, and her reading of Gayatri Spivak's 'unlearning', is significant both to Sundberg's thinking and to later discussions in this chapter, as well as to discussions of the gift in relation to a worlding pedagogy developed in Chapter 3. See: *Reshaping the University: Responsibility, Indigenous Epistemes and the Logic of the Gift*, Vancouver: University of British Columbia Press, 2008. It is also telling that Sundberg also draws on the Zapatistas ideas on a world of many worlds.

18 See also, Julietta Singh, *Unthinking Mastery: Dehumanism and Decolonial Entanglements*, Durham, NC and London: Duke University Press, 2018.

19 María Lugones, 'Toward a Decolonial Feminism', *Hypatia* 25:4, Fall 2010, pp. 742–59, p. 742. See also, María Lugones, *Pilgrimages/Perigrinajes: Theorizing Coalition against Multiple Oppressions*, Lanham, MD, Boulder, CO, New York and Oxford: Rowman and Littlefield Publishers, 2003.

20 'Purity, Impurity and Separation', in *Pilgrimages/Perigrinajes*, pp. 121–50, p. 132.
21 It is significant that Lugones called on trans subjectivity in her writing on purity to figure 'curdling', a practice of celebrating ambiguity that resists the logic of control central to the coloniality of gender. In addition, Alexis Shotwell engages in important ways with Lugones' thinking on purity and diverse bodies in her book *Against Purity: Living Ethically in Compromised Times*, Minneapolis: University of Minnesota Press, 2016, to which later sections of this chapter, and the fourth chapter of this volume in particular, will return.
22 Lugones' notion of 'world traveling' is one of the important transformational strategies identified by Chela Sandoval in her pivotal essay 'U.S. Third World Feminism: Differential Social Movement I' (1991) revised and reprinted in *Methodology of the Oppressed*, Minneapolis and London: University of Minnesota Press, 2000, pp. 41–64 (p. 61).
23 Lugones, 'Toward a Decolonial Feminism', p. 756.
24 Lugones absolutely distinguishes 'world-traveling' from 'middle-class leisurely', 'colonial and imperial' journeys – 'None of these involve risking one's ground.' See 'Playfulness, "World"-Traveling, and Loving Perception', in *Pilgrimages/Perigrinajes*, pp. 77–102, p. 98.
25 Walter D. Mignolo, 'Epistemic Disobedience, Independent Thought and Decolonial Freedom', *Theory, Culture & Society* 26, 2009, pp. 159–81. NB in borrowing the specific term 'loci of enunciation' from Mignolo, I would extend his genealogy to include earlier, important insights from many feminist scholars on situated knowledge and standpoint theory.
26 Geraldine Pratt and Victoria Rosner, *The Global and the Intimate: Feminism in Our Time*, New York: Columbia University Press, 2012; the multi-scalar coordinates (such as global/intimate) of transnational feminisms are discussed in greater depth in the first volume of this Trilogy, *Transnational Feminisms, Transversal Politics and Art: Entanglements and Intersections* (2020).
27 *Changing Places* was a partnership project between the artists and the following venues: Walker Art Gallery and Lady Lever Art Gallery, National Museums Liverpool (20 October 2007–20 April 2008); Bury Art Gallery, Museum and Archives (10 November 2007–23 February 2008); The Collection and The Tennyson Research Centre, Lincoln (2 February–27 April 2008); Leeds Art Gallery (June–September 2008).
28 Sara Ahmed, *Strange Encounters: Embodied Others in Post-Coloniality*, London and New York: Routledge, 2000, p. 164.
29 I am indebted to discussions with my colleagues Peter Yeandle and Pandora Syperek, whose work on the establishment of natural history museums, zoos and other 'infotainment' complexes in Victorian Britain breaks new ground on imperial histories and the environmental humanities. Suffice to say that the histories of provincial art museums differ from those of both aristocratic country house collections and London's British Museum and National Gallery, and they also tend to be overshadowed by their metropolitan counterparts in the scholarly literature on museum studies and connoisseurship, a point made by Sheila McGregor in 'Cross-Purposes: Looking again at Victorian collections', in Phil Sayers and Rikke Lundgreen, eds, *Changing Places*, Bury Art Gallery, Museum and Archives, 2007, pp. 9–28.
30 Anne McClintock, *Imperial Leather: Race, Gender and Sexuality in the Colonial Contest*, London and New York: Routledge, 1995. See, particularly, chapter 5, 'Soft Soaping Empire'.
31 The selection of Leighton's work by Sayers and Lundgreen was apt not only because it hearkened to the ubiquity of neo-classical female nudes in late Victorian painting and their collection and display in metropolitan museums and galleries across Britain, but, in addition, because Leighton's work was commissioned by fellow artist Alma Tadema as part of a grand decorative scheme and was designed, like Sayers' restaging, to fit within a long, thin, arched recess.

32 The tale of Psyche passed into the classical 'canon' through the work of Apuleius, a Berber living under Roman rule in what is now Algeria; her visual rendering as White is a trope that emerged through European neo-classicism, as noted in *White Psyche*, shown at the Whitworth Art Gallery in Manchester in 2021 (https://www.whitworth.manchester.ac.uk/whats-on/exhibitions/currentexhibitions/whitepsyche/). It is further interesting in the context of this chapter that the work shown in Manchester was a wallpaper design printed c. 1816 by Dufour et Cie.

33 Venus Callipyge translates as the Venus of the beautiful buttocks.

34 Dorothy Rowe (now Price), 'Disruptive Beauty', in Sayers and Lundgreen, *Changing Places*, pp. 29–46, p. 34.

35 Eliza Steinbock, 'Collecting Creative Transcestors: Trans★ Portraiture Hirstory, from Snapshots to Sculpture', in Hilary Robinson and Maria Buszek, eds, *A Companion to Feminist Art*, Oxford: Wiley Blackwell, 2019, pp. 225–42, p. 235. Steinbock used 'trans★' in the essay on transcestors, but in their compelling and closely-argued book on trans cinema, *Shimmering Images: Trans Cinema, Embodiment and the Aesthetics of Change* (Durham, NC and London: Duke University Press, 2019), opted for 'trans' (sans asterisk) as the most open, overarching term. I follow their lead here.

36 Lindsay Smith, 'To Pass, Passing and to Come', in Sayers and Lundgreen, *Changing Places*, pp. 49–66.

37 Smith, 'To Pass', p. 66.

38 Stacy Alaimo, in dialogue with Moira Gatens on Benedict Spinoza, takes transcorporeality in this direction: see 'Trans-corporeal feminisms and the ethical space of nature' in Alaimo and Susan Hekman, eds, *Material Feminisms*, Bloomington and Indianapolis: Indiana University Press, 2008, pp. 237–64.

39 Elizabeth Freeman, *Time Binds: Queer Temporalities, Queer Histories*, Durham, NC and London: Duke University Press, 2010, p. 71. Freeman's take on allegory and drag is wonderfully resonant with the artists' deployment of cross-dressing as transhistorical experimentation in *Changing Places*.

40 This is a reference to the position taken by Donna Haraway in *Staying with the Trouble: Making Kin in the Chthulucene*, Durham, NC and London: Duke University Press, 2016.

41 Dorothy Rowe notes the work of Elizabeth Prettejohn and Deborah Cherry in her essay, to which I would add Tim Barringer's studies of Victorian museum culture and Colin Cruise's ground-breaking work on queer visuality in the period. Taking this thinking more globally, the insights of Alpesh Patel on queer transnational art praxis have been especially significant to my thinking; see his *Productive Failure: Writing Queer Transnational South Asian Art Histories*, Manchester: Manchester University Press, 2017.

42 Freeman, *Time Binds*, p. 173.

43 Sayers and Lundgreen, and Dorothy Rowe responded directly to the comments from the Lady Lever Visitor Book in work made for the Leeds show and in its catalogue. In *Circe (after J. W. Waterhouse)*, Sayers changed places with the figure of the Greek enchantress from Waterhouse's 1891 painting *Circe Offering the Cup to Ulysses*, and created a patinated internal frame for the image, engraved with the hand-written comments from the Visitor Book. These were also reprinted as a double-page spread in the catalogue (pp. 26–7) within a discussion of the violence of the frame by Rowe in: 'Of Mimesis, Magic and Metamorphosis', *cf.* Sayers and Lundgreen, *Changing Places with Leeds*, Leeds City Art Gallery, 2008, pp. 8–53.

44 Olu Oguibe, 'Whiteness and "The Canon"', *Art Journal* 60:4, Winter 2001, pp. 44–7.

45 Oguibe, 'Whiteness and "The Canon"', p. 46.

46 See, George P. Landow, *Victorian Web*, June 2011, available at: http://www.victorianweb.org/sculpture/french/9.html.

47 Lugones, 'Toward a Decolonial Feminism', p. 743. She also invokes Hermaphrodites as a key instantiation of mestiza logic in 'Purity, Impurity and Separation', p. 123. Not surprisingly, her insights have been critical to more recent work on decolonizing trans studies, such as the special issue of *TSQ* ('Decolonizing Transgender'), 1:3, August

58 Storying Pluriversal Worlds

2014, edited by Aren Z. Aizura, et.al., and the article by Tjasa Kancler, 'Body Politics, Trans* Imaginary and Decoloniality', *4th Nordic Transgender Studies Symposium*, Karlstad University, Sweden, October 2016 (no pages).

48 Jane Chin Davidson's work on the formation of 'Chineseness' through European collecting practices and the significance of 'ethnographic' museums (not least the Pitt Rivers Museum in Oxford), have informed my thinking on these issues throughout this chapter. See her book *Staging Art and Chineseness: The Politics of Trans/Nationalism and Global Expositions*, Manchester; Manchester University Press, 2020.

49 It is significant that Phil Sayers has well-established links with Taiwan through feminist curator and scholar Ming Turner and is well aware of the works' address to the commodified visual construction of gender/sex exoticism.

50 This will be taken up at greater length in Chapter 4.

51 There are a number of studies that have explored the paradoxical entanglements between European Liberalism and, for example, colonial economies sustained through the enslavement and indenture of non-Europeans, racism and Indigenous genocide. See Domenico Lusordo, *Liberalism: A Counter History*, London: Verso, 2014; Lisa Lowe, *The Intimacies of Four Continents*, Durham, NC and London: Duke University Press, 2015; Gloria Wekker, *White Innocence: Paradoxes of Colonialism and Race*, Durham, NC and London: Duke University Press, 2016. Lowe makes the particular point that the very nature of the archives and records obscure '... connections between the emergence of European liberalism, settler colonialism in the Americas, the transatlantic African slave trade, and the East Indies and China trades in the late eighteenth and early nineteenth centuries' (p. 1). I would also include acts of cultural vandalism as epistemicide, such as the retributive destruction of the Old Summer Palace in Beijing during the Second Opium War by the 8th Lord Elgin, son of the 7th Lord Elgin who earlier 'removed' the Parthenon frieze.

52 I am using this term to invoke one of the earliest, and still most compelling, studies exploring the relationship between European collections and imperial expansion: Nicholas Thomas, *Possessions: Indigenous Art/Colonial Culture*, London: Thames and Hudson, 1999.

53 For more information about panoramic wallpaper generally, see the Victoria and Albert Museum: https://www.vam.ac.uk/collections/wallpaper. On *Les Sauvages*, see: Robert Futernick, 'Conservation of Scenic Wallpapers: "Sauvages de la Mer Pacifique"', *Journal of the American Institute for Conservation* 20:2, Spring 1981, pp. 139–46; Vivienne Webb, 'Les Sauvages de la Mer Pacifique: A Decorative Composition in Wallpaper', in *Lisa Reihana: Emissaries*, Auckland Art Gallery Toi o Tāmaki, New Zealand at Venice catalogue, 2017, pp. 116–23.

54 Vivienne Morrell, 'Images of Pacific Peoples in 18th Century Books, Prints and Wallpaper', 2015, https://viviennemorrell.wordpress.com/2015/07/09/images-ofpacific-peoples-in-18th-century-books-prints-and-wallpaper/.

55 The Arcadian reference is developed by Nikos Papastergiadis, 'Arcadia and the Imagined Memories', in *Lisa Reihana: Emissaries*, pp. 30–41.

56 Reihana is of mixed British and Māori (Ngāpuhi) descent, and has long experience of working with trans-Pasifika groups: David O'Donnell, 'Finding a Sense of Place in the Pacific Diaspora: Pasifika Performance in Aotearoa', *Australasian Drama Studies* 73, October 2018, pp. 276–305.On the wallpaper, Reihana frequently notes its impact – see, for example: Dee Smith, 'Lisa Reihana: A Monumental, Immersive New Artwork Reanimates the Story of Captain Cook and First Contact', *ABC News*, 2018, https://www.abc.net.au/news/2018-01-31/lisa-reihana-in-pursuit-of-venus-reimagines-australian-history/9376114.

57 On thinking through the mutuality of transcultural exchange in colonial contact histories and migrations, I am indebted both to conversations with, and the wonderful writing of Anne Ring Petersen; cf. 'Spectres of Colonialism in Contemporary Art from Denmark', *Art History* 43:2, April 2020, pp. 258–83, *Migration into Art: Transcultural Identities and Art-Making in a Globalised World*, Manchester: Manchester University Press, 2017.

58 An excellent and burgeoning literature now exists on *In Pursuit of Venus [infected]* that develops these points well. See, in particular: *Lisa Reihana: Emissaries*; Michaela Bear, 'Infecting Venus: Gazing at Pacific History through Lisa Reihana's Multi-Perspectival Lens', *Australia and New Zealand Journal of Art* 19:1, 2019, pp. 7–24; James Charisma, 'A Video Challenges a Colonialist Narrative by Reinterpreting First Contact in the Pacific', *Hyperallergic*, 8 May 2019, https://hyperallergic.com/499420/lisa-reihana-emissaries-honolulu-museum-of-art/; Diana Looser, 'Viewing Time and the Other: Visualizing Cross-cultural and Trans-temporal Encounters in Lisa Reihana's *in Pursuit of Venus [infected]*', *Theatre Journal* 69, 2017, pp. 449–75; Nicholas Thomas, 'Lisa Reihana: Encounters in Oceania', *Artlink*, 1 June 2017, https://www.artlink.com.au/articles/4595/lisa-reihana-encounters-in-oceania/; Caroline Vercoe, 'History is a place: Pacific artists reimagining colonial legacies', in *Lisa Reihana: In Pursuit of Venus*, Auckland: Auckland Art Gallery, 2015, pp. 58-64.

59 Cook and his fellow travellers, British naturalist Joseph Banks, British astronomer Charles Green and Swedish naturalist Daniel Solander, recorded the transit in June 1769 from Tahiti. The significance of this event further inspired the title of Jodi A. Byrd's ground-breaking book *The Transit of Empire: Indigenous Critiques of Colonialism*, Minneapolis and London: University of Minnesota Press, 2011.

60 On the significance of the canoe technologies, see interdisciplinary Indigenous scholar Vicente M. Diaz, 'In the Wake of Matå'pang's Canoe: The Cultural and Political Possibilities of Indigenous Discursive Flourish', in Aileen Moreton-Robinson, ed., *Critical Indigenous Studies: Engagements in First World Locations*, Tucson: University of Arizona Press, 2016, pp. 119–37. On the connectedness of people across Oceania, see the oft-cited essay: 'Our Sea of Islands' by Tongan and Fijian anthropologist Epeli Hau'ofa (*The Contemporary Pacific* 6:1, Spring 1994, pp. 148–61).

61 See Elizabeth M. DeLoughrey's discussion of the incredible increase in 'Robinsonades' (desert island fantasy tales) published in English between 1788 and 1910 in *Routes and Roots: Navigating Caribbean and Pacific Island Literatures*, Honolulu: University of Hawaii Press, 2007, pp. 12–14.

62 Lugones, 'Toward a Decolonial Feminism', p. 747.

63 Reihana is absolutely clear that the work was storied in conversation with a range of Pacific Island, Māori and Aboriginal Australians and that she is very much aware of the ethical issues of telling others' tales is made clear in both: 'Artists of Oceania: Lisa Reihana in Conversation in Conversation with Tim Marlow' (27.11.18): https://www.royalacademy.org.uk/article/oceania-video-lisa-reihana-tim-marlow and in Brook Andrew and Lisa Reihana, 'In Conversation', in *Lisa Reihana: Emissaries*, pp. 74–89.

64 Nikos Papastergiadis, 'What is the South?', *Thesis 11* 100, February 2010, pp. 141–56, p. 148. Papstergiadis' use of South is further resonant with the arguments made by Pallavi Banerjee and Raewyn Connell in 'Gender Theory as Southern Theory', Barbara J. Risman, Carissa M. Froyum and William J. Scarborough, *Handbook of the Sociology of Gender*, Switzerland: Springer International, 2018, pp. 57–68. It is significant that Banerjee and Connell note especially the work of Māori scholar Linda Tuhiwai Smith and the transnational feminisms of Chilla Bulbeck and María Lugones.

65 Reihana cited in Liza Oliver, 'Reimagining Captain Cook: Pacific Perspectives', *CAA Reviews*, 2019 http://www.caareviews.org/reviews/3596#.YGr3nejds2w.

66 Christine Lorre-Johnston, 'Unsettling Oceania, 250 Years Later: Introduction', *Commonwealth Essays and Studies* 41:1 2018, pp. 75–81. The work of Kim TallBear (Sisseton-Wahpeton Oyate) has made a very important contribution to explorations of science, technology and biopower as part of the subjugation of Indigenous people and on countering this through 'multispecies ethnography' – her focus is mainly North American, but her insights are of global relevance. See, for example 'Beyond the Life/Not Life Binary: A Feminist-Indigenous Reading of Cryopreservation, Interspecies Thinking and the New Materialisms', in Joanna Radin and Emma Kowal, eds, *Cryopolitics: Frozen Life in a Melting World*, Cambridge: MIT Press, 2017.

60 Storying Pluriversal Worlds

67 Rhana Devenport's excellent preface and expository opening essay for the catalogue *Lisa Reihana: Emissaries* detail key changes made between the first showing of *iPOV[i]* in Auckland in 2015 and the final version that opened at the Venice Biennale (later touring to Australia, the US, UK and elsewhere). She notes specifically the inclusion of Aboriginal Australians, Cook's clock, Māori, Tahitian, Hawaiian and Nootka Sound canoes, and a 'flip' scene of Cook played by a female actress. I am arguing that these strategic inclusions were interconnected and vital.

68 For an excellent overview of the development of 'racial science' and its impact on the Pacific, see: Bronwen Douglas and Chris Ballard, eds, *Foreign Bodies: Oceania and the Science of Race 1750-1940*, Canberra: ANU E-Press, 2008.

69 This convergence continued well into the 20th century with nuclear testing at Maralinga, a subject I take up in chapter 3 of *Transnational Feminisms, Transversal Politics and Art: Entanglements and Intersections* (2020), the first volume of this Trilogy.

70 Significantly, M. Jacqui Alexander recounts the tale of Balboa's men slaughtering a group of Two-Spirit people in 1513 in what is now Panama, as a founding act of possession in the Americas in *Pedagogies of Crossing: Meditations on Feminism, Sexual Politics, Memory and the Sacred*, Durham, NC and London: Duke University Press, 2005. NB – I borrow the formulation trans-Indigenous from Chadwick Allen, *Trans-Indigenous: Methodologies for Global Native Literary Studies*, Minneapolis: University of Minnesota Press, 2012.

71 Looser, 'Viewing Time and the Other', pp. 449–75. (Looser notes the banned performance on p. 474). On the Māori context – see Clive Aspin, 'Hōkakatanga – Māori sexualities', revised January 2019, *Te Ara The Encyclopedia of New Zealand*, https://teara.govt.nz/en/hokakatanga-maori-sexualities; Alison Laurie and Linda Evans, *Outlines: Lesbian and Gay Histories of Aotearoa*, Wellington: Lesbian and Gay Archives of New Zealand, 2005. I would also note Amelia Jones' recent engagement with the limits of Eurocentric categorization when exploring Pasifika concepts of gender and sexuality in her volume *In Between Subjects: A Critical Genealogy of Queer Performance*, New York and London: Routledge, 2021.

72 For excellent discussions of these questions and arguments for the significance of moving beyond essentialism for trans-Indigenous, transgender thought, see Brendan Hokowhitu, 'Monster: Post-Indigenous Studies', in *Critical Indigenous Studies*, pp. 83–101; and Maddee Clark, 'Becoming-with and Together: Indigenous Transgender and Transcultural Practices', *Artlink* 37:2, June 2017, https://www.artlink.com.au/articles/4604/becomingE28091with-and-together-indigenous-transgender-/.

73 Indigenous queer theorist Jinthana Haritawarn points out how Indigenous people have long been attacked precisely for *not* creating sufficiently rigid and fixed boundaries between genders *or species* the better to exploit both. See her 'Decolonizing the Non/Human' in 'Dossier: Theorizing Queer Inhumanisms', *GLQ: A Journal of Lesbian and Gay Studies* 21:2–3, 2015, pp. 210–3.

74 Anne Salmond points out that Cook's attitudes towards Pacific people was also more fluid than, for example, Banks, whose certitude of superiority was absolute. Salmond, 'Voyaging Worlds', in *Lisa Reihana: Emissaries*, pp. 42–65.

75 *Cf.* Rhana Devenport, 'Emissaries: A New Pacific of the Past for Tomorrow', in *Lisa Reihana: Emissaries*, pp. 16–29; Salmond, 'Voyaging Worlds'; Elizabeth M. DeLoughrey, *Routes and Roots*, pp. 161–7.

76 Deirdre Brown discusses the idea of animated worlds in relation to digitizing Māori objects in: '"Ko tō ringa ki ngā rākau ā te Pākehā" – Virtual *Taonga* Māori and Museums', *Visual Resources* 24:1, March 2008, pp. 59–75, p. 63.

77 For more detail on James Pinker's multi-layered soundtrack, see Andrew Clifford, 'Unmuting History: A Polyphonic Tableau', in *Lisa Reihana: Emissaries*, pp. 124–9. NB: Naturalists on Cook's first voyage were seeking signs of musical polyphony in the Pacific, so the soundtrack has an added historical resonance.

78 *Cf.* Bear, 'Infecting Venus', p. 14.

79 The stereotypes of the 'noble savage' and 'dusky maiden' are mentioned frequently in scholarship; see, for example, Lana Lopesi, 'Beyond Essentialism: Contemporary Moana Art from Aotearoa New Zealand', *Afterall: A Journal of Art, Context and Enquiry* 46, Autumn/Winter 2018, pp. 106–15, p. 108.

80 Alexis Shotwell, *Against Purity*, p. 5.

81 This is, of course, a nod to Donna Haraway's *Staying with the Trouble* and her brilliant exposition of the entanglements between science and Eurocentric, heteronormative colonial histories in the domination of more than human worlds.

82 Kali Simmons, 'Reorientations; Or, an Indigenous Feminist Reflection on the Anthropocene', *Journal of Cinema and Media Studies* 58:2, Winter 2019, pp. 174–9; Alexis Shotwell, *Against Purity*.

83 See RA archive: https://www.royalacademy.org.uk/exhibition/oceania; it was at the Oceania exhibition that I saw *in Pursuit of Venus [infected]*.

84 'Artists of Oceania: Lisa Reihana in Conversation in Conversation with Tim Marlow' (27.11.18).

85 Cambridge also opened a Museum of Archaeology and Anthropology (MAA) in 1884, with its first curators and field researchers being trained at Oxford. The MAA came to have a more extensive Pacific collection and was linked with the RA's *Oceania* show. Its current director, Nicholas Thomas, is undertaking an ambitions decolonizing programme at MAA that includes repatriation of objects.

86 Denise Ferreira da Silva notes Balfour's racial typologies in: *Toward a Global Idea of Race*, Minneapolis: University of Minnesota Press, 2007, p. 131.

87 There is an extensive literature on anthropology's links to this myth of Indigenous cultures being on the brink of extinction; for a moving, personal account of this systematic disavowal and the impact of its slow violence on Indigenous women, see: Shirley Green, 'Looking Back, Still Looking Forward', in Joyce Green, ed., *Making Space for Indigenous Feminisms*, Halifax and Winnipeg: Fernwood Publishing, 2nd edition, 2017, pp. 274–93.

88 Emma Gattey, 'Makereti: Māori 'Insider' Anthropology at Oxford' at https://oxfordandempire.web.ox.ac.uk/article/makereti.

89 For further details on Lever's collections, see: Oliver Impey, 'Lever as a Collector of Chinese Porcelain', *Journal of the History of Collections* 4:2, 1992, pp. 227–238; Andrew West, 'Self Help, Ethnography and Art Together: Liverpool, Lever and Port Sunlight', *Journal of Museum Ethnography*, 11, May 1999, pp. 29–42.

90 Edward Morris, 'Introduction', *Journal of the History of Collections* 4:2, 1992, pp. 169–73. Morris was curator of the Walker Art Gallery.

91 In 2006, Deball co-founded the interdisciplinary UQBAR Foundation with Argentinian artist Irene Kopelman; the project is an open platform collaboration between artists, scientists and thinkers from many other fields designed to explore how knowledges are made. See: https://www.cabinetmagazine.org/events/uqbar.php.

92 In 2018–19, the Pitt Rivers Museum hosted just such a show, *Intrepid Women: Fieldwork in Action, 1910–1957*, see: https://www.prm.ox.ac.uk/event/intrepid-women.

93 Elizabeth Grosz, *Space, Time and Perversion: Essays on the Politics of Bodies*, London and New York: Routledge, 1995, p. 37.

94 The Oxford MOMA site has a downloadable transcript available: https://www.modernartoxford.org.uk/event/making-and-knowing-something/.

95 Marisol de la Cadena and Mario Blaser use 'incommensurability' in a parallel way in 'Pluriverse: Proposals for a World of Many Worlds', in *A World of Many Worlds*, pp. 1–22, pp. 9–10.

96 Gloria Anzaldúa 'Border Arte: Nepantla, el Lugar de la Frontera' (1993), reprinted in *The Gloria Anzaldúa Reader* edited Analouise Keating, Durham, NC and London: Duke University Press, 2009, pp. 176–86.

97 There are a number of significant links that make bringing these ideas into the conversation apt – Lugones frequently cited and wrote about the work of Anzaldúa and the

62 Storying Pluriversal Worlds

term 'neplanta' was borrowed for the short-lived, but highly influential journal *Neplanta: Views from the South* (2000–03), edited by Alberto Moreiras, Walter D. Mignolo and Gabriela Nouzeilles. Readers will recognize the resonance with the earlier invocation in this chapter of Papastergiadis's 'spherical consciousness from the South'. In addition, in a cogent article considering Deball's casts of the Aztec earth goddess Coatlicue, Jennifer Reynolds-Kaye notes the significance of Anzaldúa's invocation of the goddess in this text. See Reynolds-Kaye, 'Circulating Casts of the *Coatlicue*: Mariana Castillo-Deball's Unearthing of the Aztec Earth Goddess's History Or Reproduction and Display', *Sculpture Journal* 28:3, 2019, pp. 365–80, p. 378.

 98 Anzaldúa, 'Border Arte', p. 180.
 99 Anzaldúa, 'Border Arte', p. 176.
100 Anzaldúa, 'Border Arte', p. 178.
101 Nasheli Jiménez del Val, 'A Conceptual Genealogy of "The Indigenous" in Mexican Visual Culture', in *Revista de Estudio Globales y Arte Contemporáneo* 7:1, 2020, pp. 55–90, p. 60. Jiménez del Val is in dialogue with Fernando Coronil, Aníbal Quijano and Walter Mignolo in her text.
102 This echoes a point made by Lisa Reihana in her interview with Tim Marlow concerning how much she learned from re-making the costume of the Chief Mourner for *iPOV[i]*.
103 This creative circle of scholars included African-American, Indigenous and Jewish women, a number of whom were openly lesbian or bi-sexual, and their complex negotiations within the Academy and disciplinary boundaries is resonant. See: *Hidden Scholars: Women Anthropologists and the Native American Southwest*, edited by Nancy J. Parezo, Albuquerque, NM: University of New Mexico Press, 1993; Charles King, *Gods of the Upper Air: How a Circle of Renegade Anthropologists Reinvented Race, Sex, and Gender in the Twentieth Century*, New York: Doubleday, 2019. King's book was reviewed by Ira Bashkow in 'Lines of Thought: Franz Boas: The Man Who Opened Up Anthropology in America', in *The TLS: Times Literary Supplement 6114*, 5 June 2020, pp. 4–6. *See*, also: Frank A. Salamone, 'His Eyes Were Watching Her: Papa Franz Boas, Zora Neale Hurston, and Anthropology', *Anthropos* 109:1, 2014, pp. 217–224; Cynthia Saltzman, 'Ruth Leah Bunzel', *The Jewish Women's Archive*, https://jwa.org/encyclopedia/article/bunzel-ruth-leah-bernheim.
104 Anzaldúa, 'Border Arte', p. 179.
105 Returning to the question asked by Béatrice Joyeux-Prunel in 'Art History and the Global' is instructive:

> … will we succeed in articulating narratives that are global, emancipated from the hierarchies specific to the canon (ancient/modern, fine arts/decoration, kitsch/classical), and also that eschew the other hierarchies from which even the postcolonial narrative has failed to disengage (dominant/dominated)? Can we articulate narratives that function as stories, and thus are effective and convincing?
>
> (p. 434)

PART II
Practice and Flourish

2

POETIC STORIES

Genealogies of Work and Survival with Audre Lorde

Transnational feminist thought and activism places imagination, creativity and cultural transformation at the heart of its calls for social, economic and ecological justice. To know, imagine and inhabit the world, earthwide and otherwise,[1] is both profoundly creative and deeply disobedient. Transnational feminisms frequently transgress the boundaries of established disciplines, institutional frameworks and normative conventions as they fashion the tools needed to story pluriversal worlds towards new and different futures. Their transgressions are crossings that make connections – changing not only *what* is known, but *how* and to what ends.

Practices of crossing, connecting and making knowledges otherwise have led to the emergence of a rich body of creative and experimental writing/making by feminist theorists, artists and activists. This work challenges the pre-eminence of academic norms and scholarly conventions premised upon sharp binary hierarchies between universal/objective knowledge and particular/subjective imagination.[2] Race-critical, decolonial, ecofeminist and queer interventions going back decades have unravelled these simplistic yet dominant hierarchies to reveal the structural sustenance they provide to hegemonic heteropatriarchy, racism, colonial conquest and ecological devastation on a world scale. Epistemic and disciplinary disobedience are entangled with affective and imaginative calls to action in the work of transnational feminists as they explore the radical potential of prefigurative politics storied through *poetics*, a term taken broadly here to encompass various modes of creative textuality – written, performed, and/or materialized through visual art and film. It is important to note that my focus in this chapter is not on poetry, literature or works of text-based visual art, *per se*, but on the crossings and connections forged by transnational feminist knowledge projects situated at the nexus of critical, theoretical and political/activist practices, and creative/artistic textual strategies and genres.[3]

DOI: 10.4324/9780429507816-5

66 Practice and Flourish

Transnational feminisms' poetic practices and textual transgressions perform disciplinary disobedience variously, crossing the boundaries of academic subjects and fields, moving between artistic genres, and creating dialogues between theory and practice, selves and others, individuals and communities. Refusing the transcendent fallacy of disembodied knowing, they speak from *somewhere*, taking responsibility for the position from which they reach out to connect with others, *elsewhere*. They emphasize conversation, dia- and plurilogue,[4] as mechanisms by which ethical bonds are created between diverse subjects through the agency of call and response, rather than by appeals to essential identity. One small worldview, universalized as Truth, dissolves in the polyvocality that tells the many personal-with/in-political stories of myriad interdependent worlds, past, present and yet to come.

While the terrain covered by feminist, queer and decolonial explorations through poetics is diverse and heterogeneous, particular constellations of ideas, in dialogue with the transnational genealogies of this project, are distinctly discernible. Feminist philosophical engagements with phenomenology, semiology, affect and imagination, for example, acknowledged the corporeality of theory and encouraged the articulation of multi-sensory embodied experience through visceral language connecting epistemology with ethics and aesthetics through feminist figurations and affective fictions.[5] Queer, trans and gender-fluid work riffed on these and other corporeal/material, performative and post-human theoretical trajectories, to voice the inessential excess of sexuality and subjectivity outside the boundaries of heteronormative surveillance and control.[6] Feminist interventions into science, technology, ecology and biopower further extended the reach of creative academic writing through crossovers with science/speculative fiction and Indigenous forms of storying that decentre the human subject while emphasizing the materiality of language and the productive potential of meaningful matter.[7] Black, Indigenous and feminists of colour, writing both from the Global South and the metropolitan diaspora, have long used poetics, creative text and critical fabulation to disrupt the monolingual dominance of White solipsism, interrogate the silences of the archive and decolonize the epistemic grammar that silences global majority women, gender non-conforming and colonized subjects.[8]

The turn to aesthetics/poetics in transnational feminist thought and activism is deeply resonant with recent and contemporary explorations in the arts seeking to dissolve hierarchical oppositions between theory and practice. The terrain of 'art writing' – a term deployed variously, but principally, to describe richly evocative critical writing *with* art that acknowledges the affective and imaginative dimensions of multi-sensory knowing – shares much with the race-critical, decolonial, queer and more-than-human trajectories of transnational feminisms.[9] Crossings between these areas of interest and expertise are now common: academics from disciplines traditionally positioned at some distance from the arts deploy creative visual methodologies in their research and write for exhibitions and art events; artists are brought into collaborative research projects with scholars from every subject and field; and transnational feminist activist networks have increasingly become hubs for radical interdisciplinary theorizing and creative public projects.[10]

Poetic Stories **67**

For this project, focused upon the ecologies and genealogies of transnational feminisms and the arts, exploring the radical potential of poetic storying and creative textuality to writing transhemispheric histories otherwise, is imperative. Such practices bridge transnational feminist thought, activism and the affective economies of the arts, entangling theory with practice, knowledge with imagination, and aesthetics with politics and ethics. They also focus attention, as does this volume generally, on the institutional and structural practices of production through which transnational feminist knowledge projects emerge. Exploring *how* the dominance of a limited One world story might be countered by knowing, imagining and (un) writing/(re)making new and many worlds, plays a crucial part in transforming the teleological 'truths' that currently hurtle us with ever-increasing velocity towards greater global injustice and ecological destruction. We may have the knowledge we deserve, but do we have the knowledges that we need?

In what follows, I want to explore transnational feminist genealogies as practices of poetic storying that facilitate vital possibilities for crossing and connection. I read this in particular against the divisive logic of disciplinary hierarchy and categorical purity, pursued through both epistemic and bodily forms of punishment. In this endeavour, I am 'conversing with and walking alongside'[11] Audre Lorde, whose work has long accompanied me and many others seeking to create conversations in and through difference, harness the power of the erotic, hear and voice righteous anger without creating a hierarchy of oppressions, and, in the knowledge that our silence will not protect us, fashion the tools needed to dismantle the master's house.[12] Importantly, in conversing with Lorde's work, and her legacy in and through the work of others, I neither take Lorde as the 'object' of my enquiry, nor as an exemplary 'illustration' of my theory.[13] Rather, Lorde's work acts as a catalyst for further action, a spur and an invitation to continue the crossings and connections needed to create transnational feminist genealogies of art. Lorde's legacy offers many points of departure for this project,[14] but here, I focus upon three vital insights from her practice that I will argue were, and continue to be, pivotal to the significance of poetic storying and creative textual experimentation in transnational feminist thought, activism and art: *work* both as constitutive of locational and interdependent subjectivity, and integral to the formation of transversal solidarities and kinships; *poetry* as anti-canonical, innovative and transformative language capable of voicing emergent visions and compelling ethical action; *survival* in and as inventive practices of flourishing with others through crossings and connections that make new, many, and more-than-human worlds.

Work: Finding Coordinates, Speaking Pieces

In the opening moments of Ada Gay Griffin and Michelle Parkerson's 1995 film, *A Litany for Survival: The Life and Work of Audre Lorde*, we hear the sonorous voice of Lorde speak the first lines of the poem after which the film was named: 'For those of us who live at the shoreline…'[15] Voiced over a series of panning shots taken on the Caribbean island of St Croix, where Lorde lived with her partner

68 Practice and Flourish

Gloria Joseph in the latter years of her life, Lorde goes on to describe the island as a crossing point between the Atlantic Ocean and the Caribbean Sea, and herself as 'an African-Caribbean-American woman'. For those familiar with Lorde's work, the sequence is itself a litany, an incantation of hyphenated and mobile locational identity, resonant with Lorde's oft-cited self-introductory inventory, 'Black, lesbian, mother, warrior, poet', and her mutable practices of cross-cultural self-naming, most notably as Zami and Gamba Adisa.[16]

The opening sequence of Griffin and Parkerson's documentary thus deftly situates Lorde as an historical subject whose African–Caribbean–American geographical coordinates bear witness to the transatlantic slave trade and the continuing legacies of European colonial conquest and genocide in the Americas. But it does much more as well. Lorde's words articulate a hyphenated subjectivity that is fluid and dynamic, a subject who lives at the 'shoreline', and whose agency emerges at the mercurial nexus of myriad crossings between times, places and bodies. Significantly, the emergence of this shoreline subject takes place in and through the *work* of poetics, in courageous and transformative practices of writing the hyphen and speaking the hiatus, that materialize the agency of subjects who were never meant to survive.

This very brief exegesis of the first minutes from *A Litany for Survival* sets out a key facet of the argument I am pursuing here, namely, that Lorde's historical locus was critical to her work not because it proved the truth of her subjectivity, nor underpinned the essence of her identity, but because it provided the material ground – the *somewhere* – from which the creative agency of her poetic storying could materialize imaginative crossings with others, *elsewhere*. Lorde's work was simultaneously grounded and mobile, capable of facilitating profoundly embodied dialogues across difference, of crossing boundaries of race, class and sex, of nation, culture and tradition, of discipline, field and genre.

Active in a number of transnational feminist networks and projects during her lifetime, Lorde's working practices literally crossed boundaries.[17] Lorde was a founding member of the Combahee River Collective (1974–80), a member of the editorial collective for the 'Third World Women' issue of *Heresies* (1979), co-founder of Kitchen Table: Women of Color Press (with Barbara Smith, 1980–92), helped to establish St Croix's Women's Coalition (1980) and was active in the Sisterhood in Support of Sisters in South Africa (SISA) network established by Gloria Joseph in 1984. Her long-term relationships with scholars, writers and feminist activists in Europe were pivotal to the establishment of Afro-German feminist, lesbian, queer and trans networks in Germany, and, with Gloria Wekker, the Sister Outsider group in the Netherlands. Lorde had enduring links with Mexico, the Caribbean and with Latinx feminist lesbian activists, and became increasingly motivated by issues of global Indigenous rights in the last decade of her life, working with Indigenous Australian and Māori women activists during visits to Australia and Aotearoa New Zealand, as well as with First Nations feminists in the United States.

Lorde's transnational praxis produced a body of work that continues to have a remarkable impact on feminist thought, activism and art today. Her writing remains in wide circulation, having been collected, anthologized, translated and published in many editions since her death in 1992. The influence of her work is palpable in that of other transnational feminist theorists, activists and creative practitioners; she is widely cited, her words often deployed as extended epigraphs, and her work has more than once been the subject of moving dedications.[18] Lorde's titles and the evocative motifs from her writing frequently find echoes in others' writing and in the names of festivals, organizations and events.[19] A prolific poet and a teacher, her legacy abides in the work of fellow poets in her circle, including Pat Parker, June Jordan, Adrienne Rich, Jewelle Gomez and Sapphire, but can also be felt in the creative writing, performance and art of later generations of practitioners, such as Sarah Schulman, Alexis Pauline Gumbs, Michèle Pearson Clark and Paul Maheke.[20] In addition, there is a small but significant film legacy, both in available footage of interviews, poetry readings and speeches, and in five films which came out between 1995 and 2018 in the US, the UK and Germany: Griffin and Parkerson's *Litany for Survival* (USA, 1995); Sonali Fernando's *The Body of a Poet* (UK, 1995); Jennifer Abod's *The Edge of Each Other's Battles: The Vision of Audre Lorde* (USA, 2002); Dagmar Schulz's *Audre Lorde: The Berlin Years, 1984–1992* (Germany, 2012); Lana Lin's *The Cancer Journals Revisited* (USA, 2018).[21]

It is not simply the extent of Lorde's impact on the genealogies of transnational feminisms over half a century that is significant here, but how her insights have resonated across many different times, places and practices. Lorde's work has provided both prescient and persistent inspiration to scholars, artists and activists seeking to generate transformative thought and action. More strongly, I would argue that Lorde's concept of *work* – used both as noun and verb in her writing – is a vital point of reference for many who have found fellowship in her ideas, and a critical figuration for transnational feminist explorations of poetics, stories and creative text.[22]

In Lorde's writing, *work* is not a word used lightly, but a term invoked with real passion:

> I want to live the rest of my life, however long or short, with as much sweetness as I can decently manage, loving all the people I love, and doing as much as I can of the work I still have to do. I am going to write fire until it comes out my ears, my eyes, my noseholes – everywhere. Until it's every breath I breathe. I'm going to go out like a fucking meteor![23]

Writing fire and doing 'good work'[24] define an approach to living fully on the horizon of death, facing your fears, refusing silence, invisibility and compliance, and taking the risk of 'speaking your pieces', even when you may be misunderstood or reviled.[25] *Work*, used by Lorde, does not evoke mindless, soul-destroying labour, but life's purpose; in doing your work you find your coordinates, the *somewhere* from which you can speak to any and every imaginable *elsewhere*. Work is a vital vocation that forges flourishing and dynamic subjectivity. It is a profound personal calling, but, importantly, it is also the basis of ethical relations with others beyond the limits of essential identity politics.[26] It is from the coordinates of one's own work that it

70 Practice and Flourish

is possible to call to others, or, as Lorde so compellingly framed it: 'I am a Black feminist lesbian warrior poet doing my work, and a piece of my work is asking you, how are you doing yours?'[27]

That is a call that demands a response. The response comes not by mimicking Lorde's work, but in each and all finding their coordinates and doing their own. Such *work* creates *crossings* – transversal dialogues that mobilize difference to forge transnational, transcultural, transracial, transgenerational, transgender solidarities and kinships. This *work* does not ignore the powerful locational politics of situated knowledge and embodied subjectivity, but it provides a means by which to reach across the abyss. Asked in 1986 for whom she wrote, Lorde turned the conversation away from identity to focus on the *use* of her *work*:

> My audience is *every* single person who can use the work I do... Now, I write out of who I am, all of the ways I describe myself, and so, all those people who share those aspects of me, who are Black, who are warrior women poets, lesbians... may find themselves closer to what I am doing, but I write out of who I am for everyone who can use what I'm saying.[28]

Using Lorde's *work* to find one's own is a familiar leitmotif in the writing of many transnational feminists who have heeded Lorde's call. Some have found their coordinates close to Lorde. M Jacqui Alexander, for example, wrote eloquently of the profound impact of finding and reading Lorde's bio-mythography, *Zami: A New Spelling of My Name*, as a young Afro-Caribbean scholar and lesbian activist recently relocated to the United States, whilst Sara Ahmed recalled the feeling of kinship that Lorde's words provided her as a young woman of colour, though not of African descent, growing up in a 'very white neighbourhood' in Australia.[29] By contrast, US American lesbian poet and activist Adrienne Rich shared a long friendship with Lorde that cut across racial lines, during which their work was frequently in dialogue on the politics of race, gender, class and sexuality.[30] Rich's critical work on White solipsism and the politics of location offers another form of response to Lorde's call to do your own work, where that work by needs must transform the silence of White privilege into the language and action of anti-racist alliance.

The voices and coordinates of transnational feminists are not the same, but rather, they are able to be raised, and resonate powerfully in their differences, together. Transversal solidarity is polyphonic, radical kinship is kaleidoscopic, or, in Lorde's words, once again emphasizing *work*: 'We have many different faces, and we do not have to become each other in order to work together.'[31]

Nowhere was the legacy of Lorde's eloquent and multifaceted conception of *work* expressed more compellingly than in Jennifer Abod's film, *The Edge of Each Other's Battles: The Vision of Audre Lorde* (2002). Abod's documentary focused on the conference organized by M Jacqui Alexander and Angela Bowen in Boston in 1990, *I Am Your Sister: Forging Global Connections across Differences*. Bringing together some 1200 women, men and activist youth from 23 countries for four days, the

Poetic Stories **71**

event was organized in dialogue with Lorde and was focused on *using her work* to address 'cultural experiences of race, gender, sexuality and class'.[32]

The documentary intersperses film of Lorde on-stage and in interview, with footage of the many and diverse participants who, during the course of the event, came on stage to *do their work*, voicing their coordinates through poetry, spoken-word, song, dance, manifesto, statement, testimony and memorial. In the speaking, and in the listening, there was anger and strength, courage and tears, collective joy, cheering, laughter, song and dance – calls found collective response. The film also recorded action from off-stage, charting the organization of the conference, including interviews with Alexander, Bowen and some of the many volunteers who worked tirelessly to enable such a large and complex event to take place.

Abod's documentary is a rich film historically and aesthetically, but here I want to focus closely on *work* by drawing together just a few key sequences and pivotal passages, starting with the final appearance of Lorde on stage, a few minutes before the film ends. As the conference draws to a close, the voices of women singing can be heard echoing in the hall as a still image of Lorde appears on screen with the words: 'Each of us must find our work and do it.' The action continues as Lorde gives her final address to the group, remarking that in organizing the event, Alexander and Bowen 'challenged me to do my work like no one before'. Thanking the participants for their energy, she comments that it is 'life-sustaining' to know that your work is used by others. At the end, Lorde encourages and challenges the group to deal with their fears, move against a common enemy and make a commitment to the future with the question: '... are you doing *your* work?'

The ending sequence is powerful as a singular moment, but more so in the wider context of the film, which had followed both the compelling polyphony of diverse voices, doing their own work whilst raised together in glorious chorus, and the difficult, sometimes painful *work* of solidarity- and alliance-building that underpins transnational dialogues in and across difference. Fifteen minutes into the documentary, Abod turned to a key element of the organization of the conference – the convenors' commitment to reserving half of the spaces for participants of colour. In the five minutes during which the film charts the impact of this commitment, and its fulfilment, we witness the extremes of both White feminist privilege and transracial alliance unfold. Some White feminists chivvy and berate young volunteers in attempts (some deceitful) to gain access to their 'rightful' spaces at the event, whilst others send money with their registration letters, pledging support for the process and asking that their fees become donations if they are not able to be allocated a seat. The sharp variation amongst White feminist responses to the equitable application process is not a surprise, but the film's emphasis upon the *work* of building solidarity – emotional, intellectual, personal, political labour – and the importance of this as the foundation of the 'on-stage' *work* of the event, is telling. Yet this is not the end of the tale.

At 45 minutes, the film turns to another crisis of solidarity that emerged during the course of the event, as a number of Asian-American and Latinx feminists

72 Practice and Flourish

(mainly from outside the United States), confronted the organizers with their sense that Black (particularly US-based African-American) women were dominating the conference and that they were, in turn, being silenced. It is not the crisis in itself that is interesting, though it generated a steep learning curve for the organizers, but the response made to the call. Alexander, Bowen and their team listened and took action; the final day of the event was wholly re-organized overnight to permit speak-outs for everyone seeking to say their piece on stage. Rifts were addressed openly and the *work* of crossing became visible and audible, embodied by the participants as they did their own work, differently, together. Creating the polyphonic and resonant solidarities that are crucial to transnational feminist *work* means voicing and listening, calling and responding, in turn. Lorde's final appearance on the stage in Boston in 1990 was *work*, the work of finding coordinates, of speaking from somewhere, of listening to others, elsewhere, and of adding her unique and mellifluous voice to the rising chorus that sounds at the edges of each other's battles.

Poetry: Unwriting the Dream of Europe

Time and again in her writing, Lorde stressed that *her work* was poetry.[33] Like *work*, Lorde used the word *poetry* with passion and care, as a transgressive and transformative term:

> I speak here of poetry as a revelatory distillation of experience, not the sterile word play that, too often, the white fathers distorted the word *poetry* to mean... For women, then, poetry is not a luxury. It is a vital necessity of our existence. It forms the quality of the light within which we predicate our hopes and dreams toward survival and change, first made into language, then into idea, then into more tangible action... Poetry is not only dream and vision; it is the skeleton architecture of our lives.[34]

Lorde's eloquent exposition of the power of poetry has inspired the work of many scholars, artists and writers subsequently. It is not my intention here, however, to attempt to trace every link, even if this were possible, nor to explore Lorde's legacy within the bounded terrain of poetry as a specific literary genre. Rather, I want to attend to the dynamic force of Lorde's tripartite concept of poetry as a form of emergent, anti-canonical and transdisciplinary thought, materialized through imaginative language, capable of compelling transformative change. Arguably, it is this description of the force and function of *poetry*, expressed with exceptional clarity in Lorde's creative and critical verse, that has proven so compelling to later transnational feminists seeking to mobilize *poetics* as a vital tool for thinking, making and writing otherwise.

I am using the terms 'anti-canonical' and 'transdisciplinary' to signal the deep sense of disobedience to Eurocentric knowledge- and worldmaking projects that lies at the heart of many transnational feminist explorations of poetry/poetics. Within this frame, Lorde's transgressive writing is frequently understood as part of a Caribbean/Black Radical or woman of colour intellectual tradition, within a transnational/global feminist (sometimes *womanist*) activist context, and as pivotal to the development of lesbian/queer of colour poetic politics.[35] These coordinates are significant not because they fix Lorde's insights to an essential identity politics, but because they situate her work within a feminist genealogy of decolonizing thought capable of dismantling Eurocentric knowledges from the 'shoreline', and at the 'edges of each other's battles'.

Tracing some of these threads makes this point clear. Caribbean-American literary scholar Carole Boyce Davies, for example, has written eloquently of the intimate interconnection between theoretical and creative work in the Black Caribbean intellectual tradition, bringing Lorde together with Claudia Jones, Zora Neale Hurston and Sylvia Wynter.[36] Black lesbian poet and critical theorist Rosamond S. King describes the 'radical interdisciplinarity' of the writing styles of Lorde, Gloria Anzaldúa and Leslie Marmon Silko, as a 'woman of color methodology'.[37] And, in an exceptionally cogent argument centred on the decolonizing politics of poetry/poetics in Black (particularly Afro-Caribbean) cultural theory, international relations scholar Louiza Odysseos traced a trajectory that linked the work of Lorde with Hortense Spillers' 'homilectics' and Sylvia Wynter's 'socio-poetics', through to Saidiya Hartman's critical fabulations in and of the 'afterlife of slavery' and Christina Sharpe's 'wake work'.[38] In her text, Odysseos made the salient case that this work constitutes a form of 'insurgent poetic revolt', that draws together processes of '"fabulation", world-making otherwise and resignification' to challenge the limits of the world as currently conceived in and through the genocidal violence of colonial globality.[39] These are not idle evocations of poetry as a limited form of 'sterile word play', but transformative understandings of poetry/poetics as creative modes through which canonical Eurocentric thought – steeped in the disciplining, punishment and destruction of difference – can be unravelled, *unworlded*, to story future worlds as yet unknown.

Following these genealogical threads further, I want to return to a particular invocation of poetry in Lorde's writing, as a prescient expression of the 'wake work' of 'insurgent poetic revolt', or what Denise Ferreira da Silva has latterly described as 'Black Feminist Poethics'.[40] In 1988, Lorde was invited to take part in a panel at the House of World Cultures in Berlin entitled 'The Dream of Europe: Authors Invite Authors'. The experience was not particularly positive for Lorde, but her statement was a clarion call to decolonize Eurocentric ways of knowing, imagining and inhabiting the world. Challenging the myth of Europe's 'civilizing' narrative from the standpoint of the non-White global majority, Lorde delivered a stinging indictment of Eurocentric solipsism and epistemic complacency underpinned by violence, reaching the conclusion that survival would only be achieved by 'learning to use difference for something other than destruction'.

74 Practice and Flourish

Significantly, Lorde opened her statement by staking a claim for *poetry* as critical to this task:

> I am an African-American poet and believe in the power of poetry. Poetry, like all art, has a function: to bring us closer to who we wish to be, to help us vision a future which has not yet been, and to help us survive the lack of that future.[41]

This is a powerful proposal for a race-critical, decolonial politics forged in and as poetics and has important ramifications for explorations of creative textuality in transnational feminist thought, activism and art. In this formulation, poetry/poetics have a purpose and that purpose links directly to the future of subjects who 'were never meant to survive'. Lorde concluded the 'Dream of Europe' with a visionary call that implicated *all* of her listeners in the challenge of future survival:

> Those of us who feel our star is in the ascendant do not need to diminish the efforts of others who wish to examine their own decline with grace... We have learned useful tools from Europe – and by 'we' I mean that two thirds of the world's population that are People of Color. Our survival means learning to use difference for something other than destruction. So does yours.
>
> And, with or without you, we are moving on.[42]

As I will argue in the final section of this chapter, it is not surprising that *survival* comes to the fore at this point, nor that it signals a worldmaking vision for the future borne of loving interdependence and multiscalar flourishing. 'Our' survival and 'yours', however brutal the production and deployment of those terms may have been or yet be, cannot be disentangled. There is no outside of this world from which to fashion another; we each and all must find and do our 'wake' work, however differently, together, to create the radical possibility of mutual *survival* in new and many worlds.

Survival: Flourishing Together in Interdependent Worlds

Lorde's writing spoke to *survival*, and 'more than survival',[43] in many and varied contexts, drawing on the potential of the term to act as a multifaceted signifier of the profound entanglement of the personal with the political. Time and again, Lorde stressed that Black lives are led on the horizon of death, in the wake of colonial genocide, enslavement and enduring forms of violence and incarceration, specifically devised for those who were never meant to survive.[44] She spoke likewise of endemic sexual and gender-based violence, and her expansive address to *survival* as a geopolitical imperative, led to her forging strong personal bonds of transnational solidarity with women of colour, Indigenous activists, and lesbian and gender-diverse people globally. In Lorde's work, the matter of survival was not a studied

Poetic Stories **75**

abstraction – 'Survival is not an academic skill'[45] – but a visceral, lived imperative, the understanding of which was, for Lorde, honed to razor sharpness by living the greater part of her last 15 years with cancer.

Lorde's determination to live fully and richly, in the wake of and with, breast and liver cancers, left an eloquent testimony across the breadth of her poetry, essays, speeches and journal entries. Two volumes of essays and diary entries in particular have served to crystallize the legacy of her thinking on survival: *The Cancer Journals*, first published in 1980, tracing her experience of breast cancer and recovery after mastectomy in 1978, and *A Burst of Light and Other Essays* (1988), combining essays and excerpts from diary entries written over her first three years of living with liver cancer (metastasized from her earlier breast cancer). Using her critical and creative writing as a vital space through which to define, practice and materialize *survival*, she came to terms with her personal experiences of cancer within a wide-ranging social, political, ethical and spiritual framework. This global yet intimate approach to cancer enabled her to express the depth of her fears, grief, passion and joy, whilst simultaneously broaching the silences and shame that persist around women's bodies, medicine and healthcare. Lorde further delivered prescient analyses of the geopolitics of 'environmental' cancers and the global power differentials that continue to ensure that some bodies are granted the imperative to survive over others.[46]

Her global and intimate approach to *survival* further provoked a powerful political and ethical impetus towards 'self-care', understood not as privileged pampering, but as the 'militant responsibility' of every woman to 'involve herself actively with her own heath'.[47] Lorde's writing on self-care as a radical take on the imbrication of the personal and the political in everyday practices of living, has proven to be one of her most enduring legacies to later generations of feminists. More strongly, self-care is not solipsistic, but generous and generative; it forms the critical groundwork for loving others, engaging the power and creativity of the erotic (beyond sex), and creating kinships, assemblages and solidarities with and through difference.[48] Lorde was decisive on the significance of both (self) care and love to her own *survival*, writing towards the end of *The Cancer Journals*:

> I believe it is this love of my life and my self, and the careful tending of that love which was done by women who love and support me, which has been largely responsible for my strong and healthy recovery from the effects of my mastectomy.[49]

Arguably, this militant responsibility for self-care, supported by the love of many and diverse women, extended the very limits of the notion of a 'self' invoked within Lorde's writing, to encompass loving connections and kinships with others, and critical acts of personal-with/in-political engagement. I want to take this idea a step further, in dialogue with the compelling arguments made by Tamara Lea Spira on Lorde's accounts of her travels in Mexico. Spira argued that Lorde's corporeal encounters with the creative potential of difference, figured through the colours,

76 Practice and Flourish

sounds, light, textures and tastes of Mexico (and of her lover there, Eudora), combined in her writing as a revolutionary decolonization of the regimes of knowledge and imagination that she had normalized growing up in the United States.[50] In her accounts of Mexico, Lorde was able to articulate her self as a mobile, mutable, 'shoreline' subject through intrinsically interconnected registers of experience – affective, imaginative, social, geographical and political.

Understanding Lorde's revolutionary poetic storying and globally interconnected political writing as deeply intertwined with bodily pleasure and aesthetics, has important ramifications for the argument I am pursuing here. By any measure, Lorde's ability to create palpable and poetic connections in her writing between structural racism, sexism, homophobia, xenophobia, global economic, social and political injustice, environmental poison, world-wide ecological devastation and long-term illness, is an exceptional feat.[51] But there is more. I want to extend this line of thought further to suggest that in their critical combination of multisensory and trans-scalar interconnectivities, Lorde's explorations of *survival* begin to move beyond the boundaries of a time-limited self and a human-centred universe, towards the possibility of creating many and more-than-human worlds. This is a visionary poetics of *survival* that is simultaneously grounded in the immediate and material struggles for greater global social, economic and ecological justice, but that yet remains open to the transformative potential of the radical imagination to make collective futures otherwise. This is the kernel of a visionary transnational feminist poetic politics capable of decolonizing the anthropocentric logic and impoverished notion of the human upon which Eurocentric universalism was founded.

I want to turn to two passages in Lorde's writing, separated by six years, yet resonant in tone, timbre and trope. The first comes at the very end of the Introduction to *The Cancer Journals* and is dated 29 August 1980:

> I have found that battling despair does not mean... ignoring the strength and the barbarity of the forces aligned against us. It means teaching, surviving and fighting... knowing that my work is part of a continuum of women's work, of reclaiming this earth and our power, and knowing that this work did not begin with my birth nor will it end with my death. It means trout fishing on the Missiquoi River at dawn and tasting the green silence, and knowing that this beauty is mine forever.[52]

The second was written in February of 1986, from the Caribbean island of Anguilla:

> Yet only earth and sky last forever, and the ocean joins them. I hear the water's song, feel the tides within the fluids of my body, hear the sea echoing my mothers' voices of survival from Elmina to Grenville to Harlem. I hear them resounding inside me from swish to boom – from the dark of the moon to fullness.[53]

Survival in these passages shifts decisively away from an individual body (*bios*), to the practices that sustain life itself (*zoe*), in which any sense of self can only be

Poetic Stories **77**

registered as part of a much greater continuum – a continuum comprised of women's work and power, sustained over generations by mothers' voices of survival, and of the very matter of the cosmos from which we, too, are made. *Survival* is not ego-centric, but persists rather in the extension of one's work/voice through that of others, an understanding that is intrinsically interconnected in each passage with the visceral, sensual/erotic recognition of the infinite entanglement of our bodies with/in the world. This is survival shaped through interdependent and more-than-human flourishing, as a transgressive and prefigurative politics that mobilizes a visionary poetics in the service of futures as yet unrealized but profoundly possible. Tasting the green silence, hearing the water's song, feeling the tides within the fluids of her body, Lorde articulated a shoreline subject whose *survival* would continue beyond her death, through the crossings and connections made in and through the bodies of those who would heed her call and extend her work, through their own, towards storying new and many future worlds.

Coda[54]

In 2018, artist and filmmaker Lana Lin completed and released the feature-length film *The Cancer Journals Revisited*. Over 98 minutes, the film brings the voices of 28 people, many (but not all) of whom identify as women, together around Lorde's book, reading passages and discussing their own experiences of breast cancer and the social, economic, environmental and institutional regimes through which women and gender-diverse subjects experience, seek to make sense of, and survive, cancer in their lives. The survivors assembled by Lin for this film most certainly are not alike: they are Black, White, Indigenous and people of colour, and they hail from many different parts of the world. Some read in English as an Old or a New World mother tongue; for others, the language is a recent addition to a multilingual suite acquired through a history of migration. They are lesbians, bisexual, queer, trans, gender non-conforming and cis-gendered, they are old and young, artists, scholars, activists, medical professionals and policy makers. They are friends and family of Lorde and those who never met the poet during her life, but have been transformed through deep kinship with her work.

The survivors tell tales of personal loss and political struggles in direct and disarming language – Elizabeth Lorde-Rollins speaks of her mother's 'sharpened urgency and political focus' living with cancer, Catalina Schliebener, an Argentinian reader of Lorde's work, narrates the brutal irony that unrelated medical treatment with hormones accelerated their breast cancer, and feminist filmmaker Barbara Hammer, who had just gone back into cancer treatment before the filming, ad libs 'I hope this isn't my last interview, but it could be.' The readers cry, they laugh and they speak truth to power; Kimberleigh Joy Smith from New York's Callen-Lorde Community Health Centre, explains the public policy issues at stake in providing adequate healthcare to the LGBTQ+ community in the context of systemic racism, sexism and homophobia, stating simply that 'violence is a health issue'. Black anthropologist Vanessa Agard-Jones reminds listeners that cancer is not a private

78 Practice and Flourish

or individual matter, but jumps 'across scales', such that exposure to chemical and physical carcinogens are the material effects of social and economic iniquities. As they read from *The Cancer Journals*, and speak from their own coordinates, the assembly of survivors speaking their pieces differently, together, become the 'continuum', whose power survives and is enhanced through collective love and care carried across generations and oceans.

But *The Cancer Journals Revisited* is much more than captured footage of a reading group, however eloquent these readers are as Lorde's interlocutors. It is a film, a soundscape and moving-image work that unfolds over time. It creates visual, haptic, sonic and spatial resonances that extend Lorde's textual poetics into new and different aesthetic registers. It does not copy, mimic or 'extract' from Lorde's writing, but uses it as a catalyst to 'move on', answers Lorde's call to each of us to find our own coordinates, and, in this instance, to do the work of storying 'more than survival'. Answering Lorde's 'call' is set out very early in the film when at 5 minutes, black text appears on a white screen: 'I am a queer Asian artist filmmaker, making this work partly in response to Audre Lorde's call to action.' Placing herself within the dynamics of the project again at 12 minutes, we are told in a voice-over: 'My partner shot this footage of me when I was undergoing chemotherapy. I never imagined I would use it.' The footage is intimate; we see Lin, who has lost her hair, at close range, through the loving eye/lens of her partner. She smiles gently, not *for* the camera, but *with* her lover. We are then told: 'But it is fitting that I should make myself somewhat as vulnerable as the people I have invited in front of the camera.' With these few scenes, Lin sets out her coordinates, but also expresses, beyond words, a continuum created through the on-going love, generosity and care of women, to which Lorde had so eloquently ascribed her own survival nearly four decades earlier.

There is, of course, much to say about a film as resonant as Lin's, but I want to end on the final note of the film itself, which turns to Lorde's writing on the continuum of the work of survival directly. As Lorde's passage is read – 'my work is part of a continuum of women's work, of reclaiming this earth and our power' – the screen fills with trees and dappled sunlight in a green forest. The scene becomes quiet with little more to be seen or heard than the ripple and sound of the breeze passing through the foliage. The camera pans to a woman's body, reclining in the wood, alighting upon her uncovered torso. Evidence of the woman's mastectomy is clearly visible across the soft rise and fall of her chest as she breathes. We watch and listen to her breathing, the breathing of a woman of colour in the green silence,[55] interrupted only by the lines 'Some kinds of pain are not so much expressed in words as born/e through words. Yet sometimes words escape us, and then what we have is breath.'

This final sequence arrests me. I cannot help but read its striking beauty with and through remembered images of thousands of hand-written signs and collective voices breathing together – *conspiring* – to speak, together, the words 'I can't breathe'. To breathe is to *aspire*; each breath may yet be enough to transform the future, and with our breath, to flourish together, in difference, in a world of many worlds (Figure 2.1).

FIGURE 2.1 Lana Lin, still from *The Cancer Journals Revisited*, 2018.
Image courtesy of the artist.

Notes

1 'Knowing, imagining and inhabiting, earthwide and otherwise' is a dialogue with the first volume of this Trilogy, *Transnational Feminisms, Transversal Politics and Art: Entanglements and Intersections*, London and New York: Routledge, 2020, where the phrase is used as an introductory 'strapline'. NB: there are a number of such dialogues cutting across the volumes of this Trilogy.
2 For a wonderful recent exemplar, see Alpesh Kantilal Patel and Yasmeen Siddiqui, eds, *Storytellers of Art Histories: Living and Sustaining a Creative Life*, Bristol and Chicago, IL: Intellect, 2022.
3 I am aware, as I make this distinction, that there is no hard and fast boundary to be delineated here, but, rather, that the dissolution of such boundaries is central to the argument being pursued. I take this as being akin to cross-boundary exploration of writing genres that Saidiya Hartman articulated in her interview with her former teacher and mentor Hazel Carby when she spoke of 'memoir, history, auto-theory, narrative, and poetics'. See: Hartman, 'Errant Daughters: A Conversation between Saidiya Hartman and Hazel Carby', *Paris Review*, 21 January 2020, https://www.theparisreview.org/blog/2020/01/21/errant-daughters-a-conversation-between-saidiya-hartman-and-hazel-carby/.
4 Shireen Roshanravan points out that plurilogue is not opposed to dialogue in her excellent article 'Motivating Coalition: Women of Color and Epistemic Disobedience', *Hypatia* 29:1, Winter 2014, pp. 41–58 (p. 43).
5 In this, and the following five notes, the lists are indicative of the range of work described, but by no means exhaustive. *Cf.* Hélène Cixous, 'The Laugh of the Medusa', trans. Keith and Paula Cohen, *Signs* 1:4, 1976, 875–93; Barbara Smith, ed., *Home Girls: A Black Feminist Anthology*, New York: Kitchen Table: Women of Color Press, 1983; Luce Irigaray, *Speculum of the Other Woman*, New York: Cornell University Press, 1985; Trinh T. Minh-ha, *Woman, Native, Other: Writing Postcoloniality and Feminism*, Indianapolis: Indiana University Press, 1989; Moira Gatens and Genevieve Lloyd, *Collective Imaginings: Spinoza Past and Present*, London and New York: Routledge, 1999; Rosi Braidotti, *Metamorphoses: Towards a Materialist Theory of Becoming*, Cambridge: Polity, 2002; bell hooks with Amalia Mesa-Bains, *Homegrown: Engaged Cultural Criticism*, Cambridge, MA:

80 Practice and Flourish

South End Press, 2006; Elizabeth Grosz, *Chaos, Territory, Art: Deleuze and the Framing of the Earth*, New York: Columbia University Press, 2008; Lauren Berlant, *Cruel Optimism*, Durham, NC and London: Duke University Press, 2011; Nina Lykke, ed., *Writing Academic Texts Differently: Intersectional Feminist Methodologies and the Playful Art of Writing*, London and New York: Routledge, 2014; Clare Hemmings, *Considering Emma Goldman: Feminist Political Ambivalence and the Imaginative Archive*, Durham, NC and London: Duke University Press, 2018; Saidiya Hartman, *Wayward Lives, Beautiful Experiments: Intimate Histories of Social Upheaval*, London: Norton, 2019; Erin Manning, *For a Pragmatics of the Useless (Thought in the Act)*, Durham, NC and London: Duke University Press, 2020.

6 *Cf.* Judith Butler, *Bodies That Matter: On the Discursive Limits of 'Sex'*, London and New York: Routledge, 1993; Stacy Alaimo and Susan Hekman, eds, *Material Feminisms*, Indianapolis: Indiana University Press, 2008; José Esteban Muñoz, *Cruising Utopia: The Then and There of Queer Futurity*, New York and London: NYU Press, 2009; Maggie Nelson, *The Argonauts*, New York: Melville House: 2016; Eliza Steinbock, *Shimmering Images: Trans Cinema, Embodiment and the Aesthetics of Change*, Durham, NC and London: Duke University Press, 2019.

7 *Cf.* Octavia Butler, *Xenogenesis Trilogy 1987–9* (republished as *Lilith's Brood*, Warner Books, 2000); Jewelle Gomez, *The Gilda Stories*, Ithaca, NY: Firebrand Books, 1991; Donna J. Haraway, *Modest_Witness@Second_Millennium. FemaleMan_Meets_OncoMouse: Feminism and Technoscience*, London and New York: Routledge, 1997; Marilyn Strathern, *Property, Substance and Effect. Anthropological Essays on Persons and Things*. London: Athlone Press, 1999; Karen Barad, *Meeting the Universe Halfway: Quantum Physics and the Entanglement of Matter and Meaning*, Durham, NC and London: Duke University Press, 2007; Dian Million, 'Felt Theory: An Indigenous Feminist Approach to Affect and History', *Wicazo Sa Review* 24:2, 2009, 53–76; Anna Tsing, *The Mushroom at the End of the World: On the Possibility of Life in Capitalist Ruins*, Princeton, NJ: Princeton University Press, 2015; KimTallBear, *The Critical Polyamorist*, http://www.criticalpolyamorist.com/.

8 *Cf.* Cherríe Moraga and Gloria Anzaldúa, eds, *This Bridge Called My Back: Writings by Radical Women of Color*, Watertown, MA: Persephone Press, 1981; Hortense Spillers, 'Mama's Baby, Papa's Maybe: An American Grammar Book', *Diacritics* 17:2, 1987, 65–81; Urvashi Butalia, *The Other Side of Silence: Voices from the Partition of India*, Gurgaon, India: Penguin Books India, 1998; Linda Tuhiwai Smith, *Decolonizing Methodologies: Research and Indigenous People* (1999), 3rd edition, London: Zed Books and Bloomsbury, 2021; María Lugones, *Peregrinajes/Pilgrimages: Theorizing Coalition against Multiple Oppressions*, New York: Rowman & Littlefield Press, 2003; Saidiya Hartman, 'Venus in Two Acts', *small axe* 26, June 2008, pp. 1–14; Leanne Betasamosake Simpson, *Islands of Decolonial Love: Stories & Songs*, Winnipeg: ARP Books, 2013, Janet Neigh, 'Dreams of Uncommon Languages: Transnational Feminist Pedagogy and Multilingual Poetics', *Feminist Formations* 26:1, Spring 2014, pp. 70–92; Elizabeth A. Povinelli, *Geontologies: A Requiem to Late Liberalism*, Durham, NC and London: Duke University Press, 2016; Kim Mahood, *Position Doubtful: Mapping Landscapes and Memories*, London: Scribe, 2016; Julietta Singh, *Unthinking Mastery: Dehumanism and Decolonial Entanglements*, Durham, NC and London: Duke University Press, 2018.

9 I have had the privilege of knowing (and sometimes of working closely with) a number of wonderful scholars whose practices of 'art writing' have made a great impact on my thinking, including Jane Rendell (*cf. Site Writing: The Architecture of Art Criticism*, London: IB Tauris, 2010 and Site: Reading Writing Quarterly: https://site-readingwritingquarterly.co.uk/); Kristen Kreider (*cf. Poetics of Place: The Architecture of Sign, Subjects and Site*, London: I.B. Tauris, 2014); Katve-Kaisa Kontturi (*cf. Ways of Following: Art, Materiality and Collaboration*, London: Open Humanities Press, 2018); Helen Ennis (*cf. Margaret Michaelis: Love, Loss and Photography*, Seattle: University of Washington Press, 2005); Elizabeth King (*cf. Attention's Loop: A Sculptor's Reverie on the Co-existence of Substance and Spirit*, New York: Harry N. Abrams, 1999); Catherine Grant

(*cf.* co-edited with Patricia Rubin, 'Special Issue: Creative Writing and Art History', *Art History* 34:2, 2011); Tilo Reifenstein, 'On Writing: Propositions for Art History as Literary Practice' (unpublished). Other key texts include: Yve Lomax, *Sounding the Event: Escapades in Dialogue and Matters in Art, Nature and Time*, London: I.B. Tauris, 2005; Estelle Barrett and Barbara Bolt, eds, *Carnal Knowledge: Towards a 'New Materialism' through the Arts*, London: I.B. Tauris, 2012. In addition, I have elsewhere written about projects incorporating creative text by a number of remarkable artists, including Faith Ringgold (see chapter 2 of my book *Women Making Art: History, Subjectivity, Aesthetics*, London and New York: Routledge, 2003); Jenny Holzer (see my 'Practice as Thinking: Toward Feminist Aesthetics', in Martin L. Davies and Marsha Meskimmon, eds, *Breaking the Disciplines: Reconceptions in Knowledge, Art and Culture*, London: I.B. Tauris, 2003, pp. 223–45; and in the first volume of this Trilogy, Nalima Sheikh and Joan Brassil.

10 *Cf.* World of Matter: http://worldofmatter.net/; Women Eco Artists Dialog (WEAD) https://www.weadartists.org/; ecoartspace: https://ecoartspace.org/; AWARE: https://awarewomenartists.com/.

11 Juanita Sundberg, 'Decolonizing Posthumanist Geographies', *Cultural Geographies* 21:1, 2014, pp. 33–47 (see chapter 1 of this volume for further discussion of this text).

12 Many readers will recognize my play with Lorde's work in this sentence, but it is serious play in that the essays I am echoing here are some of the most frequently cited in her oeuvre and thus are central to her transnational feminist legacy. *Cf.* Audre Lorde, 'The Master's Tools Will Never Dismantle the Master's House', in *Sister Outsider: Essays and Speeches by Audre Lorde*, Berkeley, CA: Crossing Press (1984), 2007, pp. 110–13; 'The Uses of the Erotic: The Erotic as Power', in *Sister Outsider*, pp. 53–9; 'The Uses of Anger: Women Responding to Racism', in *Sister Outsider*, pp. 124–33; 'There is no hierarchy of oppressions', *Bulletin: Homophobia and Education*. New York: Council on Interracial Books for Children, 1983; 'The Transformation of Silence into Language and Action', part I of *The Cancer Journals* (Aunt Lute Books, 1980), Penguin Random House UK, 2020, pp. 11–16.

13 There have been a number of critiques of White feminism's tendency to ignore, silence or 'extract' from the work of Black and feminists of colour, using them simply as 'diverse' case studies in a White Eurocentric narrative, which is the antithesis of the aim of this project. *Cf.* Joel Burges, Alisa V. Prince and Jeffrey Allen Tucker, 'Introduction: Black Studies Now and the Countercurrents of Hazel Carby', *In Visible Culture* 31, Fall 2020, pp. 1–32.

14 Indeed, Lorde's work played a major role in the first volume of this Trilogy, *Transnational Feminisms, Transversal Politics and Art*.

15 Audre Lorde, 'A Litany for Survival', in *The Collected Poems of Audre Lorde*, New York and London: W.W. Norton and Company, 1997, p. 255. This notion of a 'shoreline' subject is, of course, resonant with the 'archipelagic' thinking developed by Martiniquan poet and philosopher Édouard Glissant in his influential book, *Poetics of Relation* (1990; trans. Betty Wing, Ann Arbor, MI: University of Michigan Press, 1997), and with the concept of 'tidalectics' articulated by Bajan poet Edward Kamau Braithwaite in *The Arrivants: A New World Trilogy* from 1973. I return to these 'terraqueous' terrains in chapter 4.

16 *Cf. Zami: A New Spelling of My Name* (1982), London: Penguin Books, Ltd., 2018; Gamba Adisa (Warrior: She Who Makes Her Meaning Clear) was the African name she took shortly before her death, and her use of the term 'hyphenated' is beautifully articulated in her 'Dream of Europe' speech, to which this chapter will return: *cf.* 'The Dream of Europe' (1988), reprinted in Stella Bolaki and Sabine Broeck, eds, *Audre Lorde's Transnational Legacies*, Amherst and Boston, MA: University of Massachusetts Press, 2015, pp. 25–6.

17 Bolaki and Broeck, eds, *Audre Lorde's Transnational Legacies*. In their editorial introduction (pp. 1–15) to this ground-breaking collection, Bolaki and Broeck chart many of Lorde's genre-crossing, inter- and transnational creative, activist and educational networks and projects in the US American, Caribbean, Mexican, African and European contexts.

82 Practice and Flourish

18 The extent of her reach across the work of others is remarkable – indicative instances include, but are not limited to: Elizabeth Spelman, *Inessential Woman: Problems of Exclusion in Feminist Thought*, Boston, MA: Beacon Press, 1988; Patricia Hill Collins, *Black Feminist Thought: Knowledge, Consciousness and the Politics of Empowerment*, London and New York: Routledge, 1990; M. Jacqui Alexander and Chandra Talpade Mohanty, eds, *Feminist Genealogies, Colonial Legacies, Democratic Futures*, London and New York: Routledge, 1997; Gloria E. Anzaldúa and Analouise Keating, eds, *This Bridge We Call Home: Radical Visions for Transformation*, London and New York: Routledge, 2002; María Lugones, *Pilgrimages/Perigrinajes: Theorizing Coalition against Multiple Oppressions*, Lanham, MD, Boulder, CO, New York and Oxford: Rowman and Littlefield Publishers, 2003; Kim Marie Vaz and Gary L. Lemons, eds, *Feminist Solidarity at the Crossroads: Intersectional Women's Studies for Transracial Alliance*, London and New York: Routledge, 2012; Sara Ahmed, *Living a Feminist Life*, Durham, NC and London: Duke University Press, 2017; Ginetta E.B. Candelario, ed., *African Feminisms: Cartographies for the Twenty-First Century*, special issue of *Meridians: Feminism, Race, Transnationalism*, 17:2, November 2018; Tiffany Lethabo King, *The Black Shoals: Offshore Formations of Black and Native Studies*, Durham, NC and London: Duke University Press, 2019; Jennifer Nash, *Black Feminism Reimagined: After Intersectionality*, Durham, NC and London: Duke University Press, 2019.
19 A few examples will suffice: Carole Boyce Davies, 'Sisters Outside: Tracing the Caribbean/Black Radical Intellectual Tradition', *Small Axe* 13:1, March 2009, pp. 217–29; *Audre Lorde: A Burst of Light Symposium* at Medgar Evers College, 2014 (where Angela Davis gave a keynote on Audre Lorde available on YouTube: https://www.youtube.com/watch?v=EpYdfcvYPEQ&t=21s); Jack Halberstam, 'Vertiginous Capital Or, The Master's Toolkit', *Bully Bloggers*, 2 July 2018, https://bullybloggers.wordpress.com/?s=masters+toolkit; Jenna Hamed, *Poetry Is Not a Luxury*, exhibition catalogue, New York: Center for Book Arts, 2019; *Poetry Is Not a Luxury: The Poetics of Abolition*, A panel discussion with Saidiya Hartman, Canisia Lubrin, Nat Raha and Christina Sharpe, chaired by Nydia A. Swaby, organized by Arika, 10.08.2020, https://arika.org.uk/archive/items/revolution-not-one-time-event/poetry-not-luxury-poetics-abolition; and the Atlanta-based ZAMI NOBLA: National Organization of Black Lesbians on Aging.
20 Sarah Schulman and *The Lesbian Avengers Handbook* (1993): http://www.lesbianavengers.com/about/history.shtml; Alexis Pauline Gumbs, *School of Our Lorde*, a touring performance work, 2013 ff.: https://summerofourlorde.wordpress.com/tour/; Michèle Pearson Clark, *All That Is Left Unsaid*, single channel video, 2014: https://www.michelepearsonclarke.com/all-that-is-left-unsaid/; Paul Maheke, *Mutual Survival: Lorde's Manifesto*, video diptych, 2015: http://paulmaheke.com/projets/mutual-survival-lordes-manifesto.
21 A few notes on the films might be helpful here. I include Pratibha Parmar's 18-minute film *Emergence* (1986) under the umbrella of interview footage, rather than in the list of films above, which are longer documentaries and/or cinematic essays on Lorde and her legacy. Bolaki and Broeck's anthology *Audre Lorde's Transnational Legacies* was published as an accompaniment to Dagmar Schulz's *The Berlin Years* and includes both an excellent essay from Schulz on the making of the film and its transnational critical reception during its first few years on the film and feminist festival tour, and a reprinted essay by Pratibha Parmar and Jackie Kay from 1988, 'Frontier: An Interview with Audre Lorde', pp. 74–84. I would also like to thank ZAMI NOBLA and Women Make Movies for facilitating streaming access to the films.
22 I am in dialogue with Bolaki and Broeck here as well as with aspects of my own work: on the 'work' of art (*cf. Women Making Art: History, Subjectivity*) and both/and (noun and verb) of gender and drawing (*cf. Drawing Difference: Connections between Gender and Drawing*, co-authored with Phil Sawdon, London: Bloomsbury, 2016). I would also note that Zora Neale Hurston documented African-American traditions of 'verbal nouns' in her work on folklore: see Laura Odysseos, 'Stolen Life's Poetic Revolt', *Millennium: Journal of International Studies* 47:3, 2019, pp. 341–72 (p. 365).

Poetic Stories **83**

23 Audre Lorde, 'A Burst of Light: Living with Cancer', journal entry 9 December 1985, in *A Burst of Light and Other Essays* (1988), Long Island: Ixia Press edition, 2017, pp. 40–133 (p. 71).

24 See the repetition of the phrase 'I have done good work' in 'A Burst of Light', journal entry 10 June 1984, p. 54.

25 Lorde, *The Cancer Journals*.

> I am learning to speak my pieces, to inject into the living world my convictions of what is necessary and what I think is important without concern (of the enervating kind) for whether or not it is understood, tolerated, correct or heard before.
>
> (p. 40)

26 Spelman, *Inessential Woman*.

27 Audre Lorde, 'Commencement Address: Oberlin College' (1989), in Rudolph P. Byrd, Johnnetta Betsch Cole and Beverly Guy-Sheftall, eds, *I Am Your Sister: Collected and Unpublished Writings of Audre Lorde*, Oxford: Oxford University Press, 2009, p. 214. This key question is repeated by Lorde in various texts and speeches.

28 Lorde in Marion Kraft, 'Bonds of Sisterhood/Breaking of Silences: An Interview with Audre Lorde' (1986), reprinted in Bolaki and Broeck, *Audre Lorde's Transnational Legacies*, pp. 41–54, p. 52. Italics in the original.

29 M. Jacqui Alexander, 'Remembering This Bridge Called My Back' reprinted in *Pedagogies of Crossing: Meditations on Feminism, Sexual Politics, Memory and the Sacred*, Durham, NC and London: Duke University Press, 2005, pp. 257–86. Sara Ahmed, *Living a Feminist Life*.

30 'An Interview: Audre Lorde and Adrienne Rich' in Lorde, *Sister Outsider*, pp. 81–109.

31 Audre Lorde, 'I Am Your Sister: Black Women Organizing Across Sexualities', in *A Burst of Light and Other Essays*, pp. 10–17 (p. 10).

32 Throughout the film, Abod captures Lorde speaking many times about the 'use' of her work, including, at 50 minutes, an admission that she only took part in the event when Alexander and Bowen agreed that the focus would not be on 'honouring' her, but on 'using her work'.

33 Lorde in 'A Burst of Light', journal entry 10 June 1984, p. 54. This is reiterated in the (playful, but serious) anecdote with which Nancy Breano opened the 1983 'Introduction' to the collection *Sister Outsider*:

> When we began editing *Sister Outsider* – long after the book had been conceptualized, a contract signed, and new material written – Audre Lorde informed me, as we were working one afternoon, that she doesn't write theory. "I am a poet", she said.
>
> (p. 8)

34 Lorde, 'Poetry Is Not a Luxury', in *Sister Outsider*, pp. 36–9 (pp. 37/8). Italics in the original.

35 See, for example, Roshanravan, 'Motivating Coalition'; Linda Garber, *Identity Poetics: Race, Class, and the Lesbian-Feminist Roots of Queer Theory*, New York: Columbia University Press, 2001; Flávia Santos de Araújo, *Moving against Clothespins: The Poli(Poe)tics of Embodiment in the Poetry of Miriam Alves and Audre Lorde*, PhD Dissertation, University of Massachusetts, Amherst, 2017; Andréa Gill and Thula Pires, 'From Binary to Intersectional to Imbricated Approaches: Gender in a Decolonial and Diasporic Perspective', *Contexto Internacional* 41:2, May–August 2019, pp. 275–302.

36 Davies, 'Sister Outside' and 'From Masquerade to *Maskerade*: Caribbean Cultural Resistance and the Rehumanizing Project', in Katherine McKittrick, ed., *Sylvia Wynter: On Being Human as Praxis*, Durham, NC and London: Duke University Press, 2015, pp. 203–25.

37 Rosamond S. King, 'Radical Interdisciplinarity: A New Iteration of a Women of Color Methodology', *Meridians* 18:2, 2019, pp. 445–56.

38 *Cf.* Hortense J. Spillers, 'Moving on Down the Line', *American Quarterly* 40:1, 1988, pp. 83–109; Sylvia Wynter, 'Ethno or Socio Poetics', *Alcheringa: Ethnopoetics* 2:2, 1976,

pp. 78–94; Saidiya V. Hartman, *Lose Your Mother: A Journey Along the Atlantic Slave Route*, New York: Farrar, Straus and Giroux, 2007; Christina Sharpe, *In the Wake: On Blackness and Being*, Durham, NC and London: Duke University Press, 2016.

39 Odysseos, p. 366. Further following these trajectories, see Fred Moten's trilogy, collectively entitled *consent not to be a single being*, 2017–18: (*Black and Blur*, 2017; *Stolen Life*, 2018; *The Universal Machine*, 2018, all Durham, NC and London: Duke University Press) and Ashon Crawley, *Blackpentecostal Breath: The Aesthetics of Possibility*, New York: Fordham University Press, 2017.

40 Denise Ferreira Da Silva, 'Toward a Black Feminist Poethics', *The Black Scholar* 44:2, 2014, pp. 81–97. I read Ferreira Da Silva's work with two earlier uses of the term 'poethics' (though she does not note these), that of Hélène Cixous (*cf.* Merle A. Williams and Stefan Polatinsky, 'Hélène Cixous' Manna: The Face of Suffering and the Poethics of Border-Crossing', *English Studies in Africa* 52:2, 2009, pp. 63–76) and Richard Weisberg, *Poethics: And Other Strategies of Law and Literature*, New York: Columbia University Press, 1992. Weisberg, in particular, emphasizes the importance of storying and creative literary writing to the power of law to carry social weight based on an ethical relationship between subjects positioned very differently. This he counters with an increasing tendency to distance law as somehow 'scientifically objective'.

41 Lorde, 'The Dream of Europe', in Bolaki and Broeck, eds, *Audre Lorde's Transnational Legacies*.

42 Ibid.

43 I am echoing echo Adrienne Rich's endorsement of *The Cancer Journals* (1980) UK: Penguin Classics edition, 2020: 'Grief, terror, courage, the passion for survival and for more than survival, are here in the searchings of a great poet.'

44 Lorde shared with Wynter a critical conception of the racialized epistemic framework underpinning conventional 'Western' philosophical constructions of the self, that further connects European colonial genocide with global ecocide. These connections offer an added substance to the idea of the personal entangled with/in the political/cosmological. *Cf.* Sylvia Wynter and Katherine McKittrick, 'Unparalleled Catastrophe for Our Species? Or, to Give Humanness a Different Future: Conversations', in Katherine McKittrick, ed., *Sylvia Wynter: On Being Human as Praxis*, Durham, NC and London: Duke University Press, 2015, pp. 9–89; Birgit M. Kaiser and Kathrin Thiele, 'What Is Species Memory? Or, Humanism, Memory and the Afterlives of "1492"', *Parallax* 23:4, 2019, pp. 403–15.

45 Lorde, 'The Master's Tools', in *Sister Outsider*, pp. 110–13, p. 111; italics in the original.

46 In the decades following Lorde's death, it has become more common in feminist writing to connect the biopower politics of environmental damage and allostatic load with health risks, particularly for women and those populations whose economic and social positioning places them in closer proximity to poisons while making adequate access to healthcare, wholesome food and clean water more difficult (*cf.* Joni Seager, 'Rachel Carson Died of Breast Cancer: The Coming of Age of Feminist Environmentalism', *Signs: Journal of Women in Culture and Society* 28:3, 2003, pp. 945–72 and Alexander on Anzaldúa's early death from diabetes, 'Remembering This Bridge Called My Back'). It remains the case, however, that Lorde's salient expositions of these dangers – including her own factory work with toxic chemicals – broke new ground when written.

47 Lorde, 'Breast Cancer: Power vs. Prosthesis (30 March 1979)', *The Cancer Journals*, pp. 48–69, p. 65.

48 I would point readers interested in these ideas to two exceptionally insightful engagements with Lorde's work to which my thinking is indebted: In 'Practicing Love: Black Feminism, Love-Politics, and Post-Intersectionality', *Meridians* 11:2, 2011, pp. 1–24, Jennifer C. Nash argues that Lorde's work contributes to a non-identitarian and extended understanding of the self and makes a critical contribution to a radical Black feminist tradition of 'love-politics'. In addition, the explorations of Lorde's erotics by Tiffany Lethabo King in *The Black Shoals* demonstrate the potential that the work offers to

thinking through queer kinship and mutual care, as well as Black and Indigenous solidarity in the Americas around the contested issue of sovereignty.

49 Lorde, 'Breast Cancer: Power vs. Prosthesis', *The Cancer Journals*, p. 66. She further made clear that the women whose love supported her survival were not all the 'same', but shared a common cause: 'The women who sustained me through that period were Black and white, old and young, lesbian, bisexual and heterosexual, and we all shared a war against the tyrannies of silence', *cf.* 'The Transformation of Silence into Language and Action', *The Cancer Journals*, p. 13.

50 Tamara Lea Spira, 'The Geopolitics of the Erotic: Audre Lorde's Mexico and the Decolonization of the Revolutionary Imagination', in Bolaki and Broeck, pp. 177–90.

51 See Lorde, 'Breast Cancer: Power vs. Prosthesis', journal entry 30 March 1979, *The Cancer Journals*, p. 67 for one of her most sardonic connective statements:

> Was I really fighting the spread of radiation, racism, woman-slaughter, chemical invasion of our food, pollution of our environment, the abuse and psychic destruction of our young, merely to avoid dealing with my first and greatest responsibility – to be happy?

52 Lorde, 'Introduction', *The Cancer Journals*, p. 10.

53 Lorde, 'A Burst of Light: Living with Cancer', journal entry dated 'February 20, 1986, Anguilla, British West Indies', in *A Burst of Light and Other Essays*, 92.

54 There is a second coda: just four months after completing the first draft of this chapter I was diagnosed with early-stage breast cancer and began treatment. I completed the final edit with a far more intimate perspective on survival and an even greater admiration for Lorde's writing.

55 The face of the woman breathing is not shown, but I read the figure as Lin, finishing the work with a gesture that is both vulnerable and empowering; Lin later confirmed that it is she in the sequence.

3

PEDAGOGICAL WORLDS

Expansive Ecologies of Connection and Care

Transnational feminists are deeply engaged with issues of education and pedagogy throughout the world, from securing gender equity and access to education globally, to transforming learning and teaching, institutions and curricula, the better to challenge gender-based violence and inequality at many levels – physical, social, cultural, economic and ecological.[1] The gender-based obstacles to full participation in education globally are, unfortunately, as well-rehearsed as they are persistent, per UNESCO:

> 16 million girls will never set foot in a classroom – and women account for two thirds of the 750 million adults without basic literacy skills… Poverty, geographical isolation, minority status, disability, early marriage and pregnancy, gender-based violence, and traditional attitudes about the status and role of women, are among the many obstacles that stand in the way of women and girls fully exercising their right to participate in, complete and benefit from education.[2]

An abundance of evidence further demonstrates that the full participation of women and girls in education is vital to building sustainable, equitable, peaceful communities world-wide, and that women's education critically underpins both the health and the well-being of future generations and the environment.[3]

These are not abstract matters of statistics and reports. As I was writing this chapter, immersed in the hopes, aspirations, successes and failures of the generations of transnational feminist scholars, artists and activists who have worked tirelessly to establish decolonial feminist, queer, anti-racist and ecologically-responsible educational initiatives by drawing upon truly transformative pedagogical practices, Kabul fell to the Taliban.

US troops and their allies act in haste to fulfil the unilateral decision of the White House to depart from Afghanistan in a matter of weeks. British and European

DOI: 10.4324/9780429507816-6

media sources report on the rapid advance of the Taliban and the fall of cities and regions across Afghanistan. Stories emerge of Taliban units requesting lists of names of unmarried or widowed girls and women between the ages of 15 and 45; reports suggest that in more remote areas, in practice, these lists include girls from the age of 12, some of the names being generated from rosters of pupils in schools.[4] My inbox floods with desperate emails from international feminist organizations, while high-profile women's advocates, within and outside Afghanistan, speak out fearlessly and work behind the scenes to moderate the impact of a regime that has for years openly subordinated women and girls, and directly targeted outspoken and powerful women, queer and gender-diverse people with violence.[5] Closing schools and removing educational opportunities for girls was a central feature of Taliban governance in both Afghanistan and Pakistan in the past, and no one trusts the lukewarm reassurances being made by the incoming leaders that this time it will be different.

There is no room for a complacency born of geopolitical privilege in understanding these events, however. The threat to girl's education, women's autonomy and gender equity in war-torn Afghanistan does not prove the existence of two isolated worlds – a liberated West and a savage rest – and Britain and the United States, my dual 'homelands', are thoroughly enmeshed in the histories of conflict in central Asia, the Hindu Kush, and well beyond. Whilst geographical distance facilitates political and emotional disengagement from the catastrophic events befalling Afghan women and girls, another dangerous tendency begins to emerge fostered by the privilege of empowered distance, namely, casting active, vocal, articulate political subjects as victims, or, as Chandra Talpade Mohanty so aptly described it, as 'third world woman' in need of 'first world' feminist salvation.[6] That is precisely not the approach taken here. Informed and instructed by transnational feminist thought, activism and global solidarities, I follow instead the directions of scholars such as M. Jacqui Alexander, whose writing on transnational feminist intersubjectivity, relationality, and what she calls 'pedagogies of crossing', is profoundly resonant. In her words:

> What do lives of privilege look like in the midst of war and the inevitable violence that accompanies the building of empire? … One of the habits of privilege is that it spawns superiority, beckoning its owners to don a veil of false protection so that they never see themselves, the devastation they wreak or their accountability to it.[7]

I will return to Alexander's expansive explorations of pedagogies in greater detail shortly, but compelled by her question of the veil of privilege, I am reminded that the incursion of the Taliban across towns and cities in Afghanistan was not the only story of gender, violence and education to have made headlines in recent years. Closer to (my) home, in March 2021, the UK's Office for Standards in Education, Children's Services and Skills (Ofsted) launched an official enquiry into the effects of widespread sexual violence, harassment, homophobia and rape culture in British schools, and in 2017, British student Amika George's campaign against period poverty revealed gaping socio-economic disparities between girls in

88 Practice and Flourish

accessing education, a differential exacerbated by UK Government austerity policies and, more recently, the Covid-19 pandemic.[8] A carefully-worded 2019 report from the European Institute for Gender Equality (EIGE) noted that gender equity in European schools remained 'a pressing issue', explaining that gender-based violence and poverty continued to mediate against girls' access to education across the whole of the European Union.[9]

In June 2021, the traumatic legacy of Canada's Indian residential school system made international headlines again as hundreds of unmarked Indigenous graves were revealed in the grounds of former schools.[10] These schools, and their counterparts in the United States, played an intrinsic role in state-sanctioned acts of colonial genocide against Indigenous communities, and ongoing violence particularly targeting Indigenous women, girls, and Two Spirit people, across North America.[11] And as calls for abolition grow throughout the United States, race-critical feminist research, such as Monique W. Morris's acclaimed 2018 book *Pushout: The Criminalization of Black Girls in Schools*,[12] continues to expose the deep-rooted entanglement between racism and sexism in US American education and its acute failure to provide for young women of colour.

In bringing these particular examples to the fore, I am not seeking to homogenize them, nor merely to make the bland and reductive observation that the global educational gender gap is underpinned by violence and injustice against women, girls and gender-diverse subjects. As noted earlier, reams of evidence exist already to prove that claim, and make it abundantly clear why pursuing gender equity in and through education remains a vital issue for transnational feminist activists world-wide. What these examples point to, however, is a global picture marked by uneven, yet connected, inequities. A transnational feminist perspective on gender equity in global education both reveals and unravels the truncated and disconnective logic sustaining a narrative of the world that pits the West against the rest, and assumes that equity has been attained in a uniformly well-educated Global North (or among a global metropolitan elite) that now needs to reach out to teach (read 'rescue', 'liberate', 'assimilate') the Global South/developing world. Looking more attentively at the global picture discloses instead a complex and asymmetrical world in which the legacies of past and present nation- and empire-building, desired and forced migrations, genocidal violence and resource exploitation, have secured educational practices and institutions through differential operations of geopolitical power whose systemic and structural interconnections cut across the boundaries of nations, states and hemispheric polarities.

Returning to Alexander at this point is apposite. Setting out her argument in *Pedagogies of Crossing: Meditations on Feminism, Sexual Politics, Memory and the Sacred*, Alexander wrote:

> In this volume I am concerned with the multiple operations of power, of gendered and sexualized power that is simultaneously raced and classed yet not practiced within hermetically sealed or epistemically partial borders of the nation-state.[13]

Alexander continued by outlining her approach as a 'fundamentally pedagogic imperative... the imperative of making the world in which we live intelligible to ourselves and to each other – in other words, teaching ourselves'.[14]

Throughout this chapter, I am in dialogue with Alexander's expansive notion of pedagogy as a transnational feminist practice of crossing through *teaching ourselves*, a shared endeavour of mutual knowledge production that makes the world intelligible to ourselves *and* to each other. Mobilizing pedagogy in this way engenders a practice of transnational feminist worldmaking that undermines any fictive sense of mastery, emphasizing instead the critical entanglements, the crossings and connections, that constitute a politics of listening to, and learning with and from, others. For a project focused on the ecologies and genealogies, worlds and stories, of transnational feminisms and the arts, such an expanded pedagogical imperative to cross and connect is crucial.

The arts have not stood outside critical feminist engagements with pedagogy, and feminist interventions into art's histories, theories and practices have long acknowledged the centrality of education to issues of gender equity in the cultural sphere. Historians have written at length about the impediments faced by women seeking to access art education,[15] and how the conventional modes and materials of art teaching all too frequently served only to reinforce a canonical tale of Great Masters, Old and new. Such teaching marginalized the presence and significance of women as cultural producers generally, and amplified this effect through racism, colonial domination, homo- and transphobia, as well as class discrimination. More than just a Eurocentric phenomenon, research points to a global gender gap in art education that is similarly asymmetrical and iniquitous.[16]

It would be a mistake, however, to reduce feminist critiques of the histories, practices and institutions of art education to stories of despair or hopelessness in the face of persistent obstacles. Quite the contrary; for generations, feminist art scholars and artists have combined their ground-breaking research with their grounded experiences of education and training in the arts, to develop and maintain innovative and experimental teaching and learning practices, programmes and institution-building projects.[17] Many of these scholars and artists were (or are) teachers as well as feminist political activists, and the initiatives they founded frequently brought these two worlds into direct connection.

While this chapter is not a survey of feminism and art education globally, it converses with, and builds upon, the intellectual insights and practical interventions of many transnational feminist arts educators who have sought not just to teach, but also to learn with others, through the arts. It is my contention that these insights and interventions demonstrate the transformative potential of arts education and pedagogy when practised as a mode of transnational feminist worldmaking that fosters both critical connection and care. Connections are key to anti-racist, decolonial, ecofeminist knowledge projects seeking to counter practices of geopolitical and epistemic violence underpinned by disciplinary silos, silences and silencing, whilst care, understood here as loving attention and generosity, sustains both mutual learning and peaceful coexistence with others, and with/in many worlds.

90 Practice and Flourish

The pedagogical worlds of connection and care visited over the course of this chapter are inhabited by artists who transgress borders whilst drawing pluriversal maps, scholars who refuse the punitive disciplinary logic of epistemicide, activists willing to risk listening to stories told in different voices to embrace the power of the erotic and the humility of the gift. Always, at the core, are teachers who never cease to learn from myriad others in vibrant and more than human worlds.

In what follows, the argument unfolds through three propositions derived from my experience as a learning-teacher with a profound investment in the potential of creative pedagogies in the arts to engender expanded ecologies of connection and care through a transnational feminist worldmaking praxis. Each proposition brings together theory, practice and experience to engage with the co-production of knowledges and worlds through a transnational feminist ecology of art. Arguably, it is from this material-imaginative locus that we can teach ourselves practices that engender mutual flourishing.

I Pedagogies of Crossing Draw Palimpsestic Maps of Pluriversal Worlds

Two lines drawn by British officials define the borders of present-day Pakistan. To the west lies the Durand Line, named for Sir Mortimer Durand, who, in 1893, in the wake of the Second Anglo-Afghan War, delineated the border between what was then British India and Afghanistan. To the east lies the Punjabi segment of the Radcliffe Line, the product of the hasty and injudicious work led by Cyril Radcliffe to demarcate the borders between India and the new nation of Pakistan, so as to facilitate the swift departure of the British at Partition in 1947. Both were lines drawn as convenient imperial marks on a map designed to secure British interests in central and south Asia, and both have been redrawn many times in blood.

–|–

In 1948, feminist activist artist Lala Rukh was born in the ancient city of Lahore, in recently-created Pakistan. It was the city she inhabited throughout her life and to which she richly contributed as a teacher, mentor, artist and vocal political feminist, social justice and environmental activist. Lala Rukh's first four years as a teacher were spent in the Department of Fine Art at the University of the Punjab, where she witnessed at first-hand the impact of an increasingly intolerant fundamentalist regime on the institution, before joining the National College of Arts (NCA) in 1983. During her 30-year tenure at the NCA, Lala Rukh's aesthetic, intellectual and political impact was profound; many of Pakistan's most successful international artists studied at the NCA with Lala Rukh as undergraduates or on the Masters programme in Visual Art that she established in 2000. Lala Rukh combined teaching and making art with her political activism, most notably as a founding member of the Lahore branch of the Women's Action Forum (WAF), an exceptionally visible feminist organization that began in 1981 as a response to President Muhammad

Zia-ul-Haq's conservative regime (1977–88), which it challenged publicly, and successfully, on many issues of gender equity. Lala Rukh was active within a number of other political organizations, including the border-crossing Pakistan–India Peoples' Forum for Peace and Democracy (PIPFPD) and the Lahore Bachao Committee, a climate justice group with whom she was still campaigning to save green spaces in the city in 2016, only a year before her death.

Lala Rukh's engagement with feminism, art and teaching consistently crossed borders and mapped connections to think and make new worlds. Whilst embedded in the cultural, political and intellectual life of Lahore, Lala Rukh was widely travelled and cosmopolitan in her outlook, gleaning an astute view of the region through journeys within Pakistan and to India, Sri Lanka, Afghanistan, Iran and Turkey, as well as a global perspective on south and central Asia, during stays in Africa, South America, Europe and the United States.[18] Likewise, Lala Rukh's commitment to grassroots political action was informed by her conception of feminism as an expansive, transnational intellectual and political project; in her terms '... feminism really talks about a new social order... about a whole system that is going... and it addresses, now, global issues'.[19]

Lala Rukh's crossings and connections were perhaps most strikingly drawn in her art practice and pedagogy, where, in her own work, she regularly crossed genres between drawing, printmaking, photography, calligraphy, animation and music, whilst refusing the spatio-temporal distinction between modern, Western fine art and traditional, South Asian applied arts, in both theory and practice. Her innovative curriculum design for the Masters programme at the NCA continued this thread, combining Western art history, theory and studio practice with a South Asian seminar and training in traditional practices from the region, such as miniature painting, calligraphy and weaving. She was critically aware of the implicit border policing within the social and institutional frameworks of art education, critiquing everyday sexism within her own department – taking men to be 'artists' (who taught) and women to be 'teachers' (who made art), for example – but also praising the NCA for breaking down significant barriers of caste and class amongst the student body.[20] Lala Rukh also taught across borders, developing a well-known screen printing manual, *In Our Own Backyard*, and running workshops to train feminist activist groups, whose radical messages meant that they could not access professional services for their posters and printed material.[21] Of her pedagogical practice, Lala Rukh was definitive: 'I think dialogue makes all the difference you know? That has been my approach. I can't separate, I can't even use that construct of a student/teacher...'[22]

Drawing lines, crossing borders and mapping connections were intrinsic to Lala Rukh's transnational feminist thought, activism, pedagogical practice and art. In 1997, in the aftermath of the retaliatory violence that spread through India, Pakistan, Kashmir and Bangladesh following the demolition of the Babri Mosque by Hindu Nationalists in 1992, Lala Rukh produced three multi-media diptychs, *Mirror Image 1, 2 and 3* (Figure 3.1). Echoing her use of collaged newspaper accounts of femicide for the 1985 WAF poster, *Crimes Against Women*, the ground of each *Mirror*

FIGURE 3.1 Lala Rukh, *Mirror Image: 1*, 1997. Mixed media on graph paper, 48 × 60 cm. Collection of the Metropolitan Museum of Art, New York (2019.260a–c).
Image courtesy of the Estate of Lala Rukh and Grey Noise Dubai.

Image was comprised of a collage of articles on sectarian violence and the rise of right-wing political fundamentalism on both sides of the Radcliffe Line. In each work, the dual collages, darkened nearly to black by layers of thick marks drawn in conte crayon and China marker on their surfaces, are mounted as mirror images, facing one another across the lines of the graph paper, the violence on one side of the border perfectly replicating that on the other.[23] Facing mirrors visualize infinite regress, as violence begets violence: xenophobic nationalism, sectarian genocide, right-wing fundamentalism, misogynist femicide, nuclear-fuelled militarism, accelerated ecocide. If the works are a brooding reflection on the border, so too are they a palimpsestic map demonstrating how a British line drawn in brutal haste to solve the problem of an over-extended empire continues to be drawn time and again, without resolution, as the horizon line of the present.

A few years before *Mirror Image*, Lala Rukh undertook a different serial exploration of borders and horizons, entitled *River in an ocean* (1992–93) (Figure 3.2). In mixed media on exposed photographic paper, Lala Rukh's drawings combined charcoal grey washes with slender silver lines to render, on an intimate scale, the vast and fluid nexus between rivers, oceans and sky. The series was linked, for Lala Rukh, to the deeply humbling experience of travel and a life-long fascination with the immensity and dynamism of the sea. Nothing visible in the series is fixed; no

Pedagogical Worlds 93

FIGURE 3.2 Lala Rukh, *River in an ocean: 6*, 1993. Mixed media on photographic paper 24.8 × 20.9 cm.
Image courtesy of the Estate of Lala Rukh and Grey Noise, Dubai.

edge is hard, no boundary fast, the very surface of the drawings, light-sensitive and inconstant. A minimalist meditation on mutability, the works dissolve sharp borderlines into waterscapes and waves where river, ocean, light and sky meet to form liquid horizons. In this respect, it is telling that the initial impetus for the series came during a trip Lala Rukh made to Peshawar, where, from the window of the plane, she saw the sinuous movement of a river glistening beneath the night sky. That river was the Kabul, as it flows across the border between Afghanistan and Pakistan.[24]

When Durand was tasked to draw the line that now defines that border, cutting across the Kabul river valley, he referred to the geographical surveys undertaken by cartographers employed by the British East India Company. As Dilip de Cunha has so elegantly argued, these maps were designed to make a topography of nebulous water- and rainscapes, created by cyclical monsoons, intelligible to British colonial agencies, and, thus, rivers were delineated as sharp lines drawn on a defined landscape.[25] The Durand Line that came to separate Afghanistan from British India was drawn along the 'line' of the Indus River, ignoring centuries of civilization in the valley that flowed freely over and across the water. Precisely a century later, Lala Rukh's *River in an Ocean* reimagined the border, drawing the fluid lines of

94 Practice and Flourish

a pluriversal map across and over the rigid boundaries of a conquered land. The works suggest a very different way of looking at water, as courses and sheds that shape the valleys of central Asia, stream over the borders of nation-states into seas and oceans, and cross between continents, connecting worlds and stories in the ebb and flow of time and space.

–|–

In *Pedagogies of Crossing*, following a passage describing a massacre of Indigenous people by the British in the Caribbean in the 18th Century, Alexander wrote this of rivers and seas:

> For months after the massacre, Indian blood usurped the place of mud and ran into the narrow channel that led to the Caribbean Sea... The bloody river took the story to the Sea, the Wide Sargasso Sea... Water overflows with memory... Crossings are never undertaken all at once and never once and for all.[26]

Earlier in the same volume, in dialogue with Toni Morrison's call to draw maps without a mandate for conquest, Alexander wrote of palimpsestic time and space:

> On this reconfigured map of palimpsestic time, the various parchments are not positioned by opposing a distant 'then and there' to a proximate 'here and now'. Rather, I have sought to make them intelligible by bringing the 'here' and 'there' into ideological proximity within a single social formation as well as among and between social formations that have been positioned as opposites in the linear narration of time.[27]

Bringing Alexander into connection with Lala Rukh is not merely a dramatic conceit, a riff played between a few accidentally resonant images and phrases. Indeed, my argument is that there is nothing random about the fact that there are significant, material, connections between their work, and that we need to act on the 'pedagogical imperative' to teach ourselves to see just such crossings and connections if we are to counter the disciplinary and intellectual legacies of colonial genocide, epistemicide, femicide and ecocide that continue to map the course of our present.

Deploying her expansive concept of 'pedagogies of crossing', Alexander redraws the map of the world as a palimpsest where time and space overlap and multi-layered connections emerge between early-modern European imperialism, colonial conquest, enslavement and genocide, and the neo-Imperial 'world order' of the early 21st century in which an endless 'War on Terror' is pursued by global superpowers and their allies in the name of justice and equity for all. Positioning herself on the map between the Caribbean, the Congo and an Anglo-US academy, Alexander is critically aware of epistemic location and the complicity of knowledge production pursued in powerful institutions.[28] Time and again, Alexander turns to the transnational feminist classroom for insights into pedagogies of crossing and creative ways to 'map – reimagine, practice and live'[29] in a world of many, interconnected, worlds. Critical to her transnational feminist pedagogical practice of worldmaking is learning with and from others, and Alexander singles out for special criticism what she calls 'add and stir feminism' and liberal feminist 'rescue narratives' that all too easily emerge in the feminist classrooms of the Anglo-US academy.

Liberal rescue narratives protect their speakers from seeing their complicity in the epistemic violence they enact against the women they silence, and they are increasingly focused on women in central Asia and the Middle East – women such as Lala Rukh and the extraordinary feminist activists currently risking their lives in Afghanistan to protect education and the rights of girls and women under the Taliban. Lala Rukh and Alexander drew maps of an expanded pedagogical practice of transnational feminist worldmaking through crossing and connection. Creating a dialogue between their voices and tropes – rivers, oceans, maps, borders, palimpsestic time and space – enables us to follow their lead, listen to and learn from the crossings and connections their expansive pedagogies materialize against the silencing logic and anaesthetizing distance produced by the habit of privilege.

II Decolonizing Pedagogies Get the Stories Right and Tell the Stories Well

The propositional sub-heading of this section deliberately echoes the words of Māori scholar and professor of Indigenous education, Linda Tuhiwai Smith (Ngāti Awa and Ngāti Porou), who, in her ground-breaking book, *Decolonizing Methodologies: Research and Indigenous People*, made the salient point that 'An activist must get the story right as well as tell the story well, and so must a researcher.'[30] First published in 1999, *Decolonizing Methodologies* has had an extraordinary impact both within and outside the academy, most particularly upon Indigenous scholars and activists seeking to reclaim research practices and outcomes for the benefit of their communities, but also upon the work of race-critical, queer and transnational feminists seeking to develop decolonial epistemes. Its approach to methodologies is expansive:

> *Decolonizing Methodologies* is concerned not so much with the actual technique of selecting a method but much more with the context in which research problems are conceptualized and designed, and with the implications of research for its participants and their communities. It is also concerned with the institution of research, its claims, its values and practices, and its relationships to power.[31]

Tuhiwai Smith's wide-ranging account of methodology enables her to challenge knowledge production and the academy on many fronts, not least on the matter of discipline – as both noun and verb. Under the paired sub-headings 'colonizing the disciplines' and 'disciplining the colonized', Tuhiwai Smith demonstrated the intrinsic interconnections between the development of Eurocentric academic knowledge

96 Practice and Flourish

within a system of discrete disciplines, and the violent eradication of alternative Indigenous, and other 'non-Western', knowledges as part of the European imperial project. This double act of disciplining has significant ramifications, as she wrote:

> Insularity protects a discipline from the 'outside', enabling communities of scholars to distance themselves from others and, in the more extreme forms, to absolve themselves of responsibility for what occurs in other branches of their discipline, in the academy and in the world.[32]

Decolonizing research methodologies, challenging disciplinary insularity and creating alternative knowledges is not just a matter of *what* is known, but of *how, where* and *to what ends*. Knowledges act in, and make, the world; paraphrasing Brazilian philosopher and educationalist Paolo Freire, to *name* the world, is to change it.[33] Historically, colonizers claimed the sole right to name, the right to create history, to story the world through a totalizing, universal and singular narrative, silencing the myriad voices who might, together, sing the stories of many worlds. In thinking through histories, Tuhiwai Smith was in dialogue with Freire's writing on the power of naming and, significantly, with pedagogy – what she called the 'critical pedagogy of decolonization':

> *Coming to know the past* has been part of the critical pedagogy of decolonization. To hold alternative histories is to hold alternative knowledges. The pedagogical implication of this access to alternative knowledges is that they can form the basis of alternative ways of doing things.[34]

To decolonize methodology is to explore the space where power, knowledges, disciplines, and histories meet. To create alternative knowledges is to begin the process of transforming the world. Research meets methodology meets pedagogy meets activism.[35]

–|–

In 2015, I had the privilege of joining colleagues at the Michaelis School of Fine Art for a short period as an International Visiting Scholar at the University of Cape Town.[36] I arrived during a period of intense debate and action at the university, just three months after Marion Walgate's statue of Cecil Rhodes had been removed from its plinth on the main campus following the successful protests led by the Rhodes Must Fall (RMF) campaign. Looking back, the brief period between the removal of the monument and the commencement of a series of more hostile campus protests in early 2016 was like the eye of a storm. For me, it was a crucible.

Let me be clear: my brief and impressionistic account of the impact of this moment makes no grand claims to 'insider' knowledge of the RMF campaign, its later international manifestations, or the politics of higher education in South Africa. On the contrary, scholars far better placed than I, such as South African feminist art historian Brenda Schmahmann, have written exceptionally astute accounts of the events, and I am indebted to their analyses.[37] The focus of my tale resides elsewhere – not in what I can teach others about the events I experienced, but in what I learned from them.

Simply, having been invited to Cape Town to extend a number of ongoing research dialogues with colleagues at Michaelis, and to share my work on transnational feminisms and the arts more widely with scholars and students at the university, I arrived at a moment of such remarkable intellectual and political dynamism that *what* I thought I might know was wholly overshadowed by *how, from where* and *to what ends* I could make any claims to *know* at all. From vibrant exchanges with students on the post-Apartheid politics of queer performance and the challenge of bridging 'Western' feminisms and African womanist philosophy in making art,[38] to critical debates on curating, community memory and urban regeneration, including a visit to the Lewandle Migrant Labour Museum that will stay with me forever, there was no possibility of claiming the protection of disciplinary insularity, nor any retreat into the safety of an academic ivory tower available.

My brief time at UCT was marked, instead, by a palpable experience of the critical pedagogies of decolonization in practice, and I learned just how different that is from the cool theoretical conversations that too commonly attend discussions of 'decolonizing the curriculum' in Anglo-US institutions. The first signal of this came in the library on the Michaelis site where a group of students at a table proximate to mine were engaged in an animated discussion of politics and the Rhodes Must Fall campaign along with some books on their table. When they departed, I could not help but look at the titles they had left, only to find a well-worn and underlined copy of Tuhiwai Smith's *Decolonizing Methodologies*. In Cape Town, decolonizing methodologies participated in the fall of Rhodes.

A few days into my stay, my host took me to see the empty plinth on the main campus where Walgate's monument to Rhodes had stood. The site is striking: *in situ* the figure of Rhodes overlooked a vast terrain, his watchful gaze laying claim to an empire built upon the proceeds of industry and violence. Seeing the space, it was easier to understand why this particular monument had become a focal point for decolonial activism on campus, but what I was not anticipating was the extraordinary 'graffiti' that the empty plinth had attracted. The original plinth had been boxed off with plywood on which had been painted the outlines of a new plinth, decorated in traditional Ndebele patterning (Figure 3.3). Extending from the base of the new plinth, painted in swift spray can strokes along the steps and pavement, was a shadow version of the figure of Rhodes (Figure 3.4).

For me, these two elements combined to form an eloquent and elegant visual example of getting the story right and telling it well; it is necessary *both* to build a new plinth for a new history in full recognition of the African ground on which it stands, *and* to address the long shadow cast into the present by Rhodes and all that he represents. This is a story for our time and many voices are needed to tell it well, together.

98 Practice and Flourish

FIGURE 3.3 Boxed plinth with graffiti following Rhodes Must Fall demonstrations, University of Cape Town, South Africa, August 2015.
Image courtesy of the author.

FIGURE 3.4 Graffiti shadow of Rhodes at the base of the covered plinth following Rhodes Must Fall demonstrations, University of Cape Town, South Africa, August 2015.
Image courtesy of the author.

Some argue that it is time to burn down the universities, libraries, archives, museums and collections for their complacency and complicity with injustice, oppression and brutality, and perhaps 'ending the world' to rebuild anew offers a form of solution to crisis.[39] But while I stand against leaving public symbols of racism, misogyny, conquest and genocide *in situ*, unchallenged, I am not convinced that merely removing the most visible symbols of imperial violence addresses adequately its ongoing impact into the present day.[40] Rather, I find far more compelling the question asked by the shadow of Rhodes of how the past can be reconceived within the present, and, in harmony with Tuhiwai Smith, would argue that critique and negation is not enough. As she wrote in 2021:

> How does decolonizing methodologies help us when the world is in crisis? … [C]ritique is not enough. We have to continue to act, to use our own imaginations, to enhance our own institutions and forge our own pathways.[41]

Getting the story right and telling it well in the shadow of Rhodes demands more than brilliant critical thought and sharp intellectual prose, whether used with genuine purpose or as empty virtue-signalling rhetoric. It demands that we be held accountable for the material impact of our thought, stand in our word(s), and learn from those of others with whom we might begin to shape new worlds through a critical pedagogy of decolonization.

III Transnational Feminist Pedagogies Take Risks to Give Back

In the second volume of her acclaimed teaching trilogy,[42] *Teaching Community: A Pedagogy of Hope*, the late bell hooks made the compelling point that feminist pedagogies may too often have emphasized safety when they needed to value risk:

> The emphasis on safety in feminist settings often served as a barrier to cross-racial solidarity because these encounters did not feel 'safe' and were often charged with tension and conflict. Working with white students on unlearning racism, one of the principles we strive to embody is the value of risk, honoring the fact that we may learn and grow in circumstances where we do not feel safe, that the presence of conflict is not necessarily negative but rather its meaning is determined by how we cope with that conflict.[43]

This passage comes from the volume's fifth 'Teach' (hooks deployed 'teach' over 'chapter'), entitled 'What Happens When White People Change', a text focused on the radical potential of pedagogy to forge community through cross-racial and cross-gender alliance. The link between safety and community was made too in the first volume of her trilogy, where hooks stressed that a transformative pedagogy moves beyond safety to engender a 'climate of openness and intellectual rigor' that creates a truly diverse community of mutual learners.[44] And in the final volume, a

100 Practice and Flourish

return to 'radical openness' was framed as central to the creation of diverse communities through love, challenge, change and the risk of vulnerability – of being willing *not* to know, nor always to be *right*.[45]

Across all three volumes of her teaching trilogy, hooks made connections between the transformative potential of transnational feminisms, engaged pedagogy, radical openness, hope, freedom and risk. And, in her ground-breaking meditation on love, politics and justice, *All About Love: New Visions*, hooks stated categorically, that '(t)he practice of love offers no place of safety. We risk loss, hurt, pain. We risk being acted upon by forces outside our control.'[46] We risk the loss of mastery.

Long engaged with radical anti-racist, decolonial feminist activism, it is hardly surprising that hooks' understanding of critical and engaged pedagogy is not akin to the safe pedagogy of mirroring assimilation practiced in the market-driven, neo-liberal academy of the present.[47] As an African-American child growing up in the southern United States, hooks experienced both the empowerment of liberation pedagogy in her early all-Black schools, and the dehumanizing epistemic violence of c/overt racism in desegregated secondary education and high-profile US universities. If these normalizing and privileged spaces of education downplay risk in favour of safety, the better to maintain the status quo, in moments of potential crisis, at the edges and in the margins, risk re-emerges as the motor force of transformative, transnational feminist pedagogies.[48]

–|–

In 2009, my colleague, Marion Arnold, and I embarked upon the process of establishing a transnational feminist research network designed to explore relationships between gendered concepts of nation and citizenship, and the plural histories, theories and practices of photographies. The network came to be called *The Lens of Empowerment* and, during the three years of its formal convention, facilitated both a number of collaborative, international meetings and projects, as well as specific, local/regional interventions, ranging from an artists' residency and travelling exhibitions, to an international conference that formed the substance of the book *Home/Land: Women, Citizenship, Photographies*.[49]

Undoubtedly, one of the most successful projects developed through the *Lens of Empowerment* network was the eponymous teaching programme created by network partners from the University of the Fraser Valley (UFV) in British Columbia. Co-designed with elders from the Stó:lō community, on whose traditional territory the institution stands, UFV's *Lens of Empowerment* teaching programme combined Indigenous learning with feminist arts pedagogies to bring the voices of Indigenous women to narratives of nation and belonging, whilst fostering dialogue between Indigenous and non-Indigenous learners. The programme's first run in 2011–12 centred on the theme of women's citizenship and identity in Stó:lō territory (*Tel i'tsel Kwe'lo: I am from here*),[50] and, running again in 2014–15, on the pressing question of reconciliation under the broad thematic *Xwla ye toteló:met qas ye slilekwel* (*Towards understanding and harmony*).[51]

Though nearly a decade has passed since I had the privilege of hearing students from the programme's first cohort present their work at a *Lens* network event, the impact of their words and images has not lessened in intensity for me. Indeed, the work of students from both cohorts of UFV's *Lens* programme, and the four exceptional women leaders from UFV who, as members of the network, worked tirelessly to make an extraordinary pedagogical possibility into a reality, taught me innumerable lessons about the power of an engaged pedagogy driven by radical openness, generosity, love and, perhaps most profoundly, *risk*. Every aspect of UFV's *Lens* programme was entangled with risk, and, at every turn, those risks were engaged with a deep and abiding commitment to forge transnational feminist solidarities beyond assimilation, and to create learning communities through trust, respect and care.

It would be difficult to overstate the violence experienced by Indigenous women, girls and gender-diverse people in the Americas historically, or the severity of the continuing risks they face. As Mary Eberts, Canadian constitutional lawyer and counsel to the Native Women's Association of Canada (1981–2016) argued so compellingly, 'All Indian women lead a "high-risk" life because of colonialism, sexism, racism and many aspects of government policy and legislation.'[52] *Lens* students produced documentary films and photographs that took risks to tell the stories of women in Stó:lō territory, some not easy to hear: 'I didn't want to be an Indian', 'a single Aboriginal welfare mom', 'I was ashamed...'. Their tales spoke of poverty and status cards, racism, sexism and residential schools, murdered and missing women, but also, and always, of the empowerment born of community, matrilineal sovereignty and the reclamation of women's knowledge and voice, in and though the creative arts. Their work engaged with Indigenous tradition, culture, land and language, whilst making pertinent connections with contemporary activism, from Occupy to the REDress project. Simply, the students took risks. The programme was for many of the students, transformative, or, as Jessica Bennett (of the first cohort) wrote, '... when the [*Lens*] project began, my whole world changed. ... the discovery of my Aboriginal heritage has been an empowering journey.'[53]

UFV's *Lens* programme never negated the deeply complicit role of education in the historical legacies of violence against Indigenous women, girls and gender diverse subjects throughout the Americas,[54] nor the risks that educators, community leaders and students would face in making changes to the system. Risk characterized the classroom experience of those who co-designed and taught the *Lens* programme,[55] as well as the experience of senior leaders within the university and the Stó:lō community who undertook the responsibility for developing it with astonishing grace and generosity. Yet, as hooks so amply demonstrated in her work, where the risks are greatest, so too are the possibilities for imaginative and transformative worldmaking.

In 2007, shortly before we embarked upon the *Lens* network project, Ruana Kuokannen's book, *Reshaping the University: Responsibility, Indigenous Epistemes, and the Logic of the Gift*, was published. Kuokannen, a Sami scholar of Indigenous politics

102 Practice and Flourish

and law, well known for her work on Indigenous feminisms, governance and Arctic geopolitics, makes absolutely clear from the outset of her volume that the university needs to be 'reshaped' in and through an Indigenous paradigm of the gift:

> In this book, I set out to expose the ignorance and benevolent imperialism of the academy and to show how the academy is based fundamentally on a very narrow understanding of the world and human relationships... I will be suggesting a new paradigm based on the logic of the gift as it is understood in indigenous thought... The logic of the gift foregrounds a new relationship – one that is characterized by reciprocity and by a call for responsibility toward the 'other'.[56]

Kuokannen does not underestimate the complicity of the academy with the violence that secured European imperial power historically, and which is continued into the present through the dominance of the neo-liberal university in the global economy. Likewise, Kuokannen is unequivocal that the gift offers its recipients no free pass, no immunization from responsibility for injustice: 'The logic of the gift is not a cure-all for oppression and discrimination in the academy. Any suggestion that it is would belong to the colonial, arrogant mentality of universalities.'[57] Rather, the gift, as modelled through the plural epistemes of Indigenous thought, is understood as a specific, contingent and relational *practice* designed to create ecological balance between humans and a lively cosmos. The gift is not a thing you can possess, but a form of mutual agency capable of establishing an 'ongoing relationship of giving and giving back (rather than giving and taking); and if it is well maintained, responses indeed flow in both directions'.[58]

It was clear from the start that the risks taken by students and colleagues on the UFV *Lens* programme were critical to creating solidarity across the learning community and to making change within and beyond the academy. Extending this a stage further, I want to suggest that the risks were also radical practices of giving back undertaken to create the possibility of an ongoing relationship that extended well beyond the community of the classroom, the university or the nation-state, to encompass past generations, the earth and the future. UFV's Senior Advisor on Indigenous Affairs, and a respected member of the Stó:lō community, Shirley Hardman, played a key role in the international *Lens* network and to the development and success of UFV's Lens teaching programme. Her articulation of accepting risk to give back, expresses this breadth with exceptional eloquence:

> Indigenizing, including [the *Lens*] project, has meant for me a struggle for acceptance... Acceptance that Indigenous content, history telling, political movement and colonial resistance can be facilitated by what I call 'culturally allied others'. In order to honour my ancestors, to look after everything we have been given, I accept the challenges; I seek out the culturally allied others to build an Indigenised education experience for all learners. This means that I recognise the need to accept where we are and to move forward in beauty.[59]

Pedagogical Worlds **103**

Hardman and Kuokannen know the risks and yet give back; I am struck by the fact that neither are willing to concede the potential of the university yet to facilitate teaching and learning *otherwise*, if radically reconceived and reconfigured. Their determination to move forward in beauty provides yet another generative gift – of hope. Practising risk is not empty revisionism, giving back is not giving up. Rather, transnational feminist pedagogies prefigure a future politics of knowledge through practices of flourishing in love, generosity and mutuality. And this point, of course, brings us full circle to crossing, connection and care as feminist forms of worldmaking centred on listening to, and learning with, others. Transnational feminist pedagogies take risks, but do not give up; rather, they *give back*, creating new ecologies of knowledge that yet threaten to transform the world from inside out.

Notes

1 To get a sense of how extensive feminist networks are making real changes in education across the world, see the work of the UN Girl's Education Initiative (UNGEI): https://www.ungei.org/who-we-are/overview. It is important to note that women, girls, queer and gender-diverse students remain a priority in these campaigns, but that feminist initiatives towards gender equity and the elimination of sexual violence increasingly focus too on the education of men and boys.

2 See UNESCO for an overview of the scale of the issues and the significance of women's education to wider global equity: https://en.unesco.org/themes/education-and-gender-equality. Significantly, UNESCO is joined by the World Bank in both promoting and supporting education for women and girls as a priority: https://www.worldbank.org/en/topic/girlseducation.

3 For an excellent overview statement concerning the benefits of educating women and girls, see Action Aid: https://www.actionaid.org.uk/our-work/womens-rights/girls-education?gclid=EAIaIQobChMIjP-L5_r48gIVjt_tCh3Q-Af1EAAYAiAAEgJXefD_BwE.

4 Vrinda Narain, 'The World Must Not Look Away as the Taliban Sexually Enslaves Women and Girls', *The Conversation*, 15 August 2021, https://theconversation.com/the-world-must-not-look-away-as-the-taliban-sexually-enslaves-women-and-girls-165426. This has been seen elsewhere in the world, more than once, for example: Nanking in 1937–38 and Democratic Republic of Congo in 2015, *cf.* Sheng-Ping Guo, 'The Living Goddess of Mercy at the Rape of Nanking: Minnie Vautrin and the Ginling Refugee Camp in World War II (1937–38)', *Religions* 7:12, 2016 (no page numbers); Human Rights Watch (2015): https://www.hrw.org/report/2015/10/27/our-school-became-battlefield/using-schools-child-recruitment-and-military.

5 These include Pakistani-born Malala Yousafzai, the youngest ever Nobel laureate, and founder of the Malala Fund (https://malala.org/newsroom/archive/malala-funds-commitment-to-our-partners-in-afghanistan) and Pashtana Dorani, co-founder of LEARN, an NGO based in Afghanistan https://www.learnafghan.org/. NPR (National Public Radio) led with a story on Afghan women's public resistance on 17 August 2021: https://www.npr.org/2021/08/18/1029014825/afghan-women-politicians-taliban-resistance; Women Make Movies screened the Voices of Afghan Women series for free on their site: https://www.wmm.com; and The Obama Foundation also posted sites for aid for women in Afghanistan, whilst not openly decrying President Biden's unilateral withdrawal from the country: https://www.obama.org/updates/support-women-and-girls-in-afghanistan/.

6 Chandra Talpade Mohanty, 'Under Western Eyes: Feminist Scholarship and Colonial Discourses' (1984) reprinted in *Third World Women and the Politics of Feminism*, eds,

104 Practice and Flourish

Chandra Talpade Mohanty, Ann Russo and Lourdes Torres, Bloomington and Indianapolis: Indiana University Press, 1991, pp. 51–80.

7 M. Jacqui Alexander, *Pedagogies of Crossing: Meditations on Feminism, Sexual Politics, Memory and the Sacred*, Durham, NC and London: Duke University Press, 2005, pp. 1–2.

8 *Cf.* https://www.theguardian.com/society/2021/mar/29/ofsted-must-investigate-allegations-of-sexual-misconduct-in-schools-mp-says and https://www.independent.co.uk/news/uk/home-news/period-poverty-campaign-free-sanitary-schools-amika-george-a9285346.htm. Add to this the continuing impact from Ireland's Magdalen Laundries, Reformatories and Industrial Schools, and the education of women and girls in the British Isles hardly appears exemplary.

9 https://www.csee-etuce.org/en/news/education-policy/3493-new-eige-report-europe-still-struggling-with-gender-segregation-in-education.

10 *Cf.* https://www.bbc.co.uk/news/world-us-canada-57592243.

11 Final Report of the National Inquiry into Murdered and Missing Indigenous Women and Girls (2015): https://www.mmiwg-ffada.ca/final-report/; and *cf.* Georgina Lightning's new film *Somebody's Daughter 1492–2021.* https://www.somebodysdaughter-mmiw.com/. It is instructive that a damning report into the US Indian residential schools appeared as early as 1969 (the Kennedy Report), to little effect. And, of course, as Australia's 'Stolen Generation' demonstrates, the use of residential schools as agencies of Indigenous genocide has not been limited to North America.

12 Monique W. Morris, *Pushout: The Criminalization of Black Girls in Schools*, New York and London: The New Press, 2018 and *Sing a Rhythm, Dance a Blues: Education for the Liberation of Black and Brown Girls*, New York and London: The New Press, 2020. See also: Erin Debenport, Melissa Maceyko, Maywa Montenegro, S.A. Smythe and Alejandro Villalpando, 'What Do You Mean by Abolition?' *Anthropology News* website, 15 April 2021, https://politicalandlegalanthro.org/2021/04/15/what-do-you-mean-by-abolition/.

13 Alexander, *Pedagogies of Crossing*, p. 4.

14 Alexander, *Pedagogies of Crossing*, p. 6.

15 *Cf.* Germaine Greer, *The Obstacle Race: The Fortunes of Women Painters and Their Work*, New York: Farrar Straus Giroux, 1979; Laurel Lampela, 'Women's Art Education Institutions in 19th Century England', *Art Education* 46:1, 1993, pp. 64–7; Tamar Garb, *Sisters of the Brush: Women's Artistic Culture in Late Nineteenth-Century Paris*, New Haven, CT: Yale University Press, 1994; Deborah Cherry, *Beyond the Frame: Feminism and Visual Culture, Britain 1850–1900*, London and New York: Routledge, 2000; Anja Baumhoff, *The Gendered World of the Bauhaus: The Politics of Power at the Weimar Republic's Premier Art Institute, 1919–32*, Bern: Peter Lang, 2001; Elizabeth Garber, 'Social Justice and Art Education', *Visual Arts Research* 30:2, 2004, pp. 4–22; Leon Wainwright, 'Art (School) Education and Diversity', in *Beyond Cultural Diversity: The Case for Creativity*, commissioned by Arts Council England. *Third Text*, 2011; Lola Olufemi, *Feminism Interrupted: Disrupting Power*, London: Pluto Press, 2020 (chapter 6 'Art for Art's Sake', pp. 82–94); Hilary Robinson, 'Women, Feminism and Art Schools: The UK Experience', *Women's Studies International Forum* 85, 2021, pp. 1–10.

16 *Cf.* Maha Abdullah Al-Senan, 'Considerations on Society through Saudi Women's Art', *Journal of International Development Research* 5:5, May 2015, pp. 4536–4542; Ursula Tania Estrada López, 'The Entrance of Women to the Art Academies in Brazil and Mexico: A Comparative Overview', 19&20, Rio de Janeiro, X:2, July–December 2015, http://www.dezenovevinte.net/uah2/utel_en.htm; 'A Conversation with Andrea Giunta', *Princeton News*, 2019, https://plas.princeton.edu/news/2019/women-nosotras-proponemos-art-feminism-argentina; M. Nagawa, 'The Challenges and Successes of Women Artists in Uganda', in Marion Arnold, ed., *Art in Eastern Africa*, Dar-es-Salaam: Mkuki ya Nyota, 2008, pp. 151–73.

17 Instances include, but are by no means limited to: the Fine Art Department at Howard University (formally founded in 1921); Tin Sheds Gallery, Sydney (1969; joined University of Sydney 1989); The Feminist Art Program, founded 1970 by Judy Chicago, Miriam Schapiro, Rita Yokoi and others (Fresno State College and California Institute of

the Arts); Feminism and the Visual Arts MA (MAFEM), University of Leeds, founded by Griselda Pollock 1992; The Visual and Public Art Department, University of California, Monterey Bay, founded c.1994 by Judith Baca and Suzanne Lacy with Amalia Mesa-Bains; Taller Portobelo, founded in the mid-1990s by Arturo Lindsay, Spelman College; MA Visual Art, National College of the Arts, Lahore, founded 2000 by Lala Rukh and others; The Feminist Art Project, Rutgers University, co-founded 2005 by Judith K. Brodsky and Ferris Olin; Queering Yerevan, c.2006; *On Curating*, Zurich, c.2008 (OnCurating.org); from 2008, the annual course organized by Xabier Arakistain with Lourdes Méndez *Artistic Production and the Feminist Theory of Art: New Debates*, Azkuna Zentroa, Bilbao (from 2019, *The Feminist Gaze. Feminist Perspectives in Art Production and Theories of Art* at the Museo de Arte Contemporáneo del País Vasco, ARTIUM; *Critical Collective*, founded 2011 by Gayatri Sinha, Delhi; *Design for the Living World*, University of Fine Arts/HFBK in Hamburg convened by Marjetica Potrč 2011 to 2018; *AWARE: Archives of Women Artists, Research and Exhibitions*, co-founded 2014, directed by Camille Morineau; *n.paradoxa*'s MOOCs on feminism and the arts, developed by Katy Deepwell in 2017: https://nparadoxa.com/.

18 Lala Rukh gained her second MFA at the University of Chicago in 1976 and was also deeply impacted by the exhibition *Drawing Now* at MoMA in New York in the same year. For a wider discussion of the importance of drawing to feminist practice internationally, see Marsha Meskimmon and Phil Sawdon, *Drawing Difference: Connections between Gender and Drawing*, London: Bloomsbury, 2016.

19 From the interview with Lala Rukh by Maliha Noorani in 2009, no pages. Held in the Asia Art Archives; transcript available: https://aaa.org.hk/en/search/search/keywords:lala-rukh.

20 From the interview with Lala Rukh by Mariah Lookman in January 2016, no pages. Held in the Asia Art Archives; transcript available: https://aaa.org.hk/en/search/search/keywords:lala-rukh.

21 Despite Lala Rukh's work being an exemplary instance of how feminism, art and teaching so frequently entwine in radical political activism, the centrality of the Euro-US paradigm in feminist art scholarship remains strong, and outside the context of South Asian art, Lala Rukh is only beginning to garner a more global feminist reputation. See the excellent recent texts: Mariah Lookman, 'Lala Rukh, Muhanned Cader: Scripted Across the Indian Ocean' (unpublished exhibition essay), Green Cardamom Gallery, London, 2011, available at: https://www.academia.edu/25835634/Lala_Rukh_Muhanned_Cader_Scripted_Across_the_Indian_Ocean; Jyoti Dhar, 'Tranquility Amid Turmoil: Lala Rukh', *Art Asia Pacific* 102, March/April 2017 (no pages), available at http://artasiapacific.com/Magazine/102/TranquilityAmidTurmoil.

22 Interview with Mariah Lookman (2016).

23 It is telling that Lala Rukh's final trip to India before her death was to Amritsar, where she visited the Golden Temple with Indian feminist scholar Urvashi Butalia, famous for her ground-breaking work on gender and Partition, *The Other Side of Silence: Voices from the Partition of India*, Delhi: Penguin Books India, 1998.

24 It is perhaps not surprising that Peshawar is the main destination for Afghan refugees and immigrants in Pakistan, and that it has a large Pashtuk population. The river valleys continue to be connective channels despite the geopolitical borderlines that have been drawn over and across them.

25 I am indebted to scholar Rachel Murray, who made me aware of Dilip de Cunha's wonderful book, *The Invention of Rivers: Alexander's Eye and Ganga's Descent*, Philadelphia: University of Pennsylvania Press, 2018, and for inviting him to take part at a seminar at Loughborough's Institute of Advanced Studies in 2020.

26 Alexander, *Pedagogies of Crossing*, p. 290.

27 Alexander, *Pedagogies of Crossing*, p. 246.

28 It is instructive that, following his work on drawing the line at Partition, Cyril Radcliffe became the first Vice Chancellor of Warwick University, 1965–77.

29 Alexander, *Pedagogies of Crossing*, p. 253.

106 Practice and Flourish

30 Linda Tuhiwai Smith, *Decolonizing Methodologies: Research and Indigenous People* (1999), 3rd edition, London: Zed Books and Bloomsbury, 2021, pp. 282–3.
31 Tuhiwai Smith, *Decolonizing Methodologies*, p. 286.
32 Tuhiwai Smith, *Decolonizing Methodologies*, p. 77.
33 Paulo Freire, *Pedagogy of the Oppressed* (first published in English in 1970), 30th anniversary edition, London: Bloomsbury, 2000. See, in particular, chapter 3, 'Dialogics'.
34 Tuhiwai Smith, *Decolonizing Methodologies*, p. 38 (italics in the original).
35 There is a resonant convergence here with the work of Chela Sandoval, see: *Methodology of the Oppressed*, Minneapolis: University of Minnesota Press, 2000.
36 Svea Josephy was my host at UCT, and with Jean Brundrit, my closest contacts at UCT, but I must also thank Berni Searle, Michael Godby, Sue Williamson, Penny Siopsis, Nomusa Makhubu, Virginia Mackenny, Nkule Mabaso, Nancy Dantas, Fritha Langerman and Noelleen Murray for their welcoming engagement with my visit.
37 Brenda Schmahmann, 'The Fall of Rhodes: The Removal of a Sculpture from the University of Cape Town', *Public Art Dialog* 6:1, 2016, pp. 90–115.
38 Fast becoming international leaders in their fields, I am honoured to have been in dialogue with Sethembile Msezane, Anna Stielau and Olga Speakes whilst students at UCT.
39 See the cogent polemic by Edwin Mayorga, Lekey Leidecker and Daniel Orr de Gutiérrez, 'Burn It Down: The Incommensurability of the University and Decolonization', *Journal of Critical Thought and Praxis* 8:1, 2019, pp. 87–106, and Claire Colebrook's sharp analysis of world making and ending discourses: 'Creative, Speculative and World-Ending Ecologies', *Public* 32:63, September 2021, pp. 46–55.
40 For a beautiful, and succinct, meditation on this very problematic, see Dorothy Price, 'Binding Trauma', *Art History* 44:1, February 2021, pp. 8–14.
41 Tuhiwai Smith, *Decolonizing Methodologies*, p. 285.
42 See bell hooks, *Teaching to Transgress: Education as the Practice of Freedom*, London and New York: Routledge, 1994; *Teaching Community: A Pedagogy of Hope*, London and New York: Routledge, 2003; *Teaching Critical Thinking: Practical Wisdom*, London and New York: Routledge, 2010.
43 bell hooks, *Teaching Community*, p. 64 (from Teach 5 'What Happens When White People Change', pp. 55–66).
44 hooks, *Teaching to Transgress*, p. 40.
45 hooks, *Teaching Critical Thinking*, pp. 10, 45, 163.
46 bell hooks, *All About Love: New Visions*, New York: William Morrow, 2016, p. 153; NB: This is the first volume of her trilogy, *Love Song for the Nation*.
47 Dawn Rae Davis, 'Unmirroring Pedagogies: Teaching with Intersectional and Transnational Methods in the Women and Gender Studies Classroom', *Feminist Formations* 22:1, Spring 2010, pp. 136–62.
48 One of the most striking references to hooks and risk that I have come across is in the article by Patricia Ticineto Clough and Michelle Fine ('Activism and Pedagogies: Feminist Reflections', *Women's Studies Quarterly* 35:3/4, Fall 2007, pp. 255–75), in which they describe teaching and research they undertook in partnership with inmates in a women's prison. Using hooks, they discuss the space as an 'edge', a space of radical openness, where everyone involved took risks.
49 Marion Arnold and Marsha Meskimmon, eds, *Home/Land: Women, Citizenship, Photographies*, Liverpool: Liverpool University Press, 2016.
50 *Cf.* http://ufvcascade.ca/lens-of-empowerment-films-part-of-discourse-on-self-identity-acceptance-at-ufv/ and http://ufvcascade.ca/through-the-lens-of-empowerment-seeing-sitelines-in-solh-temexw/.
51 *Cf.* https://blogs.ufv.ca/blog/2014/07/ufv-lens-empowerment-project-returns-focus-womens-experience-stolo-territory/ and https://www.abbynews.com/news/stolo-stories-help-for-a-transformative-experience/.
52 Mary Eberts, 'Being an Indigenous Woman is a "High-Risk Lifestyle"', in Joyce Green, ed. *Making Space for Indigenous Feminism*, 2nd edition, Halifax and Winnipeg: Fernwood Publishing, 2017, pp. 69–102, p. 71.

Pedagogical Worlds **107**

53 Jessica Bennett, cited in Stephanie Gould, Jacqueline Nolte, Shirley Hardman and Sarah Ciurysek with Jessica Bennett, Andrea Smith and Jennifer Janik, 'Women's Citizenship and Identity in Stó:lō Territory: A Collective Essay from the University of the Fraser Valley's Lens Project', in Arnold and Meskimmon, eds, *Home/Land: Women, Citizenship, Photographies*, pp. 289–307, p. 302.

54 Referring both to the Indian residential schools and to higher education, Dean of the Arts and network member, Jacqueline Nolte, and *Lens* programme instructor, Stephanie Gould, made this point unequivocally in Gould, 'Women's Citizenship and Identity in Stó:lō Territory', pp. 292 and 299. I would further remind readers of the emphasis placed by The Final Report of Canada's National Enquiry into Missing and Murdered Indigenous Women and Girls [MMIWG], *Reclaiming Power and Place* (2019) upon co-creating curriculum with Indigenous women as a counter to violence:

> We call upon all elementary, secondary, and post-secondary institutions and education authorities to educate and provide awareness to the public about missing and murdered Indigenous women... and about the issues and root causes of violence they experience. All curriculum development and programming should be done in partnership with Indigenous Peoples, especially Indigenous women...
>
> (p. 103)

55 Photography instructor and network member Sarah Ciurysek spoke directly of having 'had much to learn' and how being willing to express this vulnerability openly to students, facilitated 'community-building and learning'. Cuirysek, cited in Gould, et al., 'Women's Citizenship and Identity in Stó:lō Territory', p. 297. Also, on education, vulnerability and mastery, see Julietta Singh, *Unthinking Mastery: Dehumanism and Decolonial Entanglements*, Durham, NC and London: Duke University Press, 2018, p. 67.

56 Ruana Kuokannen, *Reshaping the University: Responsibility, Indigenous Epistemes, and the Logic of the Gift*, Vancouver, BC: University of British Columbia Press, 2007, p. 2.

57 Kuokannen, *Reshaping the University*, p. 148.

58 Kuokannen, *Reshaping the University*, p. 119. See also her point that the logic of the gift in Indigenous thought 'cannot be formulated as preconceived models; it must be worked out *in practice* and then eventually inform the accompanying theory', p. 146.

59 Shirley Hardman, cited in Gould et al., 'Women's Citizenship and Identity in Stó:lō Territory', p. 294.

PART III

Worlding Pluriversal Stories

4

TRANS-SCALAR ECOLOGIES

Worlding Planetary Feminist Stories *with* Art

As a sensory, material and discursive assembly, art can make new worlds from old, and many worlds from One. This chapter turns to art's worldmaking potential, and, in particular, to its role within the transformative, pluriversal and ecological worlding projects of transnational feminisms. Yet, in making this turn, questions remain; for even if art's practices are worldmaking, and have the potential to foster the emergence of new, many and more-than-human worlds, how so, and why does it matter? For reasons that will become clear, addressing these questions is crucial to my explorations of transnational feminisms, ecological thinking and the arts, and, in posing them, I find myself in good company.

In his cogent and compelling volume, *Epistemologies of the South: Justice Against Epistemicide*, Portugese sociologist of law Boaventura de Sousa Santos stated categorically that '[t]his is a time of reckoning at a planetary level, involving humans and mother earth'.[1] His statement was not a conceit, but a clarion call, urging readers to recognize that there can be 'no global social justice without global cognitive justice', and that the apocalyptic trinity of colonialism, patriarchy and global capitalism ('among humans and between humans and nature') have led only to genocide, ecocide and epistemicide. What De Sousa Santos calls 'Western-centric' knowledge has had its day, and it is time to recognize and foster plural ways of knowing with/in many and diverse worlds.

Along broadly similar lines but with a different focal point, Caribbean philosopher, literary scholar and writer Sylvia Wynter connected her incisive analysis of anthropogenic climate change and species extinction with the entangled histories of global colonial conquest, enslavement, indenture, genocide and a forcibly imposed ordering of gender and sexuality. Wynter's analysis linked the new world order of the Columbian exchange, inaugurated in 1492,[2] with geological debates around the Anthropocene, focusing on 1750 and 1950 as pivotal inflection points, to argue that the global imperialism pursued by the 'West' reinvented the very category of the

DOI: 10.4324/9780429507816-8

112 Worlding Pluriversal Stories

human. Like De Sousa Santos, Wynter calls for profound epistemic change in the face of a catastrophic reckoning:

> We must now collectively undertake a rewriting of knowledge as we know it. This is a rewriting in which ... I want the West to recognize the dimensions of what it has brought into the world... [b]ecause the West *did* change the world, *totally*. And I want to suggest that it is *that* change that has made our own proposed far-reaching changes *now* as imperative as they are inevitable... [I]f we continue with our old way of thinking... we drift as a species toward an unparalleled catastrophe.[3]

The arguments made by De Sousa Santos and Wynter are hard-hitting, but not hopeless. For Wynter, the crisis provides an opportunity: '... think of the dazzling creativity of the alternative challenge that would be opened up!'[4] The opportunity centres upon thinking the human not as 'Man', but as 'homo narrans', a 'hybrid' storytelling species (*bios* and *logos/mythoi* at once) that instantiates human being not as a noun, but as a verb – as *praxis*.[5] For De Sousa Santos, the aim is 'Good Living/ Buen Vivir',[6] a socially- and epistemically-just form of interdependent and pluriversal flourishing, that, De Sousa Santos argues, can only emerge by countering the intellectual monoculture imposed by Western-centric 'lazy reason' through the development of new 'ecologies' – ecologies of knowledge, temporality, recognition, productivities and trans-scale.[7]

The intellectual breadth that Wynter and De Sousa Santos bring to their analyses of social, economic and ecological justice lends compelling force to their arguments for profound epistemic transformation. They ask us to reimagine not only *what* we think, but *how* and *for what purpose*. Thinking thus understood becomes a critical practice towards making new and many worlds – thinking *matters*. More strongly, I would argue that thinking becomes *ecological*.[8]

In her lucid writing on the politics of epistemic location, US American feminist philosopher Lorraine Code makes clear that 'ecological thinking' is related to, but more than, thinking about ecology. Ecological thinking is a complex, plural, situated and connective form of thought that resists the 'epistemological monoculture' of instrumental knowledges that pursue mastery under the reductive, universalizing 'rubric of sameness'. Like De Sousa Santos and Wynter, Code asserts epistemic transformation as crucial to answering calls for social, economic and ecological justice, and similarly finds allies in feminist, 'postcolonial' and anti-racist thought and activisms, citing them as the most sustained challenges to ingrained structures of domination. Code argues with particular force for the significance of feminisms (especially anti-essentialist ecofeminisms) to the transformative potential of ecological thinking: 'If it can establish a firm enough footing, ecological thinking – like feminism at its best – will reconceive human and natural locations and relations all the way down.'[9]

As described by Code, the practice of ecological thinking is transversal, horizontal, analogous, deliberative, collaboratively negotiated, sensitive to, and respectful of, differences. A vital form of knowing, ecological thinking is responsive and responsible to others, and aims to create interdependent flourishing – 'habitats' for 'living well together'. Significantly, Code argues that ecological thinking can be realized, practically: '… the transformative potential of ecological thinking can be realized by participants engaged in producing a viable habitat and ethos, prepared to take on the burdens and blessings of place, identity, materiality, and history…'[10]

I take Code's salient comments to suggest that ecological thinking might be realized through mutual and interdependent *worldmaking*. At this point, it is important to stress that my argument for the critical entanglement of decolonial feminisms, ecological thinking and worldmaking does not posit a vision of plenitude simply waiting to be willed into being, but, rather, suggests trajectories towards interdependent practices of survival. I would argue further that many of these trajectories on worldmaking for, and as, survival, were articulated decades ago in race-critical, queer and feminist theory that affirmed the power of love, desire and hope in fashioning new futures, without underestimating the intellectual, imaginative and affective labour that *making, unmaking* and *remaking* worlds requires.[11]

In this light, I find it particularly resonant that US American queer theorist Eve Kosofsky Sedgwick's oft-cited text on paranoid and reparative reading opens with an anecdote delineating the interconnected brutalities of racism, homophobia, militarized political violence and environmental destruction, as a means by which to ask its searching question concerning *knowledge* – 'What does knowledge do…'.[12] Sedgwick's deconstruction of 'paranoid reading' as a strong theory, leaning towards tautology as it creates knowledges already known, chimes with descriptions of Western-centric epistemic monoculture. More to the point, Sedgwick's counter-claim for 'reparative reading' as contingent, plural, accretive, ameliorative and aesthetic shares significant affinities with ecological thinking. At the very end of her text, the 'reparative impulse' is proposed as central to practices of collective survival, or 'the many ways selves and communities succeed in extracting sustenance from the objects of a culture – even of a culture whose avowed desire has often been not to sustain them'.[13]

Although Code and Sedgwick focus primarily on human agency, their arguments concerning knowledge and mutual flourishing find an echo in the increasingly prominent development of vital materialisms in ethnographic research, such as that of US American anthropologist Anna Lowenhaupt Tsing, whose examinations of more-than-human survival in the Anthropocene are apposite here. Tsing delineates succinctly the stalemate created by reductive monocultural thinking faced with the crisis of anthropogenic climate change and species extinction, stating that: 'Neither tales of progress nor of ruin tell us how to think about collaborative survival.'[14] As Tsing argues, survival is always a form of contaminated collaboration, and plural worlds are made by more than humans, at many scales and across multidimensional registers.

How can we participate in the thinking and making that foster Buen Vivir, collaborative survival, and mutual flourishing in more-than-human worlds? Arguably, by realizing ecological thinking through practices of worldmaking that

114 Worlding Pluriversal Stories

are plural (amongst diverse humans and between humans and earth others), planetary (radically connective across micro and macro scales of time and space), but never 'pure' – always complicit with, and entangled in, the worlds being made.[15] It is my proposition that to engage with such pluriversal and planetary worlding is to engage with scale, not as a singular, universal system of equivalences,[16] but as the articulation of non-linear dynamism between and across the complexity and radical alterity of plural worlds.[17] Critically, it is also to engage with transnational feminist spatial and scalar praxis.

Transnational feminisms focus a decolonial *and* feminist lens on the intrinsic imbrication of *bio* and *geo* politics, understanding race, gender and sexuality to be intimately interconnected with the violent, extractive, *spatial* and *scalar*, geo-logics of colonial conquest, imperial expansion and global capitalism. Transnational feminist geographical thinking, in connection with transnational feminist activist networks, has long challenged concepts of space as universal or homogeneous, stressing instead the complex interconnections between 'levels', such as the local, regional, national and global, whilst emphasizing the embodied, situated and locational politics of subjectivity, identification, knowledge production and the cultural imaginary.[18] Transnational feminist praxis unravels the binary spatial logic that creates categorical distinctions between local and global, centre and periphery, West and 'the rest', preferring, instead, a multidimensional and trans-scalar engagement with the mutual emergence of these (and other) concepts of space, in and through relational epistemic practices.[19] Understanding place as a process, scale as epistemology, the entanglement of the intimate with the global, and the significance of conversing with other epistemic worlds,[20] transnational feminist scalar and spatial practice is critical to the project of feminist ecological thinking and worldmaking that is the focus of this chapter. But what about art?

Not surprisingly, and with increasing frequency, art, design and architectural practices have come to the fore for scholars and activists seeking routes/roots towards collaborative survival with/in the damaged terrain of the Anthropocene. This turn to the arts reinforces, yet again, the worldmaking agency of art's particular visual, material and spatial configurations of knowledge and imagination. The work emerging in this arena is diverse, global and multi-platform, ranging from multidisciplinary exchanges between scholars, activists and artists,[21] and interdisciplinary research into the political ecologies of art, visual culture and art history,[22] to curatorial and multi-agency eco-ventions in museums, galleries and public spaces,[23] and wide-ranging, practice-led research collaborations that bridge social, economic and ecological justice agendas.[24]

As this rich terrain indicates, art's worldmaking potential *matters*. It participates, materially, with/in, and can contribute to, the most important ethical, political and epistemic debates of the present, while suggesting directions for the future. Moreover, and what drives my engagement with art's worldmaking mattering here, ecologically-engaged art practices are deeply interconnected with transnational feminist thought and activism at many levels.[25] Although some of the current discourses around ecology and art tend to occlude feminist antecedents and influences, even a brief survey of the transhemispheric histories of feminist art theory, practice and activist intervention, demonstrates how crucial they have been to the development of work on ecological art and environmental visual culture.[26] The connective thinking-in-making of feminist art theory and eco-activism has generated myriad interventions, including critiques of the gendered dynamics of techno-science and attention to the vibrant matter of a vital cosmos;[27] aesthetic explorations of ecosexuality and queer ecologies;[28] ground-breaking work by Black, Indigenous and feminist artists of colour against toxicity, population control and the 'deferred genocide' of withheld sovereignty;[29] and artist-activist campaigns around nuclear militarism, deforestation, water rights, seeds and food, often particularly focused on the Global South.[30]

Working at the interface between ecological thinking and aesthetic worldmaking in and through transnational feminisms, this chapter develops the concept of *trans-scalar ecologies* to describe practices of non-linear and non-hierarchical worlding *with* art, between and across times and spaces, bodies and histories, geographies and cosmologies.[31] Trans-scalar ecologies world pluriversal stories and tell tales of collaborative survival that are always plural and planetary, but never 'pure'. They operate beyond 'nested' scales of equivalence and fungibility, materializing intimacies and incommensurabilities *at each* and *across varied* temporal, spatial and bio/geo scales, without reducing difference to sameness. It is my contention that the connections they draw are transversal, transhemispheric and transcorporeal (more-than-human), and that art is crucial to their materialization.

Trans-scalar worldmaking *with* art[32] further challenges the disciplinary and methodological conventions of art history, particularly where these reinforce the singularity of Eurocentric/universal narratives of value and meaning. Echoing Wynter's *homo narrans*, and the storied relational ontologies of Marilyn Strathern and Donna Haraway – *it matters what stories tell stories*[33] – writing *with* art's trans-scalar ecologies moves away from defining a category of objects called 'global feminist eco-art', or providing a survey of feminist ecological remediation and activism, illustrated, instrumentalized or documented by art. In what follows, I propose instead, to story trans-scalar ecologies that are intrinsically resistant to singularity. To start, I follow a meandering, riparian route, conversing with and walking alongside,[34] two art projects, each of which connects with a specific river ecosystem: Judith F. Baca's mural, *The Great Wall of Los Angeles* (1976–83ff), painted along the concrete walls of the Tujunga Wash flood control channel that cuts through the San Fernando Valley in Los Angeles, and Wu Mali's *Art as Environment – A Cultural Action at the Plum Tree Creek* (2010–12), undertaken along a tributary of Taiwan's Danshui River.

Each project created a flourishing ecology specific to its place, whilst, together, the works tell plural and planetary tales of transhemispheric worlds in a terraqueous cosmos. Attending to the works through trans-scalar feminist figurations of art and ecological worldmaking, this chapter unfolds over three, interconnected dialogues. The first takes a 'local turn' to develop a 'global sense of place',[35] arguing that a transversal feminist politics of non-identitarian belonging can create and maintain flourishing epistemic and ecological communities with and through art.

116 Worlding Pluriversal Stories

The second dialogue signals a significant change of scale and perspective, fore-grounding oceanic and archipelagic histories of the pre- and colonial past as they impact upon the global present. This transhemispheric tale eddies across times and spaces, drawing out unexpected bio- and geopolitical connections between the Plum Tree Creek and the Tujunga Wash. As the third dialogue flows towards the final bend in the chapter's lotic route, the perspective changes from globality to planetarity, to tell a tale of the entanglement between human and more-than-human bodies (of water) in a vibrant, ethico-aesthetic cosmos. Through speculative, world-making fictions and critical fabulations, the third dialogue ends the chapter with a planetary feminist tale of collaborative survival and interdependence across many worlds, beyond the technocratic mastery of one.

My argument in this chapter deliberately engages with works that are connected with specific river ecologies. While this is not to argue that only in the instance of riparian works would it be possible to articulate a trans-scalar ecology of transnational feminisms and the arts, it is the case that river ecologies provide a remarkably useful focal point for the thinking being pursued here. River ecologies are pro-foundly diverse and trans-scalar, crossing many domains of knowledge, interest and agency, and they function in this chapter as more than mere metaphor. In particular, I am indebted to the notion of 'messy rivers', developed in the work of geologist Ellen Wohl.[36] Wohl argues that the physical complexity, or 'messiness', of river cor-ridors (meandering, multi-stream, eroded and/or blocked channels, heterogeneous plains) can frequently signal their good health, and that technical interventions designed to make rivers 'simple and uniform', often damage flourishing ecosystems.

Crucial to both human and more-than-human flourishing, rivers play a central role within the biogeomorphology of both local and global environments. At a planetary scale, rivers are as powerful they are mutable; they engender, sustain, and can destroy, terrestrial life. Telling riparian tales of meandering mattering is an apt way to enter into the trans-scalar ecologies of transnational feminisms and the arts. As this chapter ebbs and flows with rivers, across lands, through oceans and beyond, my tales gravitate towards 'messy rivers', and worlds that resist scalability, univer-sality and homogeneity. But if they do not nest easily, micro-within-macro, they nonetheless resonate, through partial and polyphonic relations at each, and across many, scales, as they world the pluriversal stories of transnational feminisms *with* art.

Two Rivers, Many Worlds: A Transversal Dialogue

In 1974, the United States Army Corps of Engineers (ACE) approached Chicana feminist artist Judith Baca with a proposal to 'beautify' the Tujunga Wash, a concrete flood control channel of the Los Angeles river, widely seen as an urban eyesore. Baca had already gained a reputation in the city for her ability to realize striking mural projects by galvanizing young people from marginalized communities and leveraging multi-agency support and funding for public art.[37] Her strong aesthetic vision, substantial technical facility and exceptional communication skills ensured that, by the end of the first painting summer of 1976, the ACE's beautification project in the Tujunga Wash drainage channel had already become the largest mural in the world, measuring 1,000 feet in length.

The first 1,000 feet of *The Great Wall* charted the story of the site from 20,000 BCE to 1910, and was painted in ten main sections of 100 feet each. In 1978, the next 350-foot portion of the mural was painted, taking the historical narrative from the First World War to the end of the 1920s. *The Great Wall* extended by a further 350 feet, and one storied decade, in each of the summers of 1980, '81 and '83, chronicling the 1930s, 1940s and 1950s respectively. To date, *The Great Wall of Los Angeles* extends to 2,754 feet, has employed and trained more than 400 young people in its teams of Mural Makers, and stands as a public monument to the diverse histories of the place that came to be called California.[38]

Flourishing for nearly half a century, *The Great Wall* is a rich project that admits of many points of engagement, but in the present dialogue, one in particular comes to the fore. I want to suggest that, in its address to the loss of the 'messy' riparian ecology of the Los Angeles river through the interconnected histories of European colonization, agricultural/industrial extraction and (sub)urban expansion, *The Great Wall* did not so much remediate the river, as engender an enduring epistemic and ecological community through a transversal politics of connection and coalition-building *with* art. In this sense, Baca's project epitomizes the transnational feminist worldmaking, ecological thinking and epistemic politics of location that are the focus of this chapter.

In a comment on *The Great Wall*, Baca drew a salient connection between the site's terraqueous and human ecologies: 'A relationship exists between the disappearance of the river and the people: if you can disappear a river, how much easier is it to disappear the history of the people?'[39] Her point is both provocative and precise; the industrial processes designed to extract maximum value from rivers as exploitable 'natural resources' are the same that have destroyed riparian ecologies and communities throughout the world, and remain the focus of many social and environmental justice campaigns. Unsurprisingly, women, Indigenous communities, and other economically- and socially-marginalized groups have commonly borne the greatest 'downstream' burden from the extractive destruction of rivers, while, at the same time, they have found their voices silenced and their worlds 'disappeared'.[40]

The construction of the Tujunga Wash flood channel by the ACE participated in just such a 'disappearance', as one of a series of infrastructural projects undertaken between the 1930s and the 1960s to secure the flood plain, and clear valuable land for property development, in the city of Los Angeles. *The Great Wall* includes scenes of a number of such infrastructural projects, including the development of suburbia, the clearance of the Chavez Ravine to make way for Dodger Stadium, and the construction of the city's freeway system. *The Great Wall's* extended riparian narrative further makes apparent the intrinsic links between mid-20th-century urban development and the continuing logic of European colonization. Along the walls of the Tujunga Wash, the mural's tales of Spanish conquest, Mexican–American conflict and Anglo expansion westward do not sustain a naturalized narrative of

118 Worlding Pluriversal Stories

'manifest destiny'. Rather, the mural's histories of multi-racial and ethnic migration and settlement are marked as much by conflict as by critical entanglements with the terraqueous environment – from the discovery of gold in the river at Sutter's Mill, to the establishment of California's agricultural industry, supported both by the construction of the California Aqueduct and extensive irrigation technologies, and by the iniquitous Bracero Program that brought more than four million migrant Mexican labourers into the state between 1942 and 1964. The scenes of *The Great Wall* provide ample evidence that the concrete control exerted over the 'messy' river ecology was deeply enmeshed within a wider context of community destruction and erasure from a 'whitewashed' version of the history of the city itself.[41]

...

Some 11,000 miles away, a second river project also told the tale of a once-vibrant and 'messy' ecology, largely 'disappeared' through technological interventions designed to support rapid industrial and urban development. Between 2010 and 2012, in partnership with the arts and cultural organization Bamboo Curtain Studio, Taiwanese ecofeminist artist and curator, Wu Mali, led the award-winning, community eco-art project, *Art as Environment – A Cultural Action at the Plum Tree Creek*.[42] The Plum Tree Creek is a 13-mile-long tributary of the Danshui,[43] Taiwan's third-longest, and, arguably, most historically significant, river. For centuries, the Plum Tree Creek supported a flourishing riparian ecology along the whole of its course, but the phenomenal expansion of Taiwan's manufacturing base under the exiled Nationalist government of the Kuomintang (KMT) during the period of Martial Law (1949–87), followed by the rapid growth of New Taipei City during the 1990s, led to the 'messy' stream being culverted, polluted and, in some places, run dry.

A Cultural Action at the Plum Tree Creek was intended to raise awareness of the watercourse, and bring the issues of its history as well as its current damaged state, to a wide range of stakeholders, from local residents along its banks, to environmental scientists, urban planners, farmers, artists and civic agencies alike. In addition to raising awareness of the stream, the objective of the project was to create long-term and locally-sustainable social and ecological change in the Zhu Wei district of New Taipei City, which it effected through a combination of education and grass-roots activism that made significant inroads into the city's urban planning policy. Wu Mali's decision to work in her own neighbourhood, in partnership with well-established local community groups and environmental organizations, including the local Green Citizen's Action Alliance, and the Women's Association for Sustainable Ecology, was central to that objective. Bringing professional artists together with these partners, while working closely with local schools, colleges, universities and planning experts, such as the bio-architects Ecoscape Formosana, the project's co-design built communication, resilience and longevity into the work from the start.

The project took place over 17 months and consisted of five, interrelated, 'cultural actions' that, in Wu Mali's words, established 'a platform for dialogue'.[44] These included actions designed specifically for residents from different areas along the

FIGURE 4.1 Wu Mali, Breakfast event with local residents (2010), from *Art as Environment: A Cultural Action at the Plum Tree Creek*, 2010–12.
Image courtesy of the artist and Bamboo Curtain Studio, New Taipei City.

water's route, including very successful monthly meetings, 'Breakfast at the Plum Tree Creek', at which discussions concerning the stream, and the issues facing communities living and working alongside it, were facilitated over meals made with locally-produced food (Figure 4.1).

These were complemented by a series of community theatre actions that further encouraged dialogue between up-, mid- and downstream neighbours of the Plum Tree Creek, by using creative storytelling and participatory performance. The platform, 'Shaping of a Village: Nomadic Museum', centred on a craft-based marketplace and community visualization project undertaken in partnership with the Department of Architecture at the artist's alma mater, Tamkang University. This platform encouraged the urban residents along the creek to create viable community spaces, share skills, and work with urban designers to imagine and visualize plans for future relationships with the Plum Tree Creek. Finally, the project's educational actions, 'Local Eco-Life: Colourful Affairs with Plants' (with Zhu Wei High School) and 'There Is a Creek in Front of My School Gate' (with Zhu Wei Elementary School), included tree planting, vegetable dye and fabric workshops, performance projects and treks along the route of the creek, and inspired long-term changes in teaching and curriculum at the partner schools.

...

I want to suggest that attending to these two very different works of art, and the flourishing 'local' worlds they made as they engaged with two very differently disappeared river ecologies, does not foreclose upon creating a dialogue between them.

120 Worlding Pluriversal Stories

Rather, it provides an opportunity to understand the 'local' as formed by trans-scalar relational practices or, echoing the words of feminist geographer Doreen Massey, through 'a really global sense of place'.[45] Massey's influential argument is particularly apt here, not only because she exploded 'reactionary' Eurocentric conventions of globalization that posited idealized notions of place as bounded, singular, unified and homogeneous, but because she did so through the compelling case study of one, decidedly 'extroverted', local place, the Kilburn High Road in London. Significantly, in Massey's vivid description, the flourishing Kilburn High Road was unapologetically messy, plural, and not at all pure – thoroughly entangled with 'half the world and a considerable amount of British imperialist history'.[46]

Massey's insights are an invitation to attend closely to the specificity of place, not to fix or reify each instance, but rather, more effectively, to amplify the relations, connections and affinities that might be drawn between differently situated places. That approach resonates with the analogous reasoning and transversal dialogue characteristic of ecological thinking.[47] *The Great Wall of Los Angeles* and *A Cultural Action at the Plum Tree Creek* each explode the local into plural and heterogeneous worlds, as they reanimate the messy, disappeared stories of communities and ecologies that once flourished in and along the vibrant edges of their respective rivers. Arguably, the trans-scalar stories they tell are *transversal*, making connections between and across diverse times, spaces and bodies as they materialize transnational feminist ecological worldmaking with and through art.

Transversal dialogues between diverse communities, histories and environments were critical to both the narrative content of *The Great Wall*, and to its physical realization along the concrete lining of the Tujunga Wash. Over 400 young people from marginalized communities, 'at risk', and/or recruited directly through the juvenile justice system, were brought together in teams under the guidance of Baca and some three dozen commissioned professional artists, to develop the technical skills needed to achieve *The Great Wall*. At a time when there was little being taught in schools about the gendered, classed and racially-diverse histories of the United States, Baca brought oral history specialists, community activists, anthropologists and historians together with the Makers for collective storying sessions for the mural. Makers were paid for their work on the project, encouraged to take on leadership responsibilities in the teams, and supported in their wider education and social development.[48] In addition, the privileges of authorship were accorded to Makers, whose names were recorded on the wall alongside the section of the mural created during their tenure. Through these transversal and dialogic practices of production, the project created an 'epistemic community' amongst the Makers, as 18-year-old Todd Ableser described so well in his comments on being a Mural Maker:

> After my first year on the mural, I left with a sense of who I was and what I could do that was unlike anything I'd ever felt before. The feeling came from encountering people of different backgrounds and outlooks, and confronting history from new perspectives … I feel now that everything on the mural is my history…[49]

If *The Great Wall* is an outstanding example of the potential of participatory community art practice to foster youth empowerment and transcultural understanding through education and transversal dialogue, it is pre-eminently an outstanding work of public art and history making.[50] The mural *worlds* pluriversal stories, focusing particularly on the occluded histories that complicate and challenge the singular narrative of seamless assimilation that long dominated US public discourse. Baca's project grappled with the legacies of patriarchy, heteronormativity and the genocidal disappearance of Black, Indigenous and people of colour from the worlds and stories of what came to be the US State of California, without simply replacing the reductive universal narrative of 'one nation, indivisible' with the essentialist and polarizing politics of reified identity.[51] The mural is underscored by a decidedly transversal politics premised upon decolonial feminist 'world-travelling', where crossings and connections between many worlds are replete with celebration, confrontation and incommensurability in turn. As a space where many diverse bodies, stories and worlds meet, *The Great Wall* tells plural tales that reject 'purity as an instrument of social control'.[52]

Significantly, the mural worlds these pluriversal stories *with* art, creating meaning through trans-scalar visual connections and disjunctions. *The Great Wall* eschews one-point perspective in favour of multiple, polyangular viewpoints, deployed alongside chromatic and compositional tropes, such as the meandering line that is variously oceans, rivers, blood, flag or banner, to suggest affinities between distinct characters and stories.[53] The imaged scenes and visual transitions within the 1940s section of the mural, a section that focuses primarily on the rise of fascism and US engagement in the Second World War, exemplify these aesthetic strategies.

The narrative combines tales of particular, local individuals, such as Mrs (Anna) Laws, Dr Charles Drew, David Gonzales and Luisa Moreno, with images of named and recognizable 'collectives', such as the 'zoot suiters' and the women who worked in munitions factories during the war, collectively titled 'Rosie the Riveter'. The visual structure is not linear, yet its radical shifts of scale, colour and contrast create conceptual connections between and across times and spaces. For instance, the racially-diverse women envisaged as many different Rosies riveting in unison, are followed directly on the wall by Dr Drew, the African-American surgeon responsible for the creation of life-saving blood banks at a time when White-only policies meant that many Black Americans were denied access to hospital care. These two scenes demonstrate the often-unsung contribution of people of colour to the nation's war effort in no uncertain terms. However, the next scene on the wall, 'Mrs Laws', complicates the narrative by creating a visual inflection point that breaks the fourth wall to address viewers directly. Mrs Laws, the African-American homeowner who successfully campaigned against discriminatory housing covenants in California, is shown on a picket line with fellow protestors, but her figure is represented looking out of the mural and pushing her placard into the time and space of its viewers. Breaking out of the 1940s and into the present, the scene makes the point that racism, sexism and fascism are not things of the past, and Mrs Laws' placard is resolute: 'We fight FASCISM abroad and AT HOME' (Figure 4.2).

FIGURE 4.2 Judith F. Baca, copyright 1983. Detail 'Mrs Laws' to 'Louisa Moreno', several panels from the 1940s section of the *Great Wall of Los Angeles* mural.
Image courtesy of the SPARC Archives SPARCinLA.org.

Mrs Laws' address is followed on the wall by the story of David Gonzales, one of many men from the local Chicano community to serve in the US Army during the Second World War, represented in uniform against a painted collection of smiling family photographs. His image segues to the spats and smart shoes of young men from the Chicano and Filipino communities, the 'zoot suiters', emerging from yellow cabs along a city curb. A newspaper headline by their feet reports on racist attacks committed by White servicemen during the 'Zoot Suit Riots'. In the next scene, by means of a striking shift of perspective, tone and scale, we are confronted, visually, by the back of a pair of towering black boots worn by a soldier whose legs frame the stripped and cowering figure of a beaten zoot suiter on the pavement. At the other side of the right boot, through another shift of scale and perspective, emerges a defiant close-up image of Guatemalan-born labour organizer, Luisa Moreno, wrapped in a sweeping spiral that reads 'El Congreso de Pueblos' (the People's Congress). Like Mrs Laws, this commanding and resistant female figure pushes forward towards viewers; sustained by the collective power of her community and trade union, Moreno stands in sharp contrast to the structural racism embodied by the toxic militarized masculinity of the black-booted soldier-thug.

The Great Wall tells transversal tales of collaborative survival along the edges of a once-messy river, conversing with some of the many worlds that were disappeared by the same forces that straightened the multi-stream watercourse into a concrete waste channel. The mural is a monumental achievement by any standard, but perhaps its greatest feat is its visual and spatial 'world-travelling' and its continuing ability to bring histories into the present as a site of reparative memory and community-building through transnational feminist worldmaking *with* art.

A Cultural Action at the Plum Tree Creek, like *The Great Wall*, sought to revitalize disappeared river ecologies and communities with art. In formal terms; however, the two projects' artmaking strategies and outcomes were very different, and my argument does not seek reductively to equate a mile-long mural with a series of participatory 'cultural actions'. Yet in their decidedly transversal approach to developing effective platforms for dialogue across many and varied communities, and in their explorations of specific, 'local', riparian ecologies through an entangled and 'global sense of place', engaging with the significant affinities between the two works adds much to a discussion of how transnational feminisms, ecological thinking and trans-scalar worldmaking can address collaborative survival amidst climate emergency.

A Cultural Action at the Plum Tree Creek focused primarily on creating transversal forms of cross-community dialogue, bringing residents from up-, mid- and downstream neighbourhoods along the creek together with extant community and environmental activists groups and local educational institutions. These communities experienced the Plum Tree Creek as many different worlds; older residents remembered the plum trees planted along the creek under Japanese rule in Taiwan, and shared stories of drinking the stream's fresh water and using it in their gardens. Some of the children taking part in the actions did not even know that there was a stream running under their feet as they walked to school. Many of the participants in the Plum Tree Creek treks were unaware of its source in the Datun mountains, or its varied uses along its course. The project facilitated imaginative travel between worlds – urban and rural, city and village, farm and factory – creating connections between old and young, and between the worlds of the Indigenous Austronesians and the 'New Taiwanese', worlds formed by centuries of multiple migrations and colonizations. These transversal dialogues engaged with the multi-ethnic diversity of Taiwan as part of the story of a disappeared ecology, but also as a critical part of a hopeful tale of collaborative survival in future, created through a transcultural and intergenerational ethic of care for a shared watercourse.

Bringing together the many worlds lived across different times and spaces alongside the Plum Tree Creek created an awareness of the history of the watercourse. But the project also sought to develop dialogues towards imaginative and transformative change, in keeping with Wu Mali's proposition: 'Social change always starts with alternative social imaginaries'.[54] *A Cultural Action at the Plum Tree Creek* was not Wu Mali's first experience with feminist, socially-engaged art seeking to foster transformative change, nor was it her first environmental art project. In the early 1990s, Wu Mali's work focused on the complex entanglements between women, labour and nation in Taiwan, drawing critical connections between the gendered histories of the archipelago's colonial past and its more recent success in the global marketplace. Towards the end of the decade, Wu Mali turned increasingly to socially-engaged and participatory art projects that moved beyond the gallery, working with women's activist groups, such as Taiwan's Awakening Association, as well as educational institutions, cultural agencies and environmental and community groups. In 2006, the artist undertook her first project on the Danshui, *By the River, On the River, Of the River*, creating a platform for education and awareness of the significance of the river and its tributaries to the histories of Taiwan and to the urgent issue of climate change. By the time she initiated *A Cultural Action at the Plum Tree Creek*, Wu Mali understood well both the expectations of local art audiences and the dynamics of ecofeminist politics within the vibrant context of what has been called elsewhere, Taiwan's 'civic eco-nationalism',[55] a broadly-based, democratizing cultural politics, focused on ecological and social justice, including gender equity and Indigenous rights.

A Cultural Action at the Plum Tree Creek operated successfully within this local cultural and political context, providing a space for participatory citizen dialogue on the collaborative survival of ecological and cultural communities along the once-flourishing stream. The transversal approach Wu Mali instituted through the work – non-hierarchical and self-organizing[56] – emphasized 'quotidian' processes of artmaking, focused on participation and dialogue, rather than the production of 'artworks', to weave socially-engaged art practices into the fabric of the daily lives of the residents of the Plum Tree Creek area, and to work effectively within the limits of the art economy in Taiwan (Figure 4.3).[57] Wu Mali's practices of creating platforms for dialogue, everyday engagements with the watercourse, and the integration of future generations into the life of the creek through education, enabled *A Cultural Action at the Plum Tree Creek* to swiftly become part of the cultural life of the Zhu Wei district and be integrated into the long-term urban planning goals of New Taipei City's Vision of Grand River.[58]

As we commenced this first dialogue, conversing with and walking alongside these two rivers in many worlds, our questions concerned not only *how* these projects materialized trans-scalar ecologies with art, but *to what ends*. Charting courses of difference-in-relation, through trans-scalar entanglements between the local and the global, these works created the possibility for flourishing lifeworlds to re-emerge in once-vibrant places, now disappeared. Indeed, it was through their attention to the material specificity of their very different 'local' communities and environments that their worldmaking with art engendered a 'global sense of place'. This is not a paradox, but an instance of ecological thinking in action that poses a profound riposte to globalization as a monocultural episteme. Collaborative survival in a time of anthropogenic climate change and species extinction is a tale not of top-down universal theories or tidy technocratic solutions, but of 'becoming both

FIGURE 4.3 Wu Mali, Shaping the village, *Art as Environment: A Cultural Action at the Plum Tree Creek*, 2010–12.

Image courtesy of the artist and Bamboo Curtain Studio, New Taipei City.

Trans-Scalar Ecologies **125**

more united and increasingly different'[59] as we engage together with the rich and vital messiness of world-travelling.

Rivers in Oceans: A Transhemispheric Dialogue

As we turn from our dialogue between two rivers in many worlds, to explore rivers as they flow into seas and oceans, we shift scales from the extroverted and mutual entanglements of the global with/in the local to the archipelagic relations,[60] and oceanic intimacies,[61] of the connective and multidirectional flows of transhemispheric histories. This is not more of the same, only greater in quantity and extent, but a change of epistemic location and aesthetic register.

Where rivers meet oceans, their courses can take surprising directions, and many tidal rivers, like Taiwan's Danshui, are known to flow both ways. The Danshui forms a wide natural harbour where it meets the South China Sea at the Taiwan Strait, on the main island of the archipelago. This navigable harbour and freshwater inland river have played a key role in Taiwan's history for thousands of years – a history of transhemispheric migrations and colonizations that have flowed both ways.

The Danshui enabled Taiwan's first human inhabitants to reach its shores, and, later, facilitated the descendants of those same Austronesian-speaking people to undertake vast maritime migrations across the Indian and Pacific Oceans, populating culturally-connected archipelagos from Madagascar to Polynesia, between 4000 and 3000 BCE. By the 10th century, the harbour provided a hub for both a flourishing jade trade and a maritime silk route, making Taiwan a central point of cross-Asian exchange in the Indian Ocean. Later, the Danshui was a key point of access for Taiwan's 'serial' colonization,[62] first by Han Chinese during the Ming and Qing Dynasties,[63] followed by short-lived incursions by the Spanish and Dutch during the 17th century, the Japanese between 1895 and 1945, and, finally, exiled Chinese nationalists who, under the Kuomintang, established Martial Law between 1949 and 1987. Taiwan's present-day geopolitical position continues to flow both ways, situated, as it is, between the imperial, industrial and military aspirations of mainland China and the United States in the Pacific.

Taiwan's geopolitical situation is paradoxical – pivotal historically to both Pacific and Indian Ocean culture and trade, and critical to 'Great Power' struggles in the wake of the Cold War, yet marginal, a small archipelago and unrecognized nationstate. This paradoxical position has, until recently, been mirrored by Taiwan's relative absence from mainstream postcolonial discourse and theories of globalization. In their ground-breaking collection, *Comparativizing Taiwan*, cultural theorists Shumei Shih and Ping-hui Liao argued that interrogating this 'paradox' reveals a clear intellectual investment:

> If we take the maritime history of Taiwan seriously, Taiwan emerges as a nodal point for maritime trade among China, Southeast Asia, Europe and the Americas, and this places Taiwan in a global map of the movement of goods and peoples... The marginalization of Taiwan in post-colonial studies

126 Worlding Pluriversal Stories

is therefore all the more surprising, although, in the final analysis, it is an illustration of the most insidious kind of Eurocentrism... (E)ven in the critique of empires, Western empires get all the attention.[64]

Taiwan's complex global geographic and cultural position was not lost on Wu Mali. Indeed, she frequently emphasized the links between Taiwan's Indigenous and multi-ethnic communities, its colonial past, global capitalist present, the emergence of feminist and ecological activisms in the 1980s and '90s, and the role played by socially-engaged art practices, in negotiating what she called 'difficult questions':

> Taiwan has a number of aboriginal communities with very different cultures. This diversity was further enriched by cultural practices introduced during Qing Dynasty, the Japanese colonization, and later the Nationalist migration, and the American influence. There are lots of difficult questions waiting for us in layers of history.[65]

Wu Mali's work never shied away from difficult questions around the social, political and economic forces that shaped Taiwan's past, and will determine its future. Contact history flows both ways in Wu Mali's work, neither negating the impact of the colonial and Cold War legacies, nor positing Taiwan as an empty vessel, receiving culture in a unidirectional flow, *from* others *to* Taiwan. On the contrary, and particularly in her ecofeminist work, Wu Mali's projects demonstrate a deep engagement with Taiwan as a globally connected archipelago worlded by trans-scalar forces: 'The form of our lifeworld is shaped by various intricately linked local and global factors.'[66] In this sense, Wu Mali's work can be understood as part of a wider oceanic mode of re-thinking the global that has begun to shift the flow of thought in new and multiple directions.

Take, for example, historian Sujit Sivasundaram's revisionist global narrative of modernity from the south, whose opening is particularly resonant here:

> There is a quarter of this planet which is often forgotten in the histories that are told in the West. This quarter is an oceanic one... The Indian and Pacific Oceans – taken as a collection of smaller seas, gulfs and bays – constitute that forgotten quarter... These watery spaces of the south, studded with small strips of land, facing gigantic landmasses... [are] the makers of world history and the modern condition.[67]

Rivers in oceans world pluriversal stories – from the Plum Tree Creek, to the Danshui River, to the South China Sea, into the Indian and Pacific Oceans and back again. Taking Wu Mali's riparian ecofeminist projects as a focal point offers the possibility to explore a transhemispheric history that jams the machinery of the Eurocentric construction of globality as somehow flowing only and ever outward from the West to the rest.[68] Tracing archipelagic relations from a small island locus worlded *with* art, Wu Mali's projects rethink the space, scale and flow of ecological thinking, and of course, of what constitutes transnational feminist worldmaking.

In an interview from 2010, Wu Mali discussed the centrality of the Danshui River and its tributaries to the cultural life of Taiwan, referencing, in particular, its critical significance to 'ancient civilizations'.[69] Her reference to the extensive maritime migrations from Taiwan of Austronesian-speaking peoples that connected vast spaces across the Indian and Pacific Oceans through archipelagic networks of trade, transit, culture and language, is a timely reminder that, in the ancient world, Taiwan was neither marginal nor insignificant. More to the point, it was the skill of Taiwan's Indigenous Austronesians in navigating the rivers and oceans surrounding the archipelago that facilitated the cultural connections and trade routes underpinning the multidirectional flow characteristic of Taiwan's heritage. These links are significant to the multiple, 'messy', trans-scalar ecologies of knowledge through which Wu Mali set out her ecofeminist and socially-engaged art practices beyond a narrowly-defined Eurocentric model, noting, for example, Indigenous Austronesian thought alongside the important influences of Taoism and Buddhism to the traditions of 'deep ecology' on which she drew,[70] as well as the patriarchal Confucian legacy against which she reacted,[71] in her work.

If Wu Mali delineated her riparian cultural actions in light of Taiwan's significance to centuries of archipelagic relations between and across the Indian and Pacific Oceans, she was no less aware of Taiwan's particular location within the dynamics of Asian-Pacific Cold War power politics. The 'difficult questions' raised by Taiwan's more recent history, caught between competing Asian and Anglophone neo-imperialisms, and the extreme threat posed by climate change to small archipelagos in the Pacific, decisively situate Wu Mali's practice through trajectories connecting transnational feminisms, socially-engaged art and ecological crisis with geopolitics in and across the region. Arguably, situating her ecofeminist art praxis – politically, intellectually, aesthetically – within these multidimensional and transhemispheric dynamics is a profoundly trans-scalar project that flows in more than one direction. I trace one in particular here: the potential of Taiwan's internationally-facing art institutions to add a feminist and archipelagic dimension to critical ecological thinking in the global art world.

In 2018, Wu Mali was appointed as co-curator of the Taipei Biennial with Francesco Manacorda, with whom she curated the event under the descriptive title *Post-Nature: A Museum as an Eco-System*. In many ways, the 2018 Taipei Biennial continued, on a different scale, her ecofeminist cultural actions on the Danshui River and The Plum Tree Creek,[72] addressing the global role that pivotal, yet too-often marginalized, archipelagos can play in rethinking the transhemispheric dynamics of globalization and environmental crisis. Wu Mali and Manacorda were not the first curators of the Taipei Biennial to recognize the geographical and geopolitical position of Taiwan as critical to these debates; in 2014, the French curator Nicholas Bourriaud curated the Taipei Biennial under the title, *The Great Acceleration: Art in the Anthropocene*. Though the exhibition was mooted as a 'cross-pollination' between

128 Worlding Pluriversal Stories

Western philosophy and its echoes in Chinese thought,[73] Bourriaud's curatorial agenda, interest in continental European theory, and favoured international artists, dominated the 2014 show.[74]

Wu Mali and Manacorda set their agenda for the 2018 Biennial in stark contrast to the 2014 event. *Post-Nature* featured a majority of work from Taiwan, focused particularly on long-term social and ecological transformation projects in the archipelago, and the role that museums might play in a transhemispheric 'eco-system' driven by gender equity, social justice and ecological balance.[75] This is to conceive the museum itself as a feminist figuration, a material map of a prefigurative politics and potential cultural shift created by acknowledging and valuing the many and different worlds that have long coexisted in the archipelago. In particular, Wu Mali and Manacorda brought Indigenous art and activist groups, such as the Indigenous Justice Classroom and the Kuroshio Ocean Education Foundation, into their curatorial figuration, alongside 30 years of Taiwanese televised documentaries on climate change and local environmental action. *Post-Nature*, like the extraordinary work of Pacific Islanders in bringing the urgency of climate change activism to a world stage,[76] addressed the trans-scalar possibilities for transformation that small island archipelagos can bring to transhemispheric histories through transnational feminist worldmaking articulated in and through the arts.

A transhemispheric tale of rivers in oceans situates *A Cultural Action at the Plum Tree Creek* as a nodal point for trans-scalar flows and counter-flows that complicate unidirectional narratives of global modernity, feminism, art and ecology, including monocultural notions of the 'West'.[77] The final turn in this dialogue crosses the Pacific, to converse with the Atlantic, arguing for the significance of an oceanic perspective on the complex confluences of time, space and bodies that meet in *The Great Wall of Los Angeles*.

Taking an oceanic look at the west coast of the United States from the perspective of a small archipelago in the South China Sea is not simply a wilful act of reversal, though the shift of perspective does have interesting ramifications for challenging the usual flow of power between the sites. There is more at stake in storying a counter-flow, as an evocative analogy drawn by Shu-Mei Shih suggests: 'Taiwan is Sinophone to a similar extent that Mexico is Hispanophone or the United States is Anglophone...'[78] The analogy drawn by Shih was part of a text on the dynamics of diaspora and transculturation in which she argued that diaspora is time- and place-limited, and that linguistic and cultural traditions are ever in flux, developing and expanding not by reification, but by 'impure' processes of hybrid mixing, or, echoing Gloria Anzaldúa, 'mestizaje' practices.[79] If Shih's analogy participates in decolonial feminist rejections of 'purity' it also signals geographical nodal points forged by vibrant, 'messy', 'difficult questions' and crossings, creole sites created by the oceanic intimacies of transhemispheric histories. In a powerful echo of just such intimate bio/geo mestizaje, *The Great Wall's* image of the establishment of the pueblo that would become the city of Los Angeles focused on the racial and ethnic mix of the inhabitants, the caption on the *Wall* reading 'Founders of Los Angeles 1781 Mulatto and Mestizo Descent'.

More to the point, I am arguing that the transnational feminist perspectives epitomized by Shih's analogy and Baca's mural, provide critical tools to reimagine the global imperialism set into play five centuries ago by European nation-states – in this particular instance, Spain and Britain – that brought the Atlantic[80] into an oceanic globality whose logic continues to hold sway over the epistemic, economic and ecological fate of the planet. It is wonderfully apt to set Mexico as the central term between Taiwan and the United States in a discussion of the oceanic intimacies of empire focused on Spain, Britain and the Pacific, not least because the principal maritime connection between Spain and China for more than two centuries was The Manila Galleon (1565–1815), which made the journey from Acapulco (in 'New Spain') to Manila twice annually. Taiwan's centuries-old jade trade with the Philippines was part of the Galleon's 'China trade' (porcelain, silks, jade), which, in return, brought silver from the Americas to East Asia. Spain controlled what is now California by 1769 and from 1777 to 1794, the Galleon stopped at Monterey. Throughout the 19th century, 'Mexico' (variously New Spain, Mexico and the southwestern United States) became an increasingly critical and contested site for bio/geo political control of the Americas and the Pacific by Spain, Britain and the United States.

The Great Wall's first 1,000 feet charts these contests – from the arrival of maritime Indigenous people, the Chumash, who flourished along the coast ('Chumash Village 1000 AD'), and the Tongva, the first inhabitants of the banks of the Tujunga river, to the arrival of Spanish Galleons, filled with European 'explorers' ('Portolá Expedition 1769'), followed by Catholic missionaries ('Junipero Serra', 'Missions') and soldiers who decimated Indigenous communities, claiming the land for Crown and Church. The victory of the Mexican Revolution ('Mexican Rule 1822'), in which Indigenous people joined with Spanish and creole settlers under Emiliano Zapata to overthrow Spanish rule, came to a brutal end when the United States government led an aggressive war against the independent nation ('Mexican–American War'), seizing the territory ('Treaty of Guadalupe Hidalgo 1848'). The signing of the Treaty is imaged on The Great Wall next to a westward flow of US mail and pioneer waggons under a sign saying 'Land Boom', and a train filled with oranges. On a transhemispheric level, this land boom/grab ensured Anglo-US access, through Pacific ports, to lucrative Asian trade.[81]

Critically, the establishment of the Pacific border of the continental United States does not end The Great Wall's global colonial narrative. Throughout the remaining sections of Baca's mural, from the mid-19th to the mid-20th centuries, the work recounts a continuing imperial tale of global oceanic intimacies, storied through a transnational feminist worlding *with* art. This tale flows in more than one direction, and across many scales, as it materializes the messy, occluded histories that comprise the creole confluences of the US national narrative as a transhemispheric tale of Anglo-imperial power. Materializing these confluences is a powerful act of disciplinary disobedience, of speaking truth to power and redrawing the contours of the nation-state as thoroughly embedded in, and complicit with, what American studies scholar Lisa Lowe eloquently termed 'the intimacies of four continents', in

130 Worlding Pluriversal Stories

her book of the same name. To explore occluded global interconnections, Lowe describes grappling with:

> ... the difficulties of conceptualizing the intimacies between settler colonialism in the Americas, transatlantic African slavery, the East Indies and China trades in goods and people, and the emergence of European liberal modernity, given the separate and asymmetrical archives in which each is represented.[82]

The separations and asymmetries of the archive are not accidental, but structural; bringing the streams together and reading against the flow is imperative for transformation, but it is not an easy task. In the case of US national history-making, it is especially difficult, as the dominant rhetoric of freedom and liberation is deeply intertwined with insular national narratives of voluntary inward migration, assimilation and manifest destiny, and a global power base that is the continuation and extension of new world Anglo-imperialism. This facilitates deeply incommensurate parallel narratives to pertain – simply, the land of the free and the home of the brave, the country that welcomes the world's 'huddled masses', is simultaneously a nexus of transatlantic and transpacific slaveries, Asian indentured labour, and Indigenous genocides.[83]

Baca's mural brings these frequently conflicting[84] parallel legacies to life, celebrating the occluded stories of collaborative, mestizaje survival, without reducing the violent incommensurabilities of the story of a transhemispheric empire. It is an act of unmaking and remaking worlds in equal measure. Indigenous people survive, but are not empowered, suffering waves of violence and injustice ('Unsigned Indian Treaties', 'Indian Assimilation'); African-Americans create flourishing communities ('The Dunbar Hotel'), and form powerful political projects ('Forebears of Civil Rights') but cannot dislodge structural racism ('California Gold Rush', 'Great Depression'). Women and queer citizens struggle for representation ('Suffragettes', 'Daughters of Bilitis', 'Mattachine Society') and the many waves of immigrants, both voluntary and coerced, are not equally welcomed.

The Mexican and Asian sequences across *The Great Wall* bring this final point to life in no uncertain terms and, in so doing, demonstrate how Wu Mali's 'difficult questions', posed from a small archipelago in the South China Sea, can engage in a transhemispheric dialogue with a mural painted along the Tujunga Wash in California some 11,000 miles away. Indeed, it is my contention that creating this dialogue epitomizes the transformative power of transnational feminisms' world(un/re)making potential *with* art.

Not surprisingly, Mexico's complex relationship with the United States, and the State of California in particular, features in many vignettes across *The Great Wall*. A number of these have been discussed already in this chapter, from the Mexican–American War to the Zoot Suit Riots and the Bracero Programme that brought migrant Mexican labourers into California for decades. But here, I turn to two particular sequences: 'Californios' in the 19th-century section of the mural, and '500,000 Mexican Americans Deported' in the 1920s section, drawing them together to create a speculative counter to the more conventional narrative of the United States as a 'melting pot'. Californios is a term used to refer to the Hispanophone community in California, whose roots in the area go back as far as the 17th century. This passage of the mural acts as a statement of enduring presence, even as it raises important questions regarding the status of the western United States as Anglophone. The brutal scene of Mexican-Americans being hoarded into trains for deportation in the 1920s sits between 'Unsigned Indian Treaties' and 'Dustbowl Migrants'. Read together, these passages create a story of United States immigration policy that runs counter to the prevailing narratives of open arms at Ellis Island on the Atlantic coast, and pioneering spirit forging westward into brave, new, and unoccupied, territory.

Another jarring pair of images completes this cycle, themselves placed next to one another on *The Great Wall*: 'Chinese Build the Railroad' and 'Chinese Massacre 1871' (Figure 4.4). This pairing has caused comment in the critical literature previously,[85] and the tale it tells is indeed shocking, as the very migrants who build the railroads that enable fluid westward passage from the East coast to California, are massacred in racist attacks when they begin to establish successful Sinophone communities in the State. What is not imaged on the wall itself, but underpins this narrative, is that it was the brutal subordination of China by the British Empire in the so-called Opium Wars of 1839–42 and 1856–60 that facilitated the movement of indentured Chinese labour across the Pacific to the United States. Baca's mural visually materializes what the work of so many US-based transnational feminists have argued for decades, often against the flow of more dominant White, liberal feminisms; namely, that there is no way to understand or challenge the inequities of race, gender and power within the United States without seeing the nation as fully embedded as an active player within global colonial histories and current neo-imperial power struggles. Or, as Anne McClintock pithily put it: 'By what fiat of historical amnesia can the United States of America, in particular, qualify as "post-colonial"...'[86]

FIGURE 4.4 Judith F. Baca, copyright 1983. Detail 'Chinese Build the Railway' to 'Chinese Massacre, 1871', several panels from the first 1000 ft. section of the *Great Wall of Los Angeles* mural.
Image courtesy of the SPARC Archives SPARCinLA.org.

Taiwan and Mexico are nodal points in a transhemispheric history shot through by what Indigenous theorist Jodi A. Byrd has so cogently described as the 'transit of empire'.[87] In this dialogue, they play the East and the South to a

132 Worlding Pluriversal Stories

Western-centric Global North that has seen over two centuries of Anglo-US domination of the Pacific as a 'laboratory' for racial science, an extractive 'buffer' zone, a 'free' market, and an 'empty' space (*terra/mare nullius*) available for the most devastating nuclear trials. The trans-scalar ecologies materialized by *The Great Wall* and *A Cultural Action at the Plum Tree Creek* enable a dialogue to flow many ways between these nodal points in the contested power dynamics of globalization. To challenge the epistemic legacies of imperialism that are hurtling us towards planetary extinction, we need to reveal the messy entanglements forged by these transits in creating the mythic purity of One world, and find ways to tell terraqueous tales of transcorporeal intimacies between many different worlds. This requires yet another scale of engagement and a very different dialogue, to both of which we now turn.

Making Kin with Messy Rivers: A Transcorporeal Dialogue

The meandering course of this chapter has been accompanied by a descriptive refrain bridging transnational feminisms, ecological thinking and trans-scalar worldmaking *with* art: *plural, planetary, but never pure*. As the refrain continues to resound, this final dialogue moves away from the human scale of the globe towards the more-than-human scale of the planet. Planetarity is not just globalization writ large, but rather, as transnational feminist literary and cultural critic Gayatri Spivak has argued: 'The planet is the species of alterity, belonging to another system; and yet we inhabit it, on loan.'[88] The scalar alterity of the planet cannot be assimilated simply into an anthropocentric episteme, despite the fact that humans, as a species, are profoundly entangled with/in planetary space and time. This seeming paradox creates an epistemic scalar rift, described eloquently by award-winning Indian writer Amitav Ghosh, as 'the unthinkable'.[89] But if planetary thinking[90] operates beyond the scale of human history, it yet remains imperative to the politics of environmental justice and inter-species ethics. More strongly, as this section will demonstrate, it plays a critical role in transnational feminist worldmaking with art, and in telling transcorporeal tales of collaborative survival with/in a terraqueous cosmos – of making kin with messy rivers. In what follows, my argument will again converse with and walk alongside *The Great Wall* and *A Cultural Action at the Plum Tree Creek*, but less to bring them into dialogue with one another than to argue that their reparative, more-than-human aesthetics, can facilitate a dialogue with the 'unthinkability' of climate change and species extinction that opens the possibility for radically transformed understandings of the politics of ecological justice and environmental ethics, premised on trans-scalar and transcorporeal relations of resistance, responsibility, attention and care.

Scholars have been swift to take up the challenge of climate change and 'unthinkability', arguing, for example, to expand radically the 'scale frames' of environmental justice,[91] the definitions of bio/geo collaborative worlding,[92] and the differentiated distribution of agency and responsibility that emerges through inter-species political praxis.[93] Arguably, these productive ripostes to the unthinkability of climate change and environmental justice demonstrate the potential of ecological thinking to move beyond the scale of the global, towards the planetary. In addition, it is my contention that the most efficacious of these emergent forms of thought draw planetarity into creative dialogue with transcorporeality,[94] by means of decolonial and queer feminist relational ontologies and the vibrant materialisms of posthumanisms and Indigenous thought. I heed the arguments made by ecofeminist scholar and activist Greta Gaard, that 'queer feminist, posthumanist climate justice perspectives... are needed to intervene and transform both our analyses and our solutions to climate change'.[95] Developing her discussions on queering environmental justice through a critical exploration of transcorporeality, Gaard reminds readers that relational ontologies engage us in a profound and visceral entanglement with/in the matter of the world:

> Feminist relational ontology suggests we are born and come into being through relationships, and these relationships are not only human-to-human but also human to more-than-human, including relations with other animals, plants, water bodies, rocks, soils and seasons.[96]

For me, it is not surprising that this confluence between transcorporeality and planetarity arises at the point of climate justice, since feminist relational ontology and ecological thinking place radical interdependency, collaborative survival and more-than-human flourishing at their core,[97] proposing the planet as a terrain with which humans (and others) are intimately intertwined, but over which 'Man' has no mastery.

Gaard's allusive reference to 'water bodies, rocks, soils and seasons' takes us back to the riparian ecologies that are the focal point of this chapter, from yet another scalar perspective. Messy rivers, meandering across alluvial plains, their courses straightened, their communities disappeared; tidal rivers, flowing in more than one direction, meeting oceans, connecting vast archipelagic networks – water cycles constitute planetarity in/as *bodies* of water, of which 'we' are always, and only ever, a part. In her evocative study of feminism and posthuman phenomenology, *Bodies of Water*, environmental humanities scholar Astrida Niemanis similarly brought transcorporeality together with planetarity, but in order to *think* with and through water. Through a deftly drawn series of watery exchanges between and across bodies on various scales, Niemanis posits the notion of a 'planetary hydrocommons' that is 'not outside of us, but quite literally channeling and cycling through us'.[98]

Thinking through water alongside the critical posthumanism of feminist philosopher Rosi Braidotti, Niemanis takes these arguments a step further to make the cogent point that:

> Currents of water are also currents of toxicity, queerness, coloniality, sexual difference, global capitalism, imagination, desire, and multispecies community. ... Again, as bodies of water, 'we' are all in this together, but 'we' are not all the same, nor are we all 'in this' in the same way.[99]

134 Worlding Pluriversal Stories

Signalling the differently positioned, and differentially responsible, 'we' who are bodies of water, raises the ethical and political tensions inherent in feminist planetary thinking. I would argue that these are productive tensions that foreground what the feminist philosopher of science Donna Haraway has memorably described as 'staying with the trouble',[100] acknowledging the deep entanglement of humans with the earth itself as the very position from which ecological thinking and ethical agency might emerge. This is a profoundly interdependent, immanent and 'impure' understanding of ethical agency that denies the possibility of claiming any kind of 'moral high ground', or 'mastery', by standing above or outside the fray. It asks, instead, echoing feminist philosopher Alexis Shotwell, how we might live ethically in compromised times:

> How, given the fact that we are constituted in relation to a thoroughly oppressive world from which we cannot stand outside as we set our course, can we ever craft worlds radically different from the world we experience now?[101]

Haraway and Shotwell are not alone in posing these questions, and their propositions for crafting radically different, more-than-human worlds by 'staying with the trouble' and 'making kin' are increasingly resonant with wide-ranging ecofeminist ethics and decolonial thinking on the politics of non-violent transitions to climate and environmental justice. Much of this thinking links ethico-political agency with responsible and relational practices of care and repair, in conditions of simultaneous complicity and resistance. María Puig de la Bellacasa, for example, brings feminist theory together with environmental science to argue for the significance of care 'as a concrete work of maintenance, with ethical and affective implications, and as a vital politics in interdependent worlds',[102] while political theorist Mihaela Mihai posits an 'aesthetics of care' as pivotal to building 'inclusive political relationships'[103] in the wake of extreme violence.

Realizing the ethico-political potential of bringing planetarity and transcorporeality together in a plural and more-than-human feminist approach to the epistemic rift (the *unthinkability*) of anthropogenic climate change requires a transformation not only in thinking, but also of imagining, inhabiting and making, many and diverse worlds.[104] It requires new forms of articulation, figuration and materialization. As we converse with, and walk alongside, *A Cultural Action at the Plum Tree Creek* and *The Great Wall of Los Angeles* for the final time in this chapter, our route unfolds a meander map that tells a terraqueous tale of making kin with messy rivers through complicity and care, repair and resistance. This is a tale that materializes strong fictions, and engages with figurations and fabulations, as it worlds planetary feminisms and ecological thinking *with* art.

As a starting point, I turn to the words of Wu Mali and Judith Baca. More than once in describing *A Cultural Action on the Plum Tree Creek*, Wu Mali and her interlocutors used the phrase 'mending the broken land with water'.[105] Likewise, Baca referred on more than one occasion to *The Great Wall* as a 'tattoo on the scar where the river once ran'.[106] For me, these repeated invocations of bodily vulnerability, care and repair, extended beyond the limits of the human to incorporate the land and the water, are more than just a matter of semantics. This is language that emphasizes transcorporeal intimacies, recognizes mutual vulnerabilities and, significantly, shared ethical responsibilities, effected through repair and care – *mending* the broken land, *attending* to the scarred river. These are not isolated statements, but demonstration of a planetary feminist phenomenological *intention* towards collaborative survival, premised on mutuality and interdependence. On this view, recognizing and responding to shared vulnerability[107] is not a weakness, but a strength. It creates kinships between diverse bodies at many scales. As bodies of water, 'we' and the earth's rivers, streams, seas, oceans and atmosphere are intimately intertwined and all of us are vulnerable to the devastating effects of anthropogenic climate change. Our complicity enables us *to care* – to respond to, and take responsibility for, more-than-human bodies – and to resist, together, our mutual devastation. Not, in either of these riparian projects, with a quick 'techno-fix', but with the slow, reparative and attentive practices of feminist ecological thinking and worldmaking *with* art.

There is a pivotal sequence in the short film made by Wu Mali with Bamboo Curtain Studio, *Mending the Broken Land with Water*, where the commentary makes explicit the project's perspectival shift: 'not just from the human perspective, but from the perspective of the creek'. Again, I am arguing that this is more than a clever semantic twist. As we have seen, Wu Mali, and her collaborators in the Plum Tree Creek project, consistently noted their engagement with deep ecology, informed by Taoism, Buddhism and Indigenous thought. These are ways of thinking that draw no sharp distinction between the human and nonhuman in imagining and inhabiting a vibrant and vital cosmos and, thus, speaking of the 'perspective of the creek' is not merely to anthropomorphize a body of water, but to acknowledge its planetary agency, and our mutual interdependency, along a continuum of collaborative survival. And in this, they are not alone; in Bolivia, Ecuador, Aotearoa/New Zealand and India, rivers have already gained status through more-than-human natural rights advocacy, much of which links the vitalism of current environmental science with Indigenous cosmologies.

Wu Mali's ecofeminist art projects reanimated these streams of thought in the context of Taiwan, where interdependent ecological thinking has a long tradition. For participants, the cultural actions of Wu Mali's project physically, spatially, imaginatively and transcorporeally, entangled the stream again with the mountains, stones, trees, farms, plants, animals and humans who live along its course (Figure 4.5). Walking, seeing, hearing, touching, tasting, eating, drinking with and from the creek, revitalized disappeared entanglements, and materialized the 'planetary hydrocommons' to restore more-than-human relationships with the bodies of water with and through which we share the planet.

The Great Wall does not enable its participant makers and viewers to drink, eat or bathe with the water of the Tujunga Wash, but it no less effectively tends to our entanglements, and responsibilities, within a vital and more than human cosmos. I start again with Baca's account of the mural as a tattoo on a scarred land. Writing in 2005,[108] Baca described *The Great Wall* as a site for 'art and community

FIGURE 4.5 Wu Mali, Walk along the Plum Tree Creek, *Art as Environment: A Cultural Action at the Plum Tree Creek*, 2010–12.

Image courtesy of the artist and Bamboo Curtain Studio, New Taipei City.

transformation' and murals as a form of 'relatedness'. In this same article, Baca recounted the story of Fernando, the Mural Maker for whom she designed a tattoo for the scars he sustained during a life-threatening knife attack. Fernando's scars, and the restorative act of care represented by the tattoo, are the impetus for the analogous description of the mural. But there is more. In the article, Fernando's story follows directly from Baca's account of being 'led to the river's edge' to create the mural as a 'public monument to interracial harmony'. She describes directly the ecological damage sustained by this site whose riverbanks, once lush, were at the heart of the Pueblo and home to the Indigenous Tongva people. In her account of the mural, Baca not only demonstrates her critical awareness environmental issues and their imbrication with technocratic modernity, but, more pointedly, that human flourishing is vitally entangled with the flourishing of the earth and that this flourishing links us to alternative cosmologies, most particularly in this instance, to the worlds of the Indigenous and mestizaje communities who once flourished in what is now California. This is an imaginative orientation, materialized through a phenomenological intention towards pluriversal worlds, that posits the creation of solidarity between and across diverse human communities, as inseparable from the attentive creation of community between humans and the earth.

Arguably, this imaginative intention towards more than human worlds also drove the aesthetics of the mural and shaped many of Baca's most striking visual motifs, both in *The Great Wall* and elsewhere. Take, for instance, the mural's evocation of the pre-conquest coast of 'California', replete with images of the species of plants and animals that preceded the Columbian Exchange and images of the Chumash people flourishing along the water's edge until the arrival of Spanish Galleons. At this point in the mural's tale, the fictional queen Califia appears amidst the clouds. Notwithstanding the Spanish narrative end of Califia as an allegory of Christian domination, the image in the mural depicts her as the legendary female leader of a powerful collective of women of colour who rise to defend a place of harmonious, terraqueous cosmic order against the brutality of European conquest, genocide, epistemicide and, inevitably, ecocide.

Across a wide range of work, Baca's iconography is replete with images of female empowerment that weave between and across historical and cosmological time and space, many times drawing on the 'womanist' traditions of the ancient civilizations of what is now Mexico, and their significant legacy in Chicana and Latinx feminist scholarly and creative praxis.[109] That this 'fictional' woman, Califia, is fully integrated within the 'historical' narrative of the mural, is meaningful. Likewise, later in *The Great Wall*, the *Chichimeca* corn goddess whispers ancient Indigenous knowledge into the ear of Thomas Alva Edison, and planetary elements attend to the actions of humans, both violent and glorious – the heavens revealing the order of the universe to Albert Einstein, while a campfire blazes out of control as Native Americans are forcibly 'assimilated' (Figure 4.6).

FIGURE 4.6 Judith F. Baca, copyright 1983. Detail 'Jewish Arts and Sciences' to 'Indian Assimilation', several panels from the 1950s section of the *Great Wall of Los Angeles* mural.
Image courtesy of the SPARC Archives SPARCinLA.org.

The earth turns red with the blood of lynched Mexicans, screaming faces emerge in engine steam as Chinese workers are massacred, the skies become dusty and brown over the internment camps holding Japanese citizens during the Second World War. Simply, *The Great Wall* is more than a tale of human agency on *terra nullius*; it is a story in which a vibrant cosmos sustains, grieves for and animates the very possibility of human life.

138 Worlding Pluriversal Stories

It is helpful at this point to return to Spivak's comment that '(t)he planet is the species of alterity, belonging to another system; and yet we inhabit it, on loan'.[110] As we have seen, planetary alterity and unthinkability open the space for a productive, trans-scalar dialogue to emerge between feminist ecological thinking and the ethics and politics of anthropogenic climate change and species extinction. Transcorporeal encounters are central to negotiating the chasm of unthinkability, but not every encounter is the same. Inhabiting, on loan, is not possession, but the 'prick tale of Humans in History' has seldom lent itself to 'meeting the universe half-way'.[111]

Moving away from narratives of possession, to story planetary inhabitation 'on loan', shifts the perspective decisively away from anthropocentric 'mastery', and the production of instrumental, universal and extractive knowledges that subordinate the earth as an inert resource for 'Man'. Intimacy and feminist relational ontologies are not mastery, reparative reading and responsibility are not mastery, ecological thinking and attentive care are not mastery; rather, these ways of knowing emphasize collaborative survival and interdependent flourishing, between and across many and more-than-human worlds. I am arguing that *The Great Wall* and *A Cultural Action at the Plum Tree Creek* world these ways of knowing, through material, visual and spatial practices of *intention* and *attention*, practices that direct embodied thought to stretch towards alterity, to accompany, care for and give heed to, others. These practices do not make us 'masters', but attendants, planetary denizens entangled with/in the elemental forces of the cosmos – listening to the earth, tending to the fire, singing with the air, and making kin with messy rivers.

The three riparian dialogues around which my argument has circled in this chapter materialize the ethical, political and aesthetic implications of transnational feminisms, ecological thinking and art *at different scales*. The worlds storied here neither preclude nor exclude one another; they do not nest, one transversal *within* another, nor are they reducible, one *to* another. As trans-scalar ecologies, these transhemispheric and transcorporeal tales pose different questions at each and between scales, but they do not exhaust the potential of the works to world otherwise. I offer these terraqueous tales of making kin with messy rivers as a speculative meander map for planetary feminisms. It is my hope that others might converse with and walk alongside them to story many and different worlds towards collaborative survival beyond the moribund logic of *unthinkability*.

Notes

1 Boaventura De Sousa Santos, *Epistemologies of the South: Justice against Epistemicide*, London and New York: Routledge, 2014, p. 10.
2 Sylvia Wynter, '1492: A New World View', in Vera Lawrence Hyatt and Rex Nettleford, eds, *Race, Discourse and the Origin of the Americas: A New World View*, Washington, DC: Smithsonian Press, 1995, pp. 5–57. NB: Wynter deployed 1750 in preference to the more usual 1610 date for the geological golden spike associated with the impact from the Columbian Exchange.
3 Sylvia Wynter and Katherine McKittrick, 'Unparalleled Catastrophe for Our Species? Or, to Give Humaness a Different Future: Conversations', in Katherine McKittrick, ed.,

Sylvia Wynter: On Being Human as Praxis, Durham, NC and London: Duke University Press, 2015, pp. 9–89, p. 18.

4 Wynter and McKittrick, 'Unparalleled Catastrophe, p. 17.

5 Wynter and McKittrick, 'Unparalleled Catastrophe, p. 25. Wynter develops these ideas across a number of texts, perhaps most notably 'Unsettling the Coloniality of Being/Power/Truth/Freedom: Towards the Human, after Man, Its Overrepresentation – An Argument', *CR: The New Centennial Review* 3:3, 2003, pp. 257–337. In addition, Walter D. Mignolo explores the decolonial ramifications of Wynter's thinking on the human in 'Sylvia Wynter: What Does It Mean to Be Human?', in McKittrick, ed., *Sylvia Wynter: On Being Human as Praxis*, pp. 106–23.

6 The start of *Epistemologies of the South* is written as a polyphonic exchange – a Manifesto for Good Living/Buen Vivir and a 'Minifesto for Intellectual-Activists'; the Manifesto further links Buen Vivir with the African concept of Ubuntu and the Andean idea of Sumak Kawsay (pp. 4, 6).

7 De Sousa Santos, *Epistemologies of the South*, pp. 175ff.

8 Lorraine Code, *Ecological Thinking: The Politics of Epistemic Location*, Oxford: Oxford University Press, 2006.

9 Code, *Ecological Thinking*, p. 21.

10 Code, *Ecological Thinking*, p. 5.

11 In particular, I am in dialogue with the *work* of mutual *survival*, so movingly described by Audre Lorde, and the simultaneity of 'decomposition and recomposition', explored by José Esteban Muñoz in his writing on Latina performance and queer worldmaking. On Lorde, see Chapter 2 of this volume; José Esteban Muñoz, 'Latina Performance and Queer Worldmaking; Or, *Chusmería* at the End of the Twentieth Century', in *Disidentifications: Queers of Color and the Performance of Politics*, Minneapolis: University of Minnesota Press, 1999, pp. 181–200.

12 Eve Kosofsky Sedgwick, 'Paranoid Reading and Reparative Reading, Or, You're So Paranoid, You Probably Think This Essay Is about You', in *Touching Feeling: Affect, Pedagogy, Performativity*, Durham, NC and London: Duke University Press, 2003, pp. 123–52, p. 124.

13 Sedgwick, 'Paranoid Reading', pp. 150–1.

14 Anna Lowenhaupt Tsing, *The Mushroom at the End of the World: On the Possibility of Life in Capitalist Ruins*, Princeton, NJ: Princeton University Press, 2015, p. 19. NB: it would be remiss not to mention here the significance to art, design and visual culture of the earlier cross-disciplinary, 'new materialist' anthropologies developed by both Sarah Pink and Tim Ingold.

15 See Chapter 1 for more on the problem of 'purity' and the canon.

16 In the opening arguments of *The Anthropocene: A Multidisciplinary Approach* (eds Julia Adeney Thomas, Mark Williams and Jan Zalasiewicz, Cambridge: Polity Press, 2020), the editors argue that any idea of one perfect 'scale of everything' is untenable in the face of the challenges of the Anthropocene (see pp. 9–11).

17 Suffice to say that cross-scalar thinking is central to debates on climate crisis, species extinction and the concept of the Anthropocene generally, and to the arguments of De Sousa Santos, Wynter, Code and Tsing already cited in this chapter.

18 *Cf.* Aneeth Kaur Hundle, Ioana Szeman and Joanna Pares Hoare, eds, *Feminist Review* 121, 2019 (special issue *Transnational Feminisms*); Sarah E. Dempsey, Patricia S. Parker and Kathleen J. Krone, 'Navigating Social-Spatial Difference, Constructing Counter-Space: Insights from Transnational Feminist Praxis', *Journal of International and Intercultural Communication* 4:3, August 2011, pp. 201–20.

19 *Cf.* Inderpal Grewal and Caren Kaplan, eds, *Scattered Hegemonies: Postmodernity and Transnational Feminist Practices*, Minneapolis: Minnesota University Press, 1994; Myra Marx Ferree and Aili Mari Tripp, eds, *Global Feminism: Transnational Women's Activism, Organizing and Human Rights*, New York and London: NYU Press, 2006; Janet Conway, 'Geographies of Transnational Feminism: Place and Scale in the Spatial Praxis of the World March of Women', *Social Politics* 15:2, 2008, pp. 207–31.

140 Worlding Pluriversal Stories

20 Doreen Massey, *For Space*, Los Angeles, CA, London, New Delhi and Singapore: Sage Publications, 2005, Katherine T. Jones, 'Scale as Epistemology', *Political Geography* 17:1, 1998, pp. 25–8; Geraldine Pratt and Victoria Rosner, eds, *The Global and the Intimate: Feminism in Our Time*, New York: Columbia University Press, 2012; Juanita Sundberg, 'Decolonizing Posthumanist Geographies', *Cultural Geographies* 21:1, 2014, pp. 33–47.

21 *Cf.* Heather Davis and Etienne Turpin, eds, *Art in the Anthropocene: Encounters among Aesthetics, Politics, Environments and Epistemologies*, London: Open Humanities Press, 2015; Anna Lowenhaupt Tsing, Heather Ann Swanson, Elaine Gan and Nils Bubandt, eds, *Arts of Living on a Damaged Planet: Ghosts and Monsters of the Anthropocene*, Minneapolis: University of Minnesota Press, 2017.

22 *Cf.* Jill H. Casid, *Sowing Empire: Landscape and Colonization*, Minneapolis: University of Minnesota Press, 2004; T.J. Demos, *Against the Anthropocene: Visual Culture and Environment Today*, New York: Sternberg Press, 2017; Andrew Patrizio, *The Ecological Eye: Assembling an Eco-Critical Art History*, Manchester: Manchester University Press, 2018; Sugata Ray and Venugopal Maddipati, eds, *Water Histories of South Asia: The Materiality of Liquescence*, London and New York: Routledge, 2020.

23 *Cf.* Angelika Fitz, Elke Krasny and Architekturzentrum Wien, eds, *Critical Care: Architecture and Urbanism for a Broken Planet*, Cambridge: MIT Press, 2019; Hou Hanru and Xi Bei, eds, *Video Art from the Pearl River Delta*, Berlin: Times Art Centre and Sternberg Press, 2019.

24 *Cf. Forensic Architecture*: https://forensic-architecture.org/ and *World of Matter*: https://worldofmatter.net/.

25 I develop this point in the third chapter of *Transnational Feminisms, Transversal Politics and Art: Entanglements and Intersections*, London and New York: Routledge, 2020.

26 I share with Eleanor Heartney a concern that feminism is all too commonly excised from the histories of ecological art as it moves into the mainstream, and to her excellent litany of US-based feminist activist artists who were key protagonists would add that this is a global pattern (note the prescient work of, inter alia, Betsy Damon, Agnes Denes, Bonita Ely, Basia Irland, Janet Laurence, Lucy Lippard, Mrinalini Mukherjee, Aviva Rahmani, Mierle Laderman Ukeles, Cecilia Vicuña, Judy Watson and Yin Xiuzhen). See Heartney, 'All Or Nothing', *Art in America*, May 2020, pp. 40–49 (the article appeared as 'How the Ecological Art Practices of Today Were Born in 1970s Feminism', *Art News* on 22 May 2020: https://www.artnews.com/art-in-america/features/ecofeminism-women-in-environmental-art-1202688298/). Likewise, curator Monika Fabijanski's *ecofeminism(s)* show of 2020 called attention to this history of connection, see: Sheila Wickouski, '"Ecofeminism(s)" Exhibition Connects Feminism, Art and Eco-Consciousness', *Ms.* 9/1/2020: https://msmagazine.com/2020/09/01/ecofeminisms-exhibition-connects-feminism-art-and-eco-consciousness/.

27 The 'technoscientific poeisis' pursued by Joan Brassil is exemplary, as is the work of Joanna Hoffmann, both discussed in the first volume of this trilogy: see, Meskimmon, *Transnational Feminisms, Transversal Politics and Art* (chapter 3). I would also note Ursula Biemann's founding role in *World of Matter*, the urban waste projects of Jakarta-based artists Tita Salina and Irwan Ahmett, and the geological drawing experiments of Ilana Halperin.

28 Important instances would include the work of Annie Sprinkle, Barbara Bolt and Kim Tallbear.

29 *Cf.* Alexis Pauline Gumbs, *Undrowned: Black Feminist Lessons from Marine Mammals*, Chico, CA: AK Press, 2020; Carolina Caycedo's 'geochoreographies': http://carolinacaycedo.com/category/performance-geochoreographies; Rebecca Belmore's, *Fountain*, 2005, Venice Biennale; *Love the Everglades Movement*: www.LoveTheEverglades.org; Mary Jo Aagerstoun, 'A Review Article: Ecological Art and Black Americans' Relationship to the Land', *WEAD Magazine*, 12 October 2021, https://directory.weadartists.org/%e2%80%8b%e2%80%8beco-art-and-black-americans-relationships-to-the-land.

Trans-Scalar Ecologies **141**

30 Including, for example, the striking work of Yhonnie Scarce in response to British nuclear testing on Indigenous lands in Australia (discussed in Meskimmon, *Transnational Feminisms, Transversal Politics and Art*, pp. 80–3); the video poems of Marshallese writer and performance artist Kathy Jetñil-Kijiner: https://www.kathyjetnilkijiner.com/videos-featuring-kathy/; Gaye Chan and Nandita Sharma's guerilla gardening and food access action *Eating in Public* (2003–13); the South African 'forest listening' project, Lalela: Conversations with the Land https://lalela.place/conversations/.

31 My thinking around 'trans-scalar ecologies' is indebted, but not equivalent, to De Sousa Santos' 'ecologies of trans-scale' (non-linear interrelationships between the global and the local), one of the five ecologies he proposes as part of his project to counter Eurocentric 'lazy reason'. On trans-scalar method, however, I am also in dialogue with the ground-breaking peace and conflict work of social scientist Gearoid Millar; see 'Trans-scalar Ethnographic Peace Research: Understanding the Invisible Drivers of Complex Conflict and Complex Peace', *Journal of Intervention and Statebuilding* 15:3, 2021, pp. 289–308.

32 I have elsewhere discussed the challenge of writing *with* art (rather than *about* art, as an object or illustration of theory) see *Women Making Art: History, Subjectivity, Aesthetics*, London and New York: Routledge, 2003, p. 6. See also the insightful points made by Trinh T. Minh-ha in interview with Nancy Chen, 'Speaking Nearby', reprinted in Trinh, *Cinema Interval*, London and New York: Routledge, 1999, pp. 209–25.

33 Further elaboration of this point can be found in the Introduction to this volume; see also, Donna Haraway, 'It Matters What Stories Tell Stories; It Matters Whose Stories Tell Stories', *a/b: Auto/Biography Studies* 34:3, 2019, pp. 565–75.

34 Readers are reminded of this phrase from Chapter 1, and its engagement with the work of feminist geographer Juanita Sundberg. See her 'Decolonizing Posthumanist Geographies', *Cultural Geographies* 21:1, 2014, pp. 33–47.

35 Doreen Massey, 'A Global Sense of Place', *Marxism Today*, June 1991, pp. 24–9; Millar, 'Trans-Scalar Ethnographic Peace Research', pp. 298, 301. Millar and Massey, in very different ways, argue for nuanced local-scale analysis, not as a parochial approach, but as key to understanding global patterns and affinities.

36 It is instructive that Wohl links the 'visual culture' of rivers, in particular, the development of an 18th-century landscape tradition in Europe, to the resistance met in some quarters to allowing rivers their 'messiness'. See her 'Messy Rivers are Healthy Rivers: The Role of Physical Complexity in Sustaining River Ecosystems', November 2020 (video lecture for the Institute of Advanced Studies at Loughborough University: https://www.lboro.ac.uk/research/ias/programmes/past-themes/water/. A note of thanks is due: I count myself fortunate to work with a number of outstanding river scientists, two of whom, Paul Wood and Steve Rice, introduced me to Wohl's work.

37 Baca is at last garnering widespread and well-deserved critical recognition for her significant contributions to Chicana feminist art and activism, public art and alternative history-making in the US, and the development of liberation pedagogies in the arts focused on social justice and community-building. *Cf.* Anna Indych-López, *Judith F. Baca*, Los Angeles, CA: UCLA Chicano Studies Research Center Press, 2018; Andrea Lepage, 'The Great Wall of Los Angeles: Bridging Divides and Mitigating Cultural Erasure', *The Latin Americanist*, September 2017, pp. 361–84; bell hooks and Amalia Mesa-Bains, *Homegrown: Engaged Cultural Criticism*, London and New York: Routledge, 2018; Gloria Anzaldúa, 'Border Arte: Neplanta, el Lugar de la Frontera', reprinted in Analouise Keatinge, ed., *The Gloria Anzaldúa Reader*, Durham, NC and London: Duke University Press, 2009, pp. 176–86. Significantly, 2021 saw the first major retrospective of Baca's work, *Judy Baca: Memorias de Nuestra Tierra*, open at the Museum of Latin American Art (MOLAA) in Long Beach, California.

38 The mural was initially entitled *The History of California*, and has received a number of prestigious awards over the years, including nomination as a National Historic

142 Worlding Pluriversal Stories

Monument, and support from the US National Endowment for the Arts, and most recently (February 2021), a three-year grant to extend the site through the Andrew W Mellon Foundation monuments initiative.

39 Judith F. Baca, 'The River', in *Great Wall of Los Angeles: Walking Tour Guide*, third edition, published by SPARC: Social and Public Art Resource Centre, no date, p. 11.

40 *Cf.* G. Peña, 'Endangered Landscapes and Disappearing Peoples: Identity, Place and Community in Ecological Politics', in Joni Adamson, Mei Mei Evans and Rachel Stein, eds, *The Environmental Justice Reader: Politics, Poetics and Pedagogy*, Tucson: University of Arizona Press, 2002, pp. 58–81; Macarena Gómez-Barris, *The Extractive Zone: Social Ecologies and Decolonial Perspectives*, Durham, NC and London: Duke University Press, 2017.

41 Baca's commitment to investigating city's 'hidden histories' (stories of women, multiracial communities and queer activism, particularly) was shared by other feminist artists in her circle at the time, including Suzanne Lacy and Sheila Levrant de Bretteville; this was referenced in the discussion De Bretteville's work, *Biddy Mason: Time and Place* (1989) in *Transnational Feminisms, Transversal Politics and Art*, pp. 62–6. Lacy's work was also featured in that volume, but not in the context of alternative US American history-making.

42 The project was awarded Taiwan's most prestigious art prize, the Taishin Art Award, in 2013.

43 Note that the Danshui is now transliterated as Tamsui (from 2011), but I follow Wu Mali's preference for Danshui here, so not to create confusion.

44 Zheng Bo, 'An Interview with Wu Mali', *Field: A Journal of Socially-Engaged Art Criticism* 3, Winter 2016, pp. 151–64, p. 160.

45 Massey, 'A Global Sense of Place', p. 28.

46 Massey 'A Global Sense of Place' (pp. 24–5 on 'reactionary' conventions of place).

47 My use of 'transversal politics' is in dialogue with the ground-breaking work of feminist scholars such as Nira Yuval-Davis and Cynthia Cockburn, developed at some length in the first volume of this trilogy, *Transnational Feminisms, Transversal Politics and Art*. In addition, in his prescient work, *The Three Ecologies* (1989), trans. Ian Pindair and Paul Sutton, New York and London: Continuum, 2008, Felix Guattari, argues for the significance of ethico-aesthetic processes of as central to the only effective action against ecological destruction (p. 45).

48 The young people were treated professionally, granted a voice within the project and, in many instances, supported when difficulties in other aspects of their lives (e.g. domestic and/or gang violence, drug addiction, pregnancy) threatened their participation in the project. A number of Makers attest to the fact that the project was key to their educational attainment through high school and, often, beyond.

49 Todd Ableser, 'Testimonials', at https://sparcinla.org/programs/the-great-wall-mural-los-angeles/ (italics added here for emphasis).

50 Much has been written about the *The Great Wall*, particularly focusing on the 'multicultural', feminist, race-critical and queer histories it articulates, as well its central role in the establishment of a flourishing culture of socially engaged mural making across the city of Los Angeles. The SPARC (Social and Public Art Resource Center, founded in 1976 by Baca with Christina Schlesinger and Donna Deitch) website contains extensive documentation: https://sparcinla.org/.

51 Nira Yuval-Davis, 'Dialogical Epistemology: An Intersectional Resistance to the "Oppression Olympics"', *Gender and Society* 26:1, February 2012, pp. 46–54.

52 María Lugones, *Pilgrimages/Peregrinages: Theorizing Coalition Against Multiple Oppressions*, Latham, MD, Boulder, CO, New York and Oxford: Rowman and Littlefield, 2003. In her refusal to reify identity, and in her demonstration of strong women's leadership, Baca's race- and class-critical feminist politics did not always sit easily with either liberal White feminisms or the more hetero-masculine, cultural nationalism of some parts of the Chicano movement; see the interview with Baca by Karen Mary Davalos in 2010, cited in Indych-López, *Judith F. Baca*, p. 149.

53 Indych-López, *Judith F. Baca*. In her astute visual analysis of the mural, Indych-López explores the 'meandering line', and, though she does not connect this word specifically to its riverine etymology, I intend my use here to extend, not counter, her excellent points.

54 Zheng Bo, 'An Interview with Wu Mali', p. 163.

55 Jane Chin Davidson specifically discusses Wu Mali within the context of ecofeminism in her insightful book, *Staging Art and Chineseness: The Politics of Trans/Nationalism and Global Expositions*, Manchester: Manchester University Press, 2020, pp. 91–104. Wu Mali's work first came to my attention when I supervised the excellent doctoral project of Ming Turner, whose work on Taiwanese feminism, posthumanism and art is outstanding; see her *Visualising Culture and Gender: Postcolonial Feminist Analyses of Women's Exhibitions in Taiwan, 1996–2003*, PhD Thesis, 2008, available at: https://repository.lboro.ac.uk/articles/thesis/Visualising_culture_and_gender_postcolonial_feminist_analyses_of_women_s_exhibitions_in_Taiwan_1996-2003/9332843?file=16940648. On Taiwan's 'eco-nationalism', see Paul Jobin, 'Environmental Movements in Taiwan's Anthropocene: A Civic Eco-nationalism'. in Paul Jobin, Ming-sho Ho and Hsin-Huang Michael Hsiao, eds, *Environmental Movements and Politics of the Asian Anthropocene*, Singapore: ISEAS, 2021, pp. 36–78.

56 Nasheli Jiménez de Val and Anna Maria Guasch, 'Indigenism(s)/Indigeneity: Towards a Visual Sovereignty', *Revista de Estudios Globales y Arte Contemporáneo* 7:1, 2020, pp. 1–12, p. 5.

57 Zheng Bo, 'An Interview with Wu Mali', p. 161; in addition, Shu-Mei Shih notes that Wu Mali produces different work when showing internationally, than in Taiwan, in awareness of the differing markets for art. See Shih, *Visuality and Identity: Sinophone Articulations across the Pacific*, Berkeley: University of California Press, 2007, pp. 176–80. The work is often considered to have a particularly Taiwanese approach to eco-art: Jane Ingram Allen, 'Green Art Rises in Taiwan', *Taiwan Review*, 1 July 2011, https://taiwantoday.tw/news.php?unit=20,29,35,45&post=26276; Corinne Purtill, 'Artist Gives New Life to a Polluted Taiwan Stream', *China Dialogue*, 29 April 2013, https://chinadialogue.net/en/cities/5832-artist-gives-new-life-to-a-polluted-taiwan-stream/.

58 Lu Pei-Yi, 'Three Approaches to Socially-Engaged Art in Taiwan', *Yishu: Journal of Contemporary Chinese Art* 15:6, November/December 2016, pp. 91–101, p. 95.

59 Guattari, *The Three Ecologies*, p. 45.

60 My use of 'archipelagic relations' here draws on Caribbean poet and philosopher Édouard Glissant's *Poetics of Relation* (1990), trans. Betsy Wing, Ann Arbor: University of Michigan Press, 1997, but is also in dialogue with the earlier notion of 'tidalectics', taken from Bajan poet Kamau Braithwaite's *The Arrivants: A New World Trilogy* (1973), Oxford: Oxford University Press, 1981, and with Fijian-Tongan scholar Epeli Hau'ofa's conception of highly connected Pacific Island culture, *cf.* 'Our Sea of Islands', *The Contemporary Pacific* 6:1, Spring 1994, pp. 148–61. Many recent scholars have developed and extended these ideas, particularly by bringing the Caribbean and Pacific conventions into dialogue to radically rethink globality: *cf.* Elizabeth DeLoughrey, *Routes and Roots: Navigating Caribbean and Pacific Islander Literatures*, Honolulu: University of Hawai'i Press, 2007; Tatiana Flores and Michelle A. Stephens, eds, *Relational Undercurrents: Contemporary Art of the Caribbean Archipelago*, Durham, NC and London: Duke University Press, 2017; Paul Carter *Decolonizing Governance: Archipelagic Thinking*, London and New York: Routledge, 2019; Elizabeth DeLoughrey and Tatiana Flores, 'Submerged Bodies: The Tidalectics of Representability and the Sea in Caribbean Art', *Environmental Humanities* 12:1, May 2020, pp. 132–65.

61 I am indebted to the emergent field of oceanic history, and, in particular, to the work of David Armitage, Alison Bashford and Sujit Sivasundaram; see their edited volume *Oceanic Histories*, Cambridge: Cambridge University Press, 2018, and Sivasundaram's award-winning *Waves across the South: A New History of Revolution and Empire*, London: William Collins, 2020. My thinking on the 'intimacies' of these oceanic links draws in particular upon the brilliant work of Jodi A. Byrd and Lisa Lowe: *cf.* Byrd, *The Transit*

144 Worlding Pluriversal Stories

of Empire: Indigenous Critiques of Colonialism, Minneapolis and London: University of Minnesota Press, 2011, and Lowe, *The Intimacies of Four Continents*, Durham, NC and London: Duke University Press, 2015. I am also grateful to the astute insights made in conversation by art historian Claire Farago on teaching globally-informed visual studies by focusing on oceans – her thinking made me think again.

62 Shu-mei Shih uses this term; see: Shu-mei Shih and Ping-hui Liao, 'Introduction: Why Taiwan? Why Comparatize?', in Shu-mei Shih and Ping-hui Liao, eds, *Comparatizing Taiwan*, London and New York: Routledge, 2015, pp. 1–10.

63 The majority of the Han Chinese who arrived into Taiwan during the Ming-Qing transitional period and up to the early 19th century, were Hokkein and Hakka speakers, and many intermarried with Indigenous Austronesians; these groups form the majority population of Taiwan and are usually referred to as Han Taiwanese (sometimes, 'local' Taiwanese) which distinguishes them from the Han Chinese who came under the leadership of the Kuomintang in the 20th century.

64 Shih and Liao, 'Introduction', in *Comparatizing Taiwan*, p. 3. It is also significant that, in her study of Sinophone cultural impacts across the Pacific, Shu Mei Shih argues for studying history at different scales: *cf.* Shih, *Visuality and Identity*, pp. 8, 12.

65 Zheng Bo, 'An Interview with Wu Mali', pp. 161–2.

66 Zheng Bo, 'An Interview with Wu Mali', p. 162.

67 Sujit Sivasundaram, *Waves across the South: A New History of Revolution and Empire*. London: William Collins, 2020, p. 1.

68 That most of the thinking on globalization is implicitly Eurocentric is a point made both by Massey, 'A Global Sense of Place' and by Millar, 'Trans-scalar Ethnographic Peace Research'.

69 Larry Shao, 'Interview with Wu Mali', 2010 Asia Art Archive, https://aaa.org.hk/en/ideas/ideas/interview-with-wu-mali/type/conversations.

70 Reiko Goto, Margaret Shiu and Wu Mali, 'Ecofeminism: Art as Environment – A Cultural Action at Plum Tree Creek', *Women's Eco Art Dialog*, 3 December 2014, https://directory.weadartists.org/plum-tree-creek-action.

71 Chin Davidson, *Staging Art and Chineseness*, p. 178.

72 It is significant that in 2008, the artist created a flourishing food harvesting garden, *Taipei Tomorrow as a Lake Again*, for the Taipei Biennial, a work intended to highlight the critical issue of climate change and sea level rise for Taiwan.

73 Per the press release for the Biennial: https://www.e-flux.com/announcements/31546/nicolas-bourriaud-selected-as-the-curator-of-taipei-biennial-2014/.

74 Tom Morton, 'Review of the Taipei Biennial', *Frieze*, 16 December 2014, https://www.frieze.com/article/taipei-biennial-2014.

75 These differences were brought to the fore in Leora Joy Jones, 'An Interview with Mali Wu, Co-curator of the 2018 Taipei Biennial', *Yishu: Journal of Contemporary Chinese Art* 18:3, May/June 2019, pp. 33–44.

76 Michelle Keown, Andrew Taylor and Mary Treagus, eds, *Anglo-American Imperialism and the Pacific: Discourses of Encounter*, London and New York: Routledge, 2018. Erin Suzuki, *Ocean Passages: Negotiating Pacific Islander and Asian American Literatures*, Philadelphia, PA: Temple University Press, 2021, pp. 65–70.

77 Tracing 'messy' streams of confluence, it is interesting to note that much of the Anglophone literature around Wu Mali and ecofeminist art in Taiwan (published within and beyond Taiwan) addresses 'Western' contexts solely in relation to US American influences, most importantly, the feminist, socially engaged projects of Suzanne Lacy (NB: Wu Mali translated Lacy's ground-breaking text on new genre public art). The crucial impact of Wu Mali's student years at the Düsseldorf Kunstakademie in the early 1980s, when Josef Beuys co-founded the Green Party with feminist, anti-nuclear, eco-activists Petra Kelly, Eva Quistorp and others, is rarely discussed. This, despite the fact that Wu Mali translated texts by Beuys, made direct reference to Kelly in her 1999

installation, *Sweeties of the Century*, and has worked with the Green Party, founded in 1996 in Taiwan. Without minimizing the substantive dialogues between Wu Mali and Suzanne Lacy in any way (in publications, podcast interviews, etc.), I am suggesting that additionally bringing in this post-war German context, creates a more diverse and less unilateral 'Western' flow of ideas, thus enriching thinking around the transnational feminisms and ecological art practices that have emerged so strongly in Taiwan, and Wu Mali's critical role within them.

78 Shih, *Visuality and Identity*, p. 189.
79 The echo here is mine; and readers will recognize that the rejection of 'purity' and 'mestizaje', in the work of María Lugones and Gloria Anzaldúa, were discussed more fully in Chapter 1.
80 David Armitage makes the point that, historically, the Atlantic comes much later into the oceanic mix, and was not seen to have a distinct 'identity' until the 19th century. *Cf.*, David Armitage, et al. eds, *Oceanic Histories*.
81 Keown, et al., demonstrate the deep connections between the British Empire and US imperialism in the Pacific in the intro to their *Anglo-American Imperialism and the Pacific*, pp. 7–10.
82 Lowe, *The Intimacies of Four Continents*, p. 136.
83 Byrd, *The Transit of Empire*, p. 59.
84 Indych-López's insightful analysis often focuses on this conflictual element – 'speaking back' – *cf.* Indych-López, *Judith F. Baca*, p. 66ff.
85 Andrea Lepage, 'The Great Wall of Los Angeles', pp. 362–3.
86 Anne McClintock, *Imperial Leather: Race, Gender and Sexuality in the Colonial Contest*, London and New York: Routledge, 1995, p. 294. Her comment is made particularly in recognition of the Indigenous protests against proposals for 'celebrations' of the 500th anniversary of Columbus landing in the Americas in 1992.
87 Byrd, *The Transit of Empire*.
88 In using planetary here, I am, like many others, indebted to Gayatri Chakravorty Spivak's thinking on planetarity, developed in the third chapter of her book, *Death of a Discipline*, New York: Columbia University Press, 2003 (chapter, pp. 71–102; quote, p. 72).
89 Amitav Ghosh, *The Great Derangement: Climate Change and the Unthinkable*, Chicago, IL: University of Chicago Press, 2016. Ghosh pursues his arguments in dialogue with the work of Dipesh Chakrabarty – see reference below.
90 Dipesh Chakrabarty, 'Climate and Capital: On Conjoined Histories', *Critical Enquiry* 41:1, Autumn 2014, 1–23 (p. 23). This article was, in part, written in response to Slavoj Žižek's critique of Chakrabarty'e earlier, and highly-influential article, 'The Climate of History: Four Theses', *Critical Enquiry* 35:2, Winter 2009, pp. 197–222. Chakrabarty is at pains to point out that his argument neither denies that humans have had a devastating impact on the earth, nor that pursuing social, economic and ecological justice is imperative. Rather, his point is that climate and species operate on a more-than-human scale and require new ways of thinking. Significantly, Chakrabarty refers directly to Spivak's formulation of planetary alterity in his work.
91 Hilda Kurtz, 'Scale Frames and Counter-Scale Frames: Constructing the Problem of Environmental Justice', *Political Geography* 22, 2003, pp. 887–916.
92 Kathryn Yusoff, *A Billion Black Anthropocenes or None*, Minneapolis: University of Minnesota Press, 2018; Myra J. Hird and Kathryn Yusoff, 'Lines of Shite: Microbial-Mineral Chatter in the Anthropocene', in Rosi Braidotti and Simone Bignall, eds, *Posthuman Ecologies: Complexity and Process after Deleuze*, New York and London: Rowman and Littlefield International, 2019, pp. 265–81.
93 Suzanne McCullagh, 'Heterogeneous Collectivity and the Capacity to Act: Conceptualizing Nonhumans in Political Space', in Braidotti and Bignall, *Posthuman Ecologies*, pp. 141–57. In addition, I had the pleasure to hear a paper by Mathias Thaler

146 Worlding Pluriversal Stories

at Loughborough's Institute of Advanced Studies in which he discussed his work with Mihaela Mihai on political theory, interspecies and ecological justice, entitled: 'Commemorating Loss in the Age of Omnicide' (28 April 2022).

94 For a good overview of transcorporeality, see: Stacy Alaimo, 'Trans-corporeal Feminisms and the Ethical Space of Nature', in Stacy Alaimo and Susan Hekman, eds, *Material Feminisms*, Bloomington: Indiana University Press, 2008, pp. 237–64. In addition, transcorporeality is discussed more fully in Chapter 3 of the first volume of this trilogy, *Transnational Feminisms, Transversal Politics and Art*.

95 Greta Gaard, *Critical Ecofeminism*, Lanham, MD: Lexington Books, 2007, p. 118.

96 Gaard, *Critical Ecofeminism*, p. 175.

97 Gaard's work is also in dialogue on this important point with Val Plumwood, *Feminism and the Mastery of Nature*, London and New York: Routledge, 1993, p. 194.

98 Astrid Niemanis, *Bodies of Water: Posthuman Feminist Phenomenology*, London and New York: Bloomsbury Academic, 2017, p. 64.

99 Niemanis, *Bodies of Water*, p. 15 (Niemanis is in dialogue with Braidotti's *Metamorphoses: Towards a Feminist Theory of Becoming*, Cambridge: Polity Press, 2002, in this passage).

100 Donna J. Haraway, *Staying with the Trouble: Making Kin in the Chthulucene*, Durham, NC and London: Duke University Press, 2016.

101 Alexis Shotwell, *Against Purity: Living Ethically in Compromised Times*, Minneapolis: University of Minnesota Press, 2016, p. 139.

102 María Puig de la Bellacasa, *Matters of Care: Speculative Ethics in More than Human Worlds*, Minneapolis: University of Minnesota Press, 2017, p. 5.

103 Mihaela Mihai, *Political Memory and the Aesthetics of Care: The Art of Complicity and Resistance*, Stanford, CA: Stanford University Press, 2022, p. 61. I note too, her wonderful formulation of the 'caring Refusenik'.

104 The invocation of aesthetics and, indeed, a turn to art, further characterizes the ethical and political explorations of transcorporeal planetarity – such as Mihai's use of literary and filmic texts (they are 'read' as 'texts'). In addition, I would note the most recent volume by Elizabeth M. DeLoughrey, *Allegories of the Anthropocene*, Durham, NC and London: Duke University Press, 2019, the inter-species writing of Mette Bryld and Nina Lykke, *Cosmodolphins: Feminist Cultural Studies of Technology, Animals and the Sacred*, London: Zed Books, 2000 and the poetic theory project by Sonja Boon, Lesley Butler and Daze Jefferies, *Autoethnography and Feminist Theory at the Water's Edge: Unsettled Islands*, London: Palgrave Macmillan, 2018. In addition, I am inspired by recent writing by feminist of colour that deploy water in truly insightful ways, including: Leanne Betasamosake Simpson, *Islands of Decolonial Love: Stories & Songs*. Winnipeg: ARP Books, 2013; Gumbs, *Undrowned: Black Feminist Lessons from Marine Mammals*; and the video poems of Marshall Islander poet and activist, Kathy Jetñil-Kijiner, bridging the oceanic, planetary and nuclear. See her website: https://www.kathyjetnilkijiner.com/.

105 *Cf.* Reiko Goto, et al., 'Ecofeminism: Art as Environment' and the short film made by the Bamboo Curtain Studio in 2013 to document the project used the line as its title: http://bambooculture.com/en/media/1151.

106 Michelle Adam, 'Judith Baca: "Censorship Rampant" Says Renowned Muralist', *Paramus* II:22, 13 August 2001, p. 7.

107 Erin Suzuki, *Ocean Passages*, pp. 70–1. Suzuki has a particularly compelling take on vulnerability that is not victimhood.

108 Judith F. Baca (corresponding author), 'The Human Story at the Intersection of Ethics, Aesthetics and Social Justice', *Journal of Moral Education* 34:2, 2005, pp. 153–69.

109 A few examples will direct readers: Baca's recent retrospective, *Judy Baca: Memorias de Nuestra Tierra*, the Museum of Latin American Art (MOLAA) in Long Beach, California (2021–22), focused particularly on the womanist contexts of her work, and Gloria Anzaldúa's very well-known text 'Border Arte: Neplanta, el Lugar de la Frontera' notes Baca's work as central to Chicana women's elemental power and community building.

110 Spivak, *Death of a Discipline*, p. 72.
111 I am, of course, nodding both to Donna Haraway, *Staying with the Trouble* and Karen Barad, *Meeting the Universe Halfway: Quantum Physics and the Entanglement of Matter and Meaning*, Durham, NC: Duke University Press, 2007.

AFTERWORD

On *Trilogics*

I am an avid gardener. I choose my adjective with care; *avid* invokes a keen interest, an abiding enthusiasm. Having come to gardening at mid-life, almost by accident, my avidity far outstrips my experience, and so I supplement the joyfully immersive work of tending to my garden with eagerly received gifts of practical magic from other gardeners. These come in many forms and can stay for many seasons. Occasionally, they extend beyond the garden, or, more fittingly, they extend 'the garden' into many other worlds.

One appeared some years ago when a friend of mine, who is an artist and a gardener, offered me some plants whose flowers I had admired in their garden. I accepted instantly and was asked how many I would like. Imagining just the right place for these flowers in my own garden, I answered, 'Two, please.' But when my friend came with the plants, they brought three. 'Two points describe a line, three create a space', they explained. 'Thinking in threes will be good for your garden.' And, of course, they were right.

Those who know me well are well acquainted with my avid gardening, and some will also be aware that I do not relish writing 'Conclusions'. I am not seeking to have the last word, even if I thought such a thing were possible, and concluding seems far too final and fixed for the continuing conversations I hope to engender through my writing. Pondering this whilst sitting in my garden, I was reminded of my friend's invitation to 'think in threes' to create space. My enthusiasm for writing the Afterword of this book, the second in a trilogy, immediately returned.

...

Thinking through the trilogy as a structural device was crucial to the inception of this project on the critical entanglement of transnational feminisms with art, and it has continued to be a significant aspect in its realization. Each volume is designed to

DOI: 10.4324/9780429507816-9

Afterword **149**

speak with the others; in writing the second, many connections were made directly with the first, both within the chapters and in the notes. Further thematic, theoretical and aesthetic affinities-in-difference, will be recognized without hesitation by readers of both books, or be *felt* as lingering after-effects. At points, artworks and texts that come to the fore in one book, provide a critical background for the discussion in the other, and geographical coordinates overlap to extend the maps drawn between the volumes.

Significantly, even though there are, at present, only two volumes in the trilogy, they create neither a linear time/space sequence nor a binary logic of either/or. Rather, their *trilogics* underpin multidimensional forms of interplay between and across each, precisely to create space. This is space *akin* to the garden, and *aspiring* towards many, flourishing, more-than-human worlds. This is an open terrain that I increasingly envisage as *breathing space*.

In the first volume, that space was configured around the transversal politics of transnational feminisms and the arts, and was invoked by the phrase 'knowing, imagining and inhabiting, earthwide and otherwise'. To the imaginative breathing space created by transversal dialogues, this second volume has contributed its 'plural, planetary, but never pure' praxis – we do not breathe in a vacuum, we do not breathe alone, and, as any gardener knows, from the flora to the fauna, the critters to the compost, the earth is alive with breath. This volume turned to the transhemispheric and the transcorporeal to meet the challenges of creating trans-scalar knowledges that connect the human-scale power and politics of globality with the more-than-human agencies that constitute planetarity. In multidimensional encounters, *with* and *through*, not just *about*, art, the decolonial, race-critical, queer/trans and ecological thinking of transnational feminisms found the breathing space to story pluriversal worlds and world pluriversal stories, otherwise. These practices of radical genealogy and ecological thinking/making are ones that aspire and conspire, in hope, with others, for a world in which many worlds might fit.

But they are also practices seeking to find the forms – the fictions, figurations, fabulations – through which these alternative knowledge projects, these worlding stories, might take root and grow. Such figurations will no longer story the unilateral tale of the progress of 'Man', but, rather, the multi-stranded, interconnected and interdependent webs of crossings and connections between palimpsestic pasts and presents towards as-yet-unimagined futures. As I draw this *trilogic* afterword to a close, if not a conclusion, and look forward to writing the third volume, I am heartened by the thought that beginnings, middles and ends may not follow a single straight line, but be marked by heterogeneous channels, shorelines and shoals, as they meander and map the mutual flourishing of all manner of times, places and bodies yet to come.

SELECTED BIBLIOGRAPHY

Aagerstoun, Mary Jo, 'A Review Article: Ecological Art and Black Americans' Relationship to the Land', *WEAD Magazine*, 12 October 2021: https://directory.weadartists. org/%e2%80%8b%e2%80%8beco-art-and-black-americans-relationships-to-the-land.

Adamson, Joni, Mei Mei Evans and Rachel Stein, eds, *The Environmental Justice Reader: Politics, Poetics and Pedagogy*, Tucson: University of Arizona Press, 2002.

Ahmed, Sara, *Strange Encounters: Embodied Others in Post-Coloniality*, London and New York: Routledge, 2000.

Aizura, Aren Z., 'Trystan Cotton, Carsten Balzer/Carla LaGata, Marcia Ochoa, Salvador Vidal-Ortiz, "Introduction", Special issue: "Decolonizing Transgender"', *TSQ: Transgender Studies Quarterly* 1:3, August 2014, pp. 308–19.

Alaimo, Stacy and Susan Hekman, eds, *Material Feminisms*, Bloomington and Indianapolis: Indiana University Press, 2008.

Alexander, M. Jacqui, *Pedagogies of Crossing: Meditations on Feminism, Sexual Politics, Memory and the Sacred*, Durham, NC and London: Duke University Press, 2005.

Alexander, M. Jacqui and Chandra Talpade Mohanty, eds, *Feminist Genealogies, Colonial Legacies, Democratic Futures*, London and New York: Routledge, 1997.

Allen, Chadwick, *Trans-Indigenous: Methodologies for Global Native Literary Studies*, Minneapolis: University of Minnesota Press, 2012.

Allen, Jane Ingram, 'Green Art Rises in Taiwan', *Taiwan Review*, 1 July 2011: https://taiwantoday.tw/news.php?unit=20,29,35,45&post=26276;

Antoinette, Michelle, *Reworlding Art History: Encounters with Contemporary Southeast Asian Art after 1990*, Amsterdam and New York: Rodopi, 2014.

Anzaldúa, Gloria, 'Border Arte: Nepantla, el Lugar de la Frontera' (1993), reprinted in *The Gloria Anzaldúa Reader* edited Analouise Keating, Durham, NC and London: Duke University Press, 2009, pp. 176–86.

Anzaldúa, Gloria E. and Analouise Keating, eds, *This Bridge We Call Home: Radical Visions for Transformation*, London and New York: Routledge, 2002.

Armitage, David, Alison Bashford and Sujit Sivasundaram, eds, *Oceanic Histories*, Cambridge: Cambridge University Press, 2018.

Arnold, Marion and Marsha Meskimmon, eds, *Home/Land: Women, Citizenship, Photographies*, Liverpool: Liverpool University Press, 2016.

Selected Bibliography 151

Aspin, Clive, 'Hōkakatanga – Māori Sexualities', revised January 2019, *Te Ara The Encyclopedia of New Zealand*: https://teara.govt.nz/en/hokakatanga-maori-sexualities.

Baca, Judith F. (corresponding author), 'The Human Story at the Intersection of Ethics, Aesthetics and Social Justice', *Journal of Moral Education* 34:2, 2005, pp. 153–69.

Banerjee, Pallavi and Raewyn Connell, 'Gender Theory as Southern Theory', *Handbook of the Sociology of Gender*, edited by Barbara J Risman, Carissa M Froyum and William J Scarborough, Cham: Springer International, 2018, pp. 57–68.

Barad, Karen, 'Getting Real: Technoscientific Practices and the Materialization of Reality', *Differences: A Journal of Feminist Cultural Studies* 10:2, 1998, pp. 87–128.

Barad, Karen, *Meeting the Universe Halfway: Quantum Physics and the Entanglement of Matter and Meaning*, Durham, NC: Duke University Press, 2007.

Barrett, Estelle and Barbara Bolt, eds, *Carnal Knowledge: Towards a 'New Materialism' through the Arts*, London: I.B. Tauris, 2012.

Baumhoff, Anja, *The Gendered World of the Bauhaus: The Politics of Power at the Weimar Republic's Premier Art Institute, 1919-32*, Bern: Peter Lang, 2001.

Bear, Michaela, 'Infecting Venus: Gazing at Pacific History through Lisa Reihana's Multi-Perspectival Lens', *Australia and New Zealand Journal of Art* 19:1, 2019, pp. 7–24.

Berlant, Lauren, ed., *Intimacy*, Chicago, IL: University of Chicago Press, 2000.

Berlant, Lauren, *Cruel Optimism*, Durham, NC and London: Duke University Press, 2011.

Bo, Zheng, 'An Interview with Wu Mali', *Field: A Journal of Socially-Engaged Art Criticism* 3, Winter 2016, pp. 151–64.

Bolaki, Stella and Sabine Broeck, eds, *Audre Lorde's Transnational Legacies*, Amherst and Boston, MA: University of Massachusetts Press, 2015.

Boon, Sonja, Lesley Butler and Daze Jefferies, *Autoethnography and Feminist Theory at the Water's Edge: Unsettled Islands*, London: Palgrave Macmillan, 2018.

Braidotti, Rosi, *Nomadic Subjects: Embodiment and Sexual Difference in Contemporary Feminist Theory*, New York: Columbia University Press, 1994.

Braidotti, Rosi, *Metamorphoses: Towards a Materialist Theory of Becoming*, Cambridge: Polity, 2002.

Braidotti, Rosi, 'A Theoretical Framework for the Critical Posthumanities', *Theory, Culture and Society*, special issue, 'Transversal Posthumanities', 36:6, May 2018, pp. 1–31.

Braidotti, Rosi and Simone Bignall, eds, *Posthuman Ecologies: Complexity and Process after Deleuze*, New York and London: Rowman and Littlefield International, 2019.

Brown, Deirdre, '"Ko tō ringa ki ngā rākau ā te Pākehā" – Virtual *Taonga* Māori and Museums', *Visual Resources* 24:1, March 2008, pp. 59–75.

Bryld, Mette and Nina Lykke, *Cosmodolphins: Feminist Cultural Studies of Technology, Animals and the Sacred*, London: Zed Books, 2000.

Brzyski, Anna, ed *Partisan Canons*, Durham, NC and London: Duke University Press, 2007.

Burges, Joel and Alisa V. Prince and Jeffrey Allen Tucker, 'Introduction: Black Studies Now and the Countercurrents of Hazel Carby', *InVisible Culture* 31, Fall 2020, pp. 1–32.

Butalia, Urvashi, *The Other Side of Silence: Voices from the Partition of India*, New Delhi: Penguin Books India, 1998.

Butler, Judith, *Bodies that Matter: On the Discursive Limits of 'Sex'*, London and New York: Routledge, 1993.

Byrd, Jodi A. *The Transit of Empire: Indigenous Critiques of Colonialism*, Minneapolis and London: University of Minnesota Press, 2011.

Byrd, Jodi A., 'A Return to the South', *American Quarterly* 66:3, September 2014, pp. 609–20.

Byrd, Rudolph P., Johnnetta Betsch Cole and Beverly Guy-Sheftall, eds, *I Am Your Sister: Collected and Unpublished Writings of Audre Lorde*, Oxford: Oxford University Press, 2009.

152 Selected Bibliography

Candelario, Ginetta E.B., ed., *African Feminisms: Cartographies for the Twenty-First Century*, special issue of *Meridians: feminism, race, transnationalism*, 17:2, November 2018.

Carby, Hazel, 'White Woman Listen! Black Feminism and the Boundaries of Sisterhood', in *The Empire Strikes Back: Race and racism in '70s Britain*, London and New York; Routledge, 1982, pp. 212–35.

Carby, Hazel, *Imperial Intimacies: A Tale of Two Islands*, London and New York: Verso, 2019.

Carter, Paul, *Decolonizing Governance: Archipelagic Thinking*, London and New York: Routledge, 2019.

Casid, Jill H., *Sowing Empire: Landscape and Colonization*, Minneapolis: University of Minnesota Press, 2004.

Chakrabarty, Dipesh, 'The Climate of History: Four Theses', *Critical Enquiry* 35:2, Winter 2009, pp. 197–222.

Chakrabarty, Dipesh, 'Climate and Capital: On Conjoined Histories', *Critical Enquiry* 41:1, Autumn 2014, 1–23.

Charisma, James, 'A Video Challenges a Colonialist Narrative by Reinterpreting First Contact in the Pacific', *Hyperallergic*, 8 May 2019: https://hyperallergic.com/499420/lisa-reihana-emissaries-honolulu-museum-of-art/.

Cherry, Deborah, *Beyond the Frame: Feminism and Visual Culture, Britain 1850–1900*, London and New York: Routledge, 2000.

Cixous, Hélène, 'The Laugh of the Medusa', trans. Keith and Paula Cohen, *Signs* 1:4, 1976, 875–93.

Clark, Maddee, 'Becoming-with and Together: Indigenous Transgender and Transcultural Practices', *Artlink* 37:2, June 2017: https://www.artlink.com.au/articles/4604/becomingE28091with-and-together-indigenous-transgender-/.

Clough, Patricia Ticineto and Michelle Fine, 'Activism and Pedagogies: Feminist Reflections', *Women's Studies Quarterly* 35:3/4, Fall 2007, pp. 255–75.

Code, Lorraine, *Ecological Thinking: The Politics of Epistemic Location*, Oxford: Oxford University Press, 2006.

Collins, Patricia Hill *Black Feminist Thought: Knowledge, Consciousness and the Politics of Empowerment*, London and New York: Routledge, 1990.

Connell, Raewyn, *Southern Theory: The Global Dynamics of Knowledge in Social Science*, Cambridge: Polity, 2007.

Conway, Janet, 'Geographies of Transnational Feminism: Place and Scale in the Spatial Praxis of the World March of Women', *Social Politics* 15:2, 2008, pp. 207–31.

Crawley, Ashon, *Blackpentecostal Breath: The Aesthetics of Possibility*, New York: Fordham University Press, 2017.

Davidson, Jane Chin, *Staging Art and Chineseness: The Politics of Trans/Nationalism and Global Expositions*, Manchester: Manchester University Press, 2020.

Cuomo, Chris J, *Feminism and Ecological Communities: An Ethic of Flourishing*, London and New York: Routledge, 1998.

Davies, Carole Boyce, 'Sisters Outside: Tracing the Caribbean/Black Radical Intellectual Tradition', *Small Axe* 13:1, March 2009, pp. 217–29.

Davies, Martin L. and Marsha Meskimmon, eds, *Breaking the Disciplines: Reconceptions in Knowledge, Art and Culture*, London: IB Tauris, 2003.

Davis, Dawn Rae, 'Unmirroring Pedagogies: Teaching with Intersectional and Transnational Methods in the Women and Gender Studies Classroom', *Feminist Formations* 22:1, Spring 2010, pp. 136–62.

Davis, Heather and Etienne Turpin, eds, *Art in the Anthropocene: Encounters Among Aesthetics, Politics, Environments and Epistemologies*, London: Open Humanities Press, 2015.

De Cunha, Dilip, *The Invention of Rivers: Alexander's Eye and Ganga's Descent*, Philadelphia: University of Pennsylvania Press, 2018.

De la Bellacasa, María Puig, *Matters of Care: Speculative Ethics in More than Human Worlds*, Minneapolis: University of Minnesota Press, 2017.

De la Cadena Marisol and Mario Blaser, eds, *A World of Many Worlds*, Durham, NC and London: Duke University Press, 2018.

DeLoughrey, Elizabeth M., *Routes and Roots: Navigating Caribbean and Pacific Island Literatures*, Honolulu: University of Hawaii Press, 2007.

DeLoughrey, Elizabeth M., *Allegories of the Anthropocene*, Durham, NC and London: Duke University Press, 2019.

DeLoughrey, Elizabeth and Tatiana Flores, 'Submerged Bodies: The Tidalectics of Representability and the Sea in Caribbean Art', *Environmental Humanities* 12:1, May 2020, pp. 132–65

Demeyer, Hans, 'Lauren Berlant on Intimacy as World-Making', *Extra Extra*, 16 Spring 2021: https://extraextramagazine.com/talk/lauren-berlant-on-intimacy-as-world-making/.

Demos, T.J., *Against the Anthropocene: Visual Culture and Environment Today*, New York: Sternberg Press, 2017.

Dempsey, Sarah E., Patricia S. Parker, Kathleen J. Krone, 'Navigating Social-Spatial Difference, Constructing Counter-Space: Insights from Transnational Feminist Praxis', *Journal of International and Intercultural Communication* 4:3, August 2011, pp. 201–20.

De Sousa Santos, Boaventura, *Epistemologies of the South: Justice Against Epistemicide*, London and New York: Routledge, 2014.

Dhar, Jyoti, 'Tranquility Amid Turmoil: Lala Rukh', *Art Asia Pacific*, 102 March/April 2017 (no pages), available at http://artasiapacific.com/Magazine/102/TranquilityAmidTurmoil.

Douglas, Bronwen and Chris Ballard, eds, *Foreign Bodies: Oceania and the Science of Race 1750–1940*, Canberra: ANU E-Press, 2008.

Falcón, Sylvanna M., 'Transnational Feminism as a Paradigm for Decolonizing the Practice of Research', *Frontiers: A Journal of Women's Studies* 37:1, 2016, pp. 174–94.

Ferree, Myra Marx and Aili Mari Tripp, eds, *Global Feminism: Transnational Women's Activism, Organizing and Human Rights*, New York and London: NYU Press, 2006.

Ferreira Da Silva, Denise, 'Toward a Black Feminist Poethics', *The Black Scholar* 44:2, 2014, pp. 81–97.

Fitz, Angelika, Elke Krasny and Architekturzentrum Wien, eds, *Critical Care: Architecture and Urbanism for a Broken Planet*, Cambridge: MIT Press, 2019.

Flores, Tatiana and Michelle A. Stephens, eds, *Relational Undercurrents: Contemporary Art of the Caribbean Archipelago*, Durham, NC and London: Duke University Press, 2017.

Foucault, Michel *Discipline and Punish: The Birth of the Prison*, New York: Random House, 1977.

Freeman, Elizabeth, *Time Binds: Queer Temporalities, Queer Histories*, Durham, NC and London: Duke University Press, 2010.

Freire, Paulo, *Pedagogy of the Oppressed* (first published in English in 1970), 30th anniversary edition, London: Bloomsbury, 2000.

Futernick, Robert, 'Conservation of Scenic Wallpapers: "Sauvages de la Mer Pacifique"', *Journal of the American Institute for Conservation* 20:2, Spring 1981, pp. 139–46.

Gaard, Greta, *Critical Ecofeminism*, Lanham, MD: Lexington Books, 2007.

Garb, Tamar, *Sisters of the Brush: Women's Artistic Culture in Late Nineteenth-Century Paris*, New Haven, CT: Yale University Press, 1994.

Garber, Elizabeth, 'Social Justice and Art Education', *Visual Arts Research* 30:2, 2004, pp. 4–22.

154 Selected Bibliography

Garber, Linda, *Identity Poetics: Race, Class, and the Lesbian-Feminist Roots of Queer Theory*, New York: Columbia University Press, 2001.

Gatens, Moira and Genevieve Lloyd, *Collective Imaginings: Spinoza Past and Present*, London and New York: Routledge, 1999.

Gattey, Emma, 'Makereti: Māori 'Insider' Anthropology at Oxford' at https://oxfordandempire. web.ox.ac.uk/article/makereti.

Geyer, Charles H., 'Creolizing the Canon: Manuel Puig, Junot Diaz, and the Latino Poetics of Relation', *The Comparatist* 43, October 2019, pp. 173–93.

Ghosh, Amitav, *The Great Derangement: Climate Change and the Unthinkable*, Chicago, IL: University of Chicago Press, 2016.

Gill, Andréa and Thula Pires, 'From Binary to Intersectional to Imbricated Approaches: Gender in a Decolonial and Diasporic Perspective', *Contexto Internacional* 41:2, May–August 2019, pp. 275–302.

Glissant, Édouard, *Poetics of Relation* (1990) trans. Betty Wing, Ann Arbor, MI: University of Michigan Press, 1997.

Gómez-Barris, Macarena, *The Extractive Zone: Social Ecologies and Decolonial Perspectives*, Durham, NC and London: Duke University Press, 2017.

Goto, Reiko, Margaret Shiu and Wu Mali, 'Ecofeminism: Art as Environment – A Cultural Action at Plum Tree Creek', *Women's Eco Art Dialog*, 3 December 2014: https://directory. weadartists.org/plum-tree-creek-action.

Grant, Catherine and Patricia Rubin, eds, 'Special Issue: Creative Writing and Art History', *Art History* 34:2, 2011, https://onlinelibrary.wiley.com/toc/14678365/2011/34/2

Green, Joyce, ed., *Making Space for Indigenous Feminism*, 2nd edition, Halifax and Winnipeg: Fernwood Publishing, 2017.

Greer, Germaine, *The Obstacle Race: The Fortunes of Women Painters and Their Work*, New York: Farrar Straus Giroux, 1979.

Grewal, Inderpal and Caren Kaplan, eds, *Scattered Hegemonies: Postmodernity and Transnational Feminist Practices*, Minneapolis: Minnesota University Press, 1994.

Grosz, Elizabeth, *Space, Time and Perversion: Essays on the Politics of Bodies*, London and New York: Routledge, 1995.

Grosz, Elizabeth, *Chaos, Territory, Art: Deleuze and the Framing of the Earth*, New York: Columbia University Press, 2008.

Guattari, Félix, *The Three Ecologies* (1989), trans. Ian Pindair and Paul Sutton, New York and London: Continuum, 2008.

Gumbs, Alexis Pauline, *Undrowned: Black Feminist Lessons from Marine Mammals*, Chico, CA: AK Press, 2020.

Haraway, Donna, *Staying with the Trouble: Making Kin in the Chthulucene*, Durham, NC and London: Duke University Press, 2016.

Haraway, Donna, 'It Matters What Stories Tell Stories; It Matters Whose Stories Tell Stories', *a/b: Auto/Biography Studies* 34:3, 2019, pp. 565–75.

Haritawarn, Jinthana, '"Decolonizing the Non/Human" in "Dossier: Theorizing Queer Inhumanisms"', *GLQ: A Journal of Lesbian and Gay Studies* 21:2–3, 2015, pp. 210–13.

Hartman, Saidiya, *Lose Your Mother: A Journey Along the Atlantic Slave Route*, New York: Farrar, Straus and Giroux, 2007.

Hartman, Saidiya, 'Venus in Two Acts', *small axe* 26, June 2008, pp. 1–14.

Hartman, Saidiya, *Wayward Lives, Beautiful Experiments: Intimate Histories of Social Upheaval*; London: Norton, 2019.

Hartman, Saidiya, 'Errant Daughters: A Conversation between Saidiya Hartman and Hazel Carby', *Paris Review*, 21 Jan 2020: https://www.theparisreview.org/blog/2020/01/21/ errant-daughters-a-conversation-between-saidiya-hartman-and-hazel-carby/.

Selected Bibliography 155

Hau'ofa, Epeli, 'Our Sea of Islands', *The Contemporary Pacific* 6:1, Spring 1994, pp. 148–61.

Heartney, Eleanor, 'All Or Nothing', *Art in America*, May 2020, pp. 40–49; the article appeared as 'How the Ecological Art Practices of Today Were Born in 1970s Feminism' in *Art News* on 22 May 2020: https://www.artnews.com/art-in-america/features/ecofeminism-women-in-environmental-art-1202688298/.

Hemmings, Clare, *Considering Emma Goldman: Feminist Political Ambivalence and the Imaginative Archive*, Durham, NC and London: Duke University Press, 2018.

hooks, bell *Teaching to Transgress: Education as the Practice of Freedom*, London and New York: Routledge, 1994.

hooks, bell, *Teaching Community: A Pedagogy of Hope*, London and New York: Routledge, 2003; *Teaching Critical Thinking: Practical Wisdom*, London and New York: Routledge, 2010.

hooks, bell *All About Love: New Visions*, New York: William Morrow, 2016.

hooks, bell with Amalia Mesa-Bains, *Homegrown: Engaged Cultural Criticism*, Cambridge, MA: South End Press, 2006.

Hou, Hanru and Xi Bei, eds, *Video Art from the Pearl River Delta*, Berlin: Times Art Centre and Sternberg Press, 2019.

Hundle, Aneeth Kaur, Ioana Szeman and Joanna Pares Hoare, eds, *Feminist Review* 121, 2019 (special issue *Transnational Feminisms*).

Hunter, James Davison *Culture Wars: The Struggle to Define America*, New York: Basic Books, 1991.

Impey, Oliver, 'Lever as a Collector of Chinese Porcelain', *Journal of the History of Collections* 4:2, 1992, pp. 227–238.

Indych-López, Anna, *Judith F. Baca*, Los Angeles, CA: UCLA Chicano Studies Research Center Press, 2018.

Irigaray, Luce, *Speculum of the Other Woman*, New York: Cornell University Press, 1985.

Iskin, Ruth E. ed., *Re-envisioning the Contemporary Art Canon: Perspectives in a Global World*, New York and London: Routledge, 2017.

Jiménez del Val, Nasheli, 'A Conceptual Genealogy of "The Indigenous" in Mexican Visual Culture', *Revista de Estudio Globales y Arte Contemporáneo* 7:1, 2020, pp. 55–90.

Jobin, Ming-sho Ho and Hsin-Huang Michael Hsiao, eds, *Environmental Movements and Politics of the Asian Anthropocene*, Singapore: ISEAS, 2021.

Jones, Amelia, *In Between Subjects: A Critical Genealogy of Queer Performance*, New York and London: Routledge, 2021.

Jones, Katherine T., 'Scale as Epistemology', *Political Geography* 17:1, 1998, pp. 25–8.

Jones, Leora Joy, 'An Interview with Mali Wu, Co-curator of the 2018 Taipei Biennial', *Yishu: Journal of Contemporary Chinese Art* 18:3, May/June 2019, pp. 33–44.

Joyeux-Prunel, Béatrice, 'Art History and the Global: Demonstrating the Latest Canonical Narrative', *Journal of Global History* 14:3, 2019, pp. 413–35.

Kaiser, Birgit M. and Kathrin Thiele, 'What Is Species Memory? Or, Humanism, Memory and the Afterlives of "1492"', *Parallax* 23:4, 2019, pp. 403–15.

Keown, Michelle, Andrew Taylor and Mary Treagus, eds, *Anglo-American Imperialism and the Pacific: Discourses of Encounter*, London and New York: Routledge, 2018.

King, Charles, *Gods of the Upper Air: How a Circle of Renegade Anthropologists Reinvented Race, Sex, and Gender in the Twentieth Century*, New York: Doubleday, 2019a.

King, Rosamond S., 'Radical Interdisciplinarity: A New Iteration of a Women of Color Methodology', *Meridians* 18:2, 2019b, pp. 445–56.

King, Tiffany Lethabo, *The Black Shoals: Offshore Formations of Black and Native Studies*, Durham, NC and London: Duke University Press, 2019c.

156 Selected Bibliography

King, Tiffany Lethabo, Jewell Navarro and Andrea Smith, eds, *Otherwise Worlds: Against Settler Colonialism and Anti-Blackness*, Durham, NC and London: Duke University Press, 2020.

Kuokannen, Rauna, *Reshaping the University: Responsibility, Indigenous Epistemes and the Logic of the Gift*, Vancouver: University of British Columbia Press, 2008.

Kurtz, Hilda, 'Scale Frames and Counter-Scale Frames: Constructing the Problem of Environmental Justice', *Political Geography* 22, 2003, pp. 887–916.

Lampela, Laurel, 'Women's Art Education Institutions in 19th Century England', *Art Education* 46:1, 1993, pp. 64–7.

Laurie, Alison and Linda Evans, *Outlines: Lesbian and Gay Histories of Aotearoa*, Wellington: Lesbian and Gay Archives of New Zealand, 2005.

Lepage, Andrea, 'The Great Wall of Los Angeles: Bridging Divides and Mitigating Cultural Erasure', *The Latin Americanist*, 61:3, September 2017, pp. 361–84.

Lisa Reihana: Emissaries, Auckland Art Gallery Toi o Tāmaki, New Zealand at Venice exhibition catalogue, 2017.

Lomax, Yve, *Sounding the Event: Escapades in Dialogue and Matters in Art, Nature and Time*, London: I.B. Tauris, 2005.

Lookman, Mariah, 'Lala Rukh, Muhanned Cader: Scripted across the Indian Ocean' (unpublished exhibition essay), Green Cardamom Gallery, London, 2011, available at: https://www.academia.edu/25835634/Lala_Rukh_Muhanned_Cader_Scripted_Across_the_Indian_Ocean.

Looser, Diana, 'Viewing Time and the Other: Visualizing Cross-Cultural and Trans-Temporal Encounters in Lisa Reihana's *in Pursuit of Venus [infected]*', *Theatre Journal* 69, 2017, pp. 449–75.

Lopesi, Lana, 'Beyond Essentialism: Contemporary Moana Art from Aotearoa New Zealand', *Afterall: A Journal of Art, Context and Enquiry* 46, Autumn/Winter 2018, pp. 106–15.

Lorde, Audre, *Sister Outsider: Essays and Speeches by Audre Lorde*, Berkeley, CA: Crossing Press (1984), 2007.

Lorde, Audre, *The Collected Poems of Audre Lorde*, New York and London: W.W. Norton and Company, 1997.

Lorde, Audre, *Zami: A New Spelling of My Name* (1982), London: Penguin Books, Ltd., 2018.

Lorde, Audre, *The Cancer Journals* (Aunt Lute Books, 1980), San Francisco, California: Penguin Random House, 2020.

Lorre-Johnston, Christine, 'Unsettling Oceania, 250 Years Later: Introduction', *Commonwealth Essays and Studies* 41:1 2018, pp. 75–81.

Lowe, Lisa, *The Intimacies of Four Continents*, Durham, NC and London: Duke University Press, 2015.

Lu, Pei-Yi, 'Three Approaches to Socially-Engaged Art in Taiwan', *Yishu: Journal of Contemporary Chinese Art* 15:6, November/December 2016, pp. 91–101.

Lugones, María, *Pilgrimages/Perigrinajes: Theorizing Coalition Against Multiple Oppressions*, Lanham, MD, Boulder, CO, New York and Oxford: Rowman and Littlefield Publishers, 2003.

Lugones, María, 'Toward a Decolonial Feminism', *Hypatia* 25:4, Fall 2010, pp. 742–59.

Lugones, María C. and Elizabeth V. Spelman, 'Have We Got a Theory for You! Feminist Theory, Cultural Imperialism and the Demand for "the Woman's Voice"', *Women's Studies International Forum* 6:6, 1983, pp. 573–81.

Lusordo, Domenico, *Liberalism: A Counter History*, London: Verso, 2014.

Lykke, Nina, ed., *Writing Academic Texts Differently: Intersectional Feminist Methodologies and the Playful Art of Writing*, London and New York: Routledge, 2014.

Selected Bibliography 157

Mahood, Kim, *Position Doubtful: Mapping Landscapes and Memories*, London: Scribe, 2016.

Manning, Erin, *For a Pragmatics of the Useless (Thought in the Act)*, Durham, NC and London: Duke University Press, 2020.

Massey, Doreen, 'A Global Sense of Place', *Marxism Today*, June 1991, pp. 24–9.

Massey, Doreen, *For Space*, Los Angeles, CA, London, New Delhi and Singapore: Sage Publications, 2005.

Mayorga, Edwin, Lekey Leidecker and Daniel Orr de Gutiérrez, 'Burn it Down: The Incommensurability of the University and Decolonization', *Journal of Critical Thought and Praxis* 8:1, 2019, pp. 87–106.

McClintock, Anne, *Imperial Leather: Race, Gender and Sexuality in the Colonial Contest*, London and New York: Routledge, 1995.

McKittrick, Katherine, ed., *Sylvia Wynter: On Being Human as Praxis*, Durham, NC and London: Duke University Press, 2015.

Meskimmon, Marsha, *Women Making Art: History, Subjectivity, Aesthetics*, London and New York: Routledge, 2003.

Meskimmon, Marsha, *Contemporary Art and the Cosmopolitan Imagination*, London and New York: Routledge, 2010.

Meskimmon, Marsha *Transnational Feminisms, Transversal Politics and Art: Entanglements and Intersections*, London and New York: Routledge, 2020.

Mignolo, Walter D., 'Epistemic Disobedience, Independent Thought and Decolonial Freedom', *Theory, Culture & Society* 26, 2009, pp. 159–81.

Mihai, Mihaela, *Political Memory and the Aesthetics of Care: The Art of Complicity and Resistance*, Stanford, CA: Stanford University Press, 2022.

Millar, Gearoid, 'Trans-scalar Ethnographic Peace Research: Understanding the Invisible Drivers of Complex Conflict and Complex Peace', *Journal of Intervention and Statebuilding* 15:3, 2021, pp. 289–308.

Million, Dian, 'Felt Theory: An Indigenous Feminist Approach to Affect and History', *Wicazo Sa Review* 24:2, 2009, 53–76.

Mohanty, Chandra Talpade, Ann Russo and Lourdes Torres, eds, *Third World Women and the Politics of Feminism*, Bloomington and Indianapolis: Indiana University Press, 1991.

Moraga, Cherríe and Gloria Anzaldúa, eds, *This Bridge Called My Back: Writings by Radical Women of Color*, Watertown, MA: Persephone Press, 1981.

Moreton-Robinson, Aileen, ed., *Critical Indigenous Studies: Engagements in First World Locations*, Tucson: University of Arizona Press, 2016.

Morton, Tom 'Review of the Taipei Biennial', *Frieze* 16 December 2014: https://www.frieze.com/article/taipei-biennial-2014.

Moten, Fred, *Black and Blur*, Durham, NC and London: Duke University Press, 2017.

Moten, Fred, *Stolen Life*, Durham, NC and London: Duke University Press, 2018.

Moten, Fred, *The Universal Machine*, Durham, NC and London: Duke University Press, 2018.

Muñoz, José Esteban, *Disidentifications: Queers of Color and the Performance of Politics*, Minneapolis: University of Minnesota Press, 1999.

Muñoz, José Esteban, *Cruising Utopia: The Then and There of Queer Futurity*, New York and London: NYU Press, 2009.

Nash, Jennifer C., 'Practicing Love: Black Feminism, Love-Politics, and Post-Intersectionality', *Meridians* 11:2, 2011, pp. 1–24.

Nash, Jennifer C., *Black Feminism Reimagined: After Intersectionality*, Durham, NC and London: Duke University Press, 2019.

Neigh, Janet, 'Dreams of Uncommon Languages: Transnational Feminist Pedagogy and Multilngual Poetics', *Feminist Formations* 26:1, Spring 2014, pp. 70–92.

158 Selected Bibliography

Niemanis, Astrida, *Bodies of Water: Posthuman Feminist Phenomenology*, London and New York: Bloomsbury Academic, 2017.

O'Donnell, David, 'Finding a Sense of Place in the Pacific Diaspora: Pasifika Performance in Aotearoa', *Australasian Drama Studies*, 73, October 2018, pp. 276–305.

Odysseos, Laura, 'Stolen Life's Poetic Revolt', *Millennium: Journal of International Studies* 47:3, 2019, pp. 341–72.

Oguibe, Olu, 'Whiteness and "The Canon"', *Art Journal* 60:4, Winter 2001, pp. 44–7.

Oliver, Liza, 'Reimagining Captain Cook: Pacific Perspectives', *CAA Reviews*, 2019: http://www.caareviews.org/reviews/3596#.YGr3nejds2w.

Olufemi, Lola, *Feminism Interrupted: Disrupting Power*, London: Pluto Press, 2020.

Ong, Aihwa, *Flexible Citizenship: The Cultural Logics of Transnationality*, Durham, NC and London: Duke University Press, 1999.

Papastergiadis, Nikos, 'What Is the South?', *Thesis* 11:100, February 2010, pp. 141–56.

Papasteriadis, Nikos, 'Cosmos and Nomos: Cosmopolitanism in Art and Political Philosophy', *Journal of Aesthetics and Culture* 13:1, 2021, pp. 1–14.

Patel, Alpesh Kantilal, *Productive Failure: Writing Queer Transnational South Asian Art Histories*, Manchester: Manchester University Press, 2017.

Patel, Alpesh Kantilal and Yasmeen Siddiqui, eds, *Storytellers of Art Histories: Living and Sustaining a Creative Life*, Bristol and Chicago, IL: Intellect, 2022.

Patrizio, Andrew, *The Ecological Eye: Assembling an Eco-Critical Art History*, Manchester: Manchester University Press, 2018.

Perry, Gill and Colin Cunningham, eds, *Academies, Museums and Canons of Art*, New Haven, CT and London: Yale University Press, 1999.

Petersen, Anne Ring, *Migration into Art: Transcultural Identities and Art-Making in a Globalised World*, Manchester: Manchester University Press, 2017.

Petersen, Anne Ring, 'Spectres of Colonialism in Contemporary Art from Denmark', *Art History* 43:2, April 2020, pp. 258–83.

Piotrowski, Piotr, 'Toward a Horizontal History of the European Avant-Garde', in *European Avant-Garde and Modernism Studies*, edited by Sascha Bru and Peter Nicholls, Berlin: De Gruyter, 2009, pp. 49–58.

Plumwood, Val, *Feminism and the Mastery of Nature*, London and New York: Routledge, 1993.

Povinelli, Elizabeth A., *Geontologies: A Requiem to Late Liberalism*, Durham, NC and London: Duke University Press, 2016.

Pratt, Geraldine and Victoria Rosner, *The Global and the Intimate: Feminism in Our Time*, New York: Columbia University Press, 2012.

Price, Dorothy and Catherine Grant, eds, 'Decolonizing Art History', *Art History* 43:1, February 2020, pp. 8–66.

Pollock, Griselda, *Differencing the Canon: Feminist Desire and the Writing of Art's Histories*, New York and London: Routledge, 1999.

Purtill, Corinne, 'Artist Gives New Life to a Polluted Taiwan Stream', *China Dialogue*, 29 April 2013: https://chinadialogue.net/en/cities/5832-artist-gives-new-life-to-a-polluted-taiwan-stream/.

Rahim, Jennifer with Barbara Lalla, eds, *Beyond Borders: Cross Culturalism and the Caribbean Canon*, Jamaica: University of the West Indies Press, 2009.

Ray, Sugata and Venugopal Maddipati, eds, *Water Histories of South Asia: The Materiality of Liquescence*, London and New York: Routledge, 2020.

Rehm, L., J. Kemner and O. Kaltmeier, eds, *Politics of Entanglement in the Americas: Connecting Transnational Flows and Local Perspectives*, InterAmerican Studies, vol. 19, Trier: WVT, 2017.

Reiter, Bernd, ed., *Pluriverse: The Geopolitics of Knowledge*, Durham, NC and London: Duke University Press, 2018.

Reynolds-Kaye, Jennifer, 'Circulating Casts of the *Coatlicue*: Mariana Castillo-Deball's Unearthing of the Aztec Earth Goddess's History Or Reproduction and Display', *Sculpture Journal* 28:3, 2019, pp. 365–80.

Rich, Adrienne, *On Lies, Secrets, and Silence*, New York: W.W. Norton, 1979.

Richter, Dorothee and Ronald Kolb, eds, *Decolonizing Art Institutions*, issue 35 of *On Curating*, December 2017.

Robinson, Hilary, 'Women, Feminism and Art Schools: The UK Experience', *Women's Studies International Forum* 85, 2021, pp. 1–10.

Roshanravan, Shireen, 'Motivating Coalition: Women of Color and Epistemic Disobedience', *Hypatia* 29:1, Winter 2014, pp. 41–58.

Salamone, Frank A., 'His Eyes Were Watching Her: Papa Franz Boas, Zora Neale Hurston, and Anthropology', *Anthropos* 109:1, 2014, pp. 217–224.

Sandoval, Chela, *Methodology of the Oppressed*, Minneapolis and London: University of Minnesota Press, 2000.

Sayers, Phil and Rikke Lundgreen, *Changing Places*, Bury Art Gallery, Museum and Archives, 2007.

Schmahmann, Brenda, 'The Fall of Rhodes: The Removal of a Sculpture from the University of Cape Town', *Public Art Dialog* 6:1, 2016, pp. 90–115.

Seager, Joni, 'Rachel Carson Died of Breast Cancer: The Coming of Age of Feminist Environmentalism', *Signs: Journal of Women in Culture and Society* 28:3, 2003, pp. 945–72.

Sedgwick, Eve Kosofsky, *Touching Feeling: Affect, Pedagogy, Performativity*, Durham, NC and London: Duke University Press, 2003.

Shao, Larry, 'Interview with Wu Mali', 2010 Asia Art Archive: https://aaa.org.hk/en/ideas/ideas/interview-with-wu-mali/type/conversations.

Sharpe, Christina, *In the Wake: On Blackness and Being*, Durham, NC and London: Duke University Press, 2016.

Shih, Shu-mei and Ping-hui Liao, eds, *Comparatizing Taiwan*, London and New York: Routledge, 2015.

Shohat, Ella, ed., *Talking Visions: Multicultural Feminism in a Transnational Age*, Cambridge, MA: MIT Press, 1999.

Shotwell, Alexis, *Against Purity: Living Ethically in Compromised Times*, Minneapolis: University of Minnesota Press, 2016.

Simmons, Kali, 'Reorientations; Or, an Indigenous Feminist Reflection on the Anthropocene', *Journal of Cinema and Media Studies* 58:2, Winter 2019, pp. 174–9.

Simpson, Audra and Andrea Smith, eds, *Theorizing Native Studies*, Durham, NC and London: Duke University Press, 2014.

Simpson, Leanne Betasamosake, *Islands of Decolonial Love: Stories & Songs*, Winnipeg: ARP Books, 2013.

Singh, Julietta, *Unthinking Mastery: Dehumanism and Decolonial Entanglements*, Durham, NC and London: Duke University Press, 2018.

Sivasundaram, Sujit, *Waves across the South: A New History of Revolution and Empire*. London: William Collins, 2020.

Smith, Barbara, ed., *Home Girls: A Black Feminist Anthology*, New York: Kitchen Table: Women of Color Press, 1983.

Smith, Dee, 'Lisa Reihana: A Monumental, Immersive New Artwork Reanimates the Story of Captain Cook and First Contact', *ABC News*, 2018: https://www.abc.net.au/news/2018-01-31/lisa-reihana-in-pursuit-of-venus-reimagines-australian-history/9376114.

160 Selected Bibliography

Smith, Linda Tuhiwai, *Decolonizing Methodologies: Research and Indigenous People* (1999), 3rd edition, London: Zed Books and Bloomsbury, 2021.

Spelman, Elizabeth, *Inessential Woman: Problems of Exclusion in Feminist Thought*, Boston, MA: Beacon Press, 1988.

Spillers, Hortense, 'Mama's Baby, Papa's Maybe: An American Grammar Book', *Diacritics* 17:2, 1987, 65–81.

Spillers, Hortense J., 'Moving on Down the Line', *American Quarterly* 40:1, 1988, pp. 83–109.

Spivak, Gayatri Chakravorty, 'The Making of Americans, the Teaching of English, and the Future of Cultural Studies', *New Literary History* 21, 1990, pp. 781–98.

Spivak, Gayatri Chakravorty, *Death of a Discipline* New York: Columbia University Press, 2003.

Steinbock, Eliza, 'Collecting Creative Transcestors: Trans★ Portraiture Hirstory, from Snapshots to Sculpture', in *A Companion to Feminist Art*, edited by Hilary Robinson and Maria Buszek, Oxford: Wiley Blackwell, 2019a, pp. 225–42.

Steinbock, Eliza, *Shimmering Images: Trans Cinema, Embodiment and the Aesthetics of Change*, Durham, NC and London: Duke University Press, 2019b.

Stoler, Ann Laura, *Carnal Knowledge and Imperial Power: Race and the Intimate in Colonial Rule*, Los Angeles and London: University of California Press, 2002.

Stryker, Susan, '"Transing the Queer (In)Human", in "Dossier: Theorizing Queer Inhumanisms"', *GLQ: A Journal of Lesbian and Gay Studies* 21:2–3, 2015, pp. 227–30.

Sundberg, Juanita, 'Decolonizing Posthumanist Geographies', *Cultural Geographies* 21:1, 2014, pp. 33–47.

Suzack, Cheryl, Shari M. Huhndorf, Jeanne Perreault and Jean Barman, eds, *Indigenous Women and Feminism: Politics, Activism, Culture*, Vancouver and Toronto: UBC Press, 2010.

Suzuki, Erin, *Ocean Passages: Negotiating Pacific Islander and Asian American Literatures*, Philadelphia, PA: Temple University Press, 2021.

TallBear, Kim, 'Beyond the Life/Not Life Binary: A Feminist-Indigenous Reading of Cryopreservation, Interspecies Thinking and the New Materialisms', in *Cryopolitics: Frozen Life in a Melting World*, edited by Joanna Radin and Emma Kowal, Cambridge, MA: MIT Press, 2017.

TallBear, Kim, *The Critical Polyamorist*, http://www.criticalpolyamorist.com/.

Thomas, Julia Adeney, Mark Williams and Jan Zalasiewicz, eds, *The Anthropocene: A Multidisciplinary Approach*, Cambridge: Polity Press, 2020.

Thomas, Nicholas, *Possessions: Indigenous Art/Colonial Culture*, London: Thames and Hudson, 1999.

Thomas, Nicholas, 'Lisa Reihana: Encounters in Oceania', *Artlink* 01 June 2017: https://www.artlink.com.au/articles/4595/lisa-reihana-encounters-in-oceania/.

Tlostanova, Madina, Suruchi Thapar-Björkert and Redi Koobak, 'Border Thinking and Disidentification: Postcolonial and Postsocialist Feminist Dialogues', *Feminist Theory* 17:2 2016, pp. 211–28.

Trinh, T. Minh-ha, *Woman, Native, Other: Writing Postcoloniality and Feminism*, Indianapolis: Indiana University Press, 1989.

Trinh, T Minh-ha, *Cinema Interval*, London and New York: Routledge, 1999.

Tsing, Anna Loewenhaupt, *The Mushroom at the End of the World: On the Possibility of Life in Capitalist Ruins*, Princeton, NJ: Princeton University Press, 2015.

Tsing, Anna Lowenhaupt, Heather Ann Swanson, Elaine Gan and Nils Bubandt, eds, *Arts of Living on a Damaged Planet: Ghosts and Monsters of the Anthropocene*, Minneapolis: University of Minnesota Press, 2017.

Turner, Caroline and Michelle Antoinette, eds, *Contemporary Asian Art and Exhibitions: Connectivities and World-making*, Canberra: ANU Press, 2014.

Van Robbroeck, Lize, 'Unsettling the Canon: Some Thoughts on the Design of *Visual Century: South African Art in Context*', *Third Text Africa* 3:1, November 2013, pp. 27–37.

Vercoe, Caroline, 'History is a place: Pacific artists reimagining colonial legacies', in *Lisa Reihana: In Pursuit of Venus*, Auckland: Auckland Art Gallery, 2015, pp. 58–64.

Vaz, Kim Marie and Gary L. Lemons, eds, *Feminist Solidarity at the Crossroads: Intersectional Women's Studies for Transracial Alliance*, London and New York: Routledge, 2012.

Wainwright, Leon, 'Art (School) Education and Diversity', in *Beyond Cultural Diversity: The Case for Creativity*, commissioned by Arts Council England. *Third Text*, 2011.

Weisberg, Richard, *Poethics: And Other Strategies of Law and Literature*, New York: Columbia UP, 1992.

Wekker, Gloria, *White Innocence: Paradoxes of Colonialism and Race*, Durham, NC and London: Duke University Press, 2016.

West, Andrew, 'Self Help, Ethnography and Art Together: Liverpool, Lever and Port Sunlight', *Journal of Museum Ethnography* 11, May 1999, pp. 29–42.

West, Cornel, 'Minority Discourse and the Pitfalls of Canon Formation', *Yale Journal of Criticism* 1:1, Fall 1987, pp. 193–207.

Williams, Merle A. and Stefan Polatinsky, 'Hélène Cixous' Manna: The Face of Suffering and the Poethics of Border-Crossing', *English Studies in Africa* 52:2, 2009, pp. 63–76.

Wynter, Sylvia, 'Ethno Or Socio Poetics', *Alcheringa: Ethnopoetics* 2:2, 1976, pp. 78–94.

Wynter, Sylvia, '1492: A New World View', in *Race, Discourse and the Origin of the Americas: A New World View*, edited by Vera Lawrence Hyatt and Rex Nettleford, Washington, DC: Smithsonian Press, 1995, pp. 5–57.

Wynter, Sylvia, 'Unsettling the Coloniality of Being/Power/Truth/Freedom: Towards the Human, after Man, Its Overrepresentation – An Argument', *CR: The New Centennial Review* 3:3, 2003, pp. 257–337.

Yuval-Davis, Nira, 'Dialogical Epistemology: An Intersectional Resistance to the "Oppression Olympics"', *Gender and Society* 26:1, February 2012, pp. 46–54.

Yusoff, Kathryn, *A Billion Black Anthropocenes Or None*, Minneapolis: University of Minnesota Press, 2018.

INDEX

Pages followed by n refer notes.

Abod, Jennifer 69–70; documentary film 71
African–Caribbean–American geographical
  coordinates 68
Agard-Jones, Vanessa 77
Ahmed, Sara 24, 70
Alexander, M. Jacqui 70–2, 83n29;
  explorations of pedagogies 87;
  fundamentally pedagogic imperative 89;
  multiple operations of power 88; socio-
  economic disparities 87
Andrade, Silvia 48
anti-racist 70, 86, 89, 100, 112
Anzaldúa, Gloria 73; concept of 'neplanta,'
  50; explorations of Chicana art 50
Army Corps of Engineers (ACE) 116–17
Arnold, Marion: *The Lens of Empowerment*
  100; transnational feminist research 100
*Art as Environment–A Cultural Action at the
  Plum Tree Creek* 118
The Art of a Continent (1995) 43
Audre Lorde: The Berlin Years, 1984–1992
  (Germany, 2012) 69
Aztecs (2002) 43
AZTEC: The World of Moctezuma 50

Baca, Judith 116, 134, *137*; critical
  awareness environmental issues 136;
  mural 129; Mural Maker 136
Baca, Judith F., *The Great Wall of Los
  Angeles* (1976–83*ff*) 115, 117
Balfour, Henry 43
Banerjee, Pallavi 5–6

Banks, Joseph 39–40
The Bath of Psyche 26, *27*
Benedict, Ruth Fulton 52
Black Caribbean intellectual tradition 73
Black feminisms 9
Black Feminist Poethics 73, 84n40
Boas, Franz 52
The Body of a Poet (UK, 1995) 69
Bowen, Angela 70–2
Braidotti, Rosi 133
British East India Company 34, 93
Bunzel, Ruth Leah 52
A Burst of Light and Other Essays (1988) 75
Byrd, Jodi A. 3; decolonial feminist
  interventions 4; 'laboratory' for racial
  science 132; mapping trans-scalar
  intimacies 4; racialized geopolitics of
  colonial conquest 4; transit of empire
  131; trans-scalar ecologies 132

Callen-Lorde Community Health Centre 77
The Cancer Journals 75
The Cancer Journals Revisited (USA, 2018)
  69, 78, *79*
Captive and *Captivated* (both 2007) 33
Carby, Hazel 5, 79n3
Changing Places 23–6, 28
Charvet, Jean-Gabriel 36
China: The Three Emperors, 1662–1795
  (2005) 43
civic eco-nationalism 123, 143n55
Clark, Michele Pearson 69

Index **163**

Code, Lorraine: ecological thinking 113; epistemic transformation 112; mutual and interdependent worldmaking 113; 'postcolonial' and anti-racist thought 112
collaborative survival 7, 9, 113–16, 122, 124, 133, 135, 138
coloniality of gender 22, 32–3, 39
colonization 3, 38–9, 117, 123, 125–26
Combahee River Collective (1974–80) 68
commodity racism 25
comte de La Pérouse, Jean-François de Galaup 36
Connell, Raewyn 5–6
Cook, James 36–7, 39–41
Covid-19 pandemic 88
critical ecofeminism 3, 12n13, 14n36, 146n95
Cultural Action at the Plum Tree Creek 122–23, 128, 132, 134, 138

Darwin, Erasmus 34
da Silva, Denise Ferreira 73, 84n40
Davies, Carole Boyce 73
Deball, Mariana Castillo 45; anthropological fieldwork 52; *Between making and knowing something 53*; practices of art and anthropology 51
decolonial feminist 86
de Cunha, Dilip 93
de la Bellacasa, María Puig 134
Deloria, Ella 52
del Val, Nasheli Jiménez: colonizing the imaginary of dominated people 51; genealogy of 'the Indigenous' in Mexican visual culture 51
de Saint-Saveur, Jacques Grasset 36
de Sousa Santos, Boaventura: Good Living/ Buen Vivir 112; intellectual breadth 112; no global social justice without global cognitive justice 111; Western-centric knowledge 111
Differencing the Canon: Feminist Desire and the Writing of Art's Histories 20
Drew, Charles 121
Durand, Sir Mortimer 90

Eberts, Mary: Canadian constitutional lawyer 101; Native Women's Association of Canada 101
The Edge of Each Other's Battles: The Vision of Audre Lorde (USA, 2002) 69–70
Epistemologies of the South: Justice Against Epistemicide 111
Euro and anthropocentric universalism 6

Eurocentric universalism 1, 6, 22, 54, 76
European colonial conquest 68
European imperial project 8, 22, 96
European Institute for Gender Equality (EIGE) 88

Fernando, Sonali 69
Ferrary, Desiré Maurice: blatant emphasis upon raw sexuality 32; *Salambo* (1899) 32
Freeman, Elizabeth 30
Freire, Paolo 96

Gaard, Greta 133
gender equity 86–9, 91, 123, 128
gender theory 5, 12n15, 13n22
geopolitical privilege 87
George, Amika 87
Ghosh, Amitav 132
girl's education 87
Gladstone, William Ewart 34
global feminist eco-art 115
Gomez, Jewelle 69
Gonzales, David 121; local Chicano community 122; Zoot Suit Riots 122
Grasset, Jacques 36
The Great Wall 117–18, 121, 129, 134–35, 137
Griffin, Ada Gay 67–9
Grosz, Elizabeth 46
Gumbs, Alexis Pauline 69

Haraway, Donna 7, 115, 134
Hartman, Saidiya 73, 79n3, 83n38
heterosexual gender politics 27
historical violences of slavery 3
Hurston, Zora Neale 52

(neo)imperialism 4
In Pursuit of Venus [infected] (*iPOV[i]*, 2015–17) 35
intellectual insights 89
Iskin, Ruth E. 21, 55n14–5

Jennifer C. Nash 84n48
Jones, Claudia 73
Jordan, June 69

King, Rosamond S. 73, 83n37
Kraft, Marion 83n28
Kuokannen, Ruana 22; Indigenous politics and law 101–02; *Reshaping the University: Responsibility, Indigenous Epistemes, and the Logic of the Gift* 101; transnational feminist pedagogies 103

164 Index

Lady Lever Art Gallery 24, *25*, 32–3
Lahore Bachao Committee 91
Leighton, Frederick 26
Les Sauvages de la Mer Pacifique 35
Lever, William Hesketh 24
Lewandle Migrant Labour Museum 97
LGBTQ+ community 77
Lin, Lana 69, 77–8
Litany for Survival (USA, 1995) 69
A Litany for Survival: The Life and Work of Audre Lorde 67
logic of epistemicide 90
Lorde, Audre 83n27, 83n30–4, 84n44–7, 85n49–85n55; bio-mythography 70; Black lives 74; collaborative survival 7; cultural experiences of race, gender, sexuality and class 71; documentary intersperses film of 71; Dream of Europe 74; explorations of *survival* 76; familiar leitmotif 70; final appearance on the stage in Boston 72; historical locus 68; oppression Olympics 6; practices of cross-cultural self-naming 68; revolutionary poetic storying 76; transatlantic slave trade 68; transgressive writing 73; transnational feminisms and art's transhemispheric histories 7; transnational feminist networks and projects 68; transnational praxis 68–9; tripartite concept of poetry 72; Western liberal epistemologies 6
Lorde-Rollins, Elizabeth 77
Lugones, María: the coloniality of gender 22, 32; hybrid imagination 23; logic of purity 22; lover of purity 22–3; trans and queer subjects 32; world traveling 23
Lunar Society of Birmingham 34
Lundgreen, Rikke 23; gender identifications 30

Maheke, Paul 69
Makereti: criticized by later European scholars 48; cultural concert party 44; fieldwork 46; marrying an Oxfordshire 44; material 46; Māori songs 44
Mali, Wu 118, 123–24, 134–35; appointed as co-curator of the Taipei Biennial 127; and Manacorda 128; projects 126; riparian cultural actions 127; work 126
manifest destiny 51, 118, 130
The Manila Galleon 129
Marjoribanks, Dudley Coutts 34
Marmon Silko, Leslie 73
Massey, Doreen 120

McClintock, Anne 24
McDougall, Elsie Colsell 45, 52
McKittrick, Katherine 83n36, 84n44
Mexican–American conflict 117
Michaelis School of Fine Art 96
Mignolo, Walter D. 1
Mohanty, Chandra Talpade 87
Moreno, Luisa 121
Morris, Monique W.: global educational gender gap 88; *Pushout: The Criminalization of Black Girls in Schools* 88; *teaching ourselves* 89; transnational feminist perspective on gender equity 88
Morrison, Toni 93
multi-epistemic practices of thinking 7
Museum of Modern Art 45

National College of Arts (NCA) 90–1
National Gallery of Australia 36
Nationalist government of the Kuomintang (KMT) 118
Neale Hurston, Zora 73
Niemanis, Astrida 133

Odysseos, Louiza 73
On Reflection (2007) 25–6
ontological purification 22, 31, 42, 50
Orrock, James 33
Oxford Natural History Museum 49

Pakistan–India Peoples' Forum for Peace and Democracy (PIPFPD) 91
Parker, Pat 69
Parkerson, Michelle 67–9
parochial universalism 8
Patel, Alpesh Kantilal 79n2
Pedagogies of Crossing: Meditations on Feminism, Sexual Politics, Memory and the Sacred 88
pious universalism 5, 13n23
Pitt Rivers Museum 43
Polk, James K. 51
Pollock, Griselda: compelling study of the sexual politics 20; concept of *transcanons* 21; role of Eurocentric literary 20; teleological narratives 20
Price, Dorothy 27
public philanthropy 25
Pueblo, Zuni 52

racial and sexual purity 25
racialization 3
Radcliffe, Cyril 90
radical interdisciplinarity 66, 73, 83n37
Ravine, Chavez 117

Reihana, Lisa 35; gender and sexual politics 37; panoramic video installation 37; *In Pursuit of Venus [infected]*, 2015–17 38; *In Pursuit of Venus [infected]*, detail: Mourning, 2015–17 42; *In Pursuit of Venus [infected]*, detail: Stars, 2015–17 41; transnational feminist genealogies of art 36
Rhodes, Cecil 96; Graffiti shadow of 98
Rhodes Must Fall (RMF) campaign 96
Rich, Adrienne 69–70, 83n30, 84n43
Rivers, Pitt 48
Roman figure of Antinous 32
Rukh, Lala: aesthetic, intellectual and political impact 90; cultural, political and intellectual life of Lahore 91; engagement with feminism, art and teaching 91; expanded pedagogical practice 95; *Mirror Image:* 1, 1997 92; pedagogies of crossing 94; *River in an ocean* (1992–93) 93; serial exploration of borders and horizons 92; transnational feminist thought 91; Women's Action Forum 90

Sapphire 69
Sayers, Phil 23; *Captivated*, 2007 34; gender identifications 30; large-scale digital 25; *On Reflection*, 2007 29; transgender transpositions 33
Schliebener, Catalina 77
Schmahmann, Brenda: critical pedagogies of decolonization 97; decolonizing the curriculum 97; at UCT 97
Schulman, Sarah 69
Schulz, Dagmar 69
Second Opium War (1856–60) 34, 58n51
Sedgwick, Eve Kosofsky 139n12–3; paranoid and reparative reading 113
Self-Help (1859) 34
self-reflexive *unlearning* 22
Sharpe, Christina 73
Shih, Shu-Mei: analogy 128–29
Shotwell, Alexis 134
Sivasundaram, Sujit 126
Sloane, Sir Hans 43
Smiles, Samuel 34
Smith, Kimberleigh Joy 67
Smith, Linda Tuhiwai: *Decolonizing Methodologies: Research and Indigenous People* 95; decolonizing research methodologies 95–7; development of Eurocentric academic knowledge 95–6
Smith, Lindsay: significance of Hermaphrodite 28; *tableaux vivant* 29
Society of Dilletanti 39

Southern theory 3, 5
Spelman, Elizabeth V. 5–6
Spillers, Hortense 73
Spira, Tamara Lea 75, 85n50
Spivak, Gayatri 19, 132, 138
St Croix's Women's Coalition (1980) 68
Steinbock, Eliza 28; figure of Hermaphrodite 28; figure trans subjectivity 28
Stevenson, Matilda Coxe 45, 52
storying: ecologies and genealogies 7–9; pluriversal worlds 9–11
Strathern, Marilyn 115
Sundberg, Juanita 55n16–7; ongoing processes of ontological purification 22
Support of Sisters in South Africa (SISA) 68

Tableau of the Discoveries of Captain Cook and La Perouse (1798–99) 36
Tadema, Lawrence Alma 25
Taipei Biennial 127
Taiwan's: characteristic of 127; Danshui 125; Indigenous and multi-ethnic communities 126; Indigenous Austronesians 127
Tamkang University 119
transhemispheric thinking 4–5
transnational feminisms 65, 100; aesthetic explorations of ecosexuality and queer ecologies 115; aesthetics/poetics in 66; and art's transhemispheric histories 2, 7; art writing 66; binary spatial logic 114; creative textual experimentation in transnational feminist 67; critical ecofeminism 3; critical entanglement of 148; decolonial *and* feminist lens 114; decolonial and race-critical trajectories of 2–3; ecological thinking of 149; ecological worlding projects of 111; ecologies and genealogies of 67; epistemologies of the South 3; feminist theory 2; gendered dynamics of techno-science 115; poetic practices and textual transgressions 66; and practices of genealogy 8–9; project of feminist ecological thinking 114; queer and decolonial explorations 66; transnational feminist activist networks 114; transversal politics of 149; trilogy on 9
transnationality 10, 16n60
trans-scalar ecologies 10–1, 111–38
Tsing, Anna Lowenhaupt 113

University of Cape Town 96
University of the Fraser Valley (UFV) 100; *Lens* programme 101–02

166 Index

Venus Callipyge 26, 57n33
visual tropes of Victorian art 25

Walgate, Marion 96; monument to
Rhodes 97
Wedgwood, Josiah 34
Western-centric feminist theory 6
Western Universality, imperial project of 1, 4
White solipsism 5, 66, 70
Wilberforce, Samuel 43
Wohl, Ellen 116
woman of color methodology 73, 83n37

Women's Action Forum (WAF) 90
women's autonomy 87
Wu Mali's *Art as Environment—A Cultural
Action at the Plum Tree Creek* (2010–12)
115
Wynter, Sylvia 73, 83n34, 83n38, 84n44;
analysis of anthropogenic climate
change 111; catastrophic reckoning 112;
intellectual breadth 112

Zapata, Emiliano 129
Zia-ul-Haq, Muhammad 90–1